GOLD RUSH LEGACY

Marian,

You are part of the legacy!

"God's children are
worth their weight
in Gold!" Lam 4:2

Greg Roth

GOLD RUSH LEGACY

W. W. Brier

Pioneer Presbyterian Pastor

Dr. Greg Roth

To order additional copies of this book, contact:
Xlibris Corporation
1-888-795-4274
www.Xlibris.com
Orders@Xlibris.com
28827

CONTENTS

My journey began in a graveyard. As the new pastor at Centerville Presbyterian Church, I began working with a restoration committee to clean the overgrown cemetery site that surrounded our original 1850's church. The small chapel that birthed our congregation had burned two years earlier, leaving a gaping hole in its original site. The site was overgrown with weeds, and there were a number of tombstones already knocked to the ground.

The Brier Tombstone in Fremont, California
Credit: Photo by author

It was hard to miss. Near the entrance of the site stands an imposing tombstone, a gray monolithic block of granite eight feet tall by five feet wide that celebrates the founding pastor, the Reverend William Wallace Brier. I read the inscription that celebrated his ministry:

William Wallace Brier
Born November 6, 1821, died June 3, 1887.
From this home he went forth to organize churches at: Marysville, Centerville, Alvarado,
Mt. Eden, San Leandro, Pleasanton, Livermore, Milpitas, Red Bluff, East Oakland; in
the state of Nevada: Carson City, Virginia City, and Elko. It is said that he had a
personal hand in organizing 27 churches throughout his lifetime.
"To Him who overcomes I will make a pillar in the temple of my God, and he will go
out no more."

The inscription peaked my curiosity, and I wanted to learn more about this man who had such a remarkable ministry in the gold rush era. He must have been a remarkable pastor and pioneer. I began inquiring about him at the churches listed on his tombstone, tracing backwards to find the clues about the length and breadth of his ministry.

I was told that the gold rush was formed in the minds of hungry men. It began with a dream of easy riches, a vision of a flash of color in the gold pan, and a beckoning call to search the countryside for the sake of God, country, and personal gain. But the miners never had a clue of what they were getting into they were captured by this dream.

This biography began as my own gold rush. I was hungry for answers about the history, and I dug for clues. The riches I was prospecting for were the dreams of history—the history of California, my congregation, and the pastor who guided it during difficult years to minister to the 49'ers.

The journey I was about to embark upon would ultimately bring me to the verge of both exhilaration and exhaustion. Staking a claim to this gold involved a long and winding journey of tedious work. Now and then, there was a fleck of color in my gold pan, soon to be assembled with other flecks, scraped out of the riverbank of libraries around the country. I found a great deal of information scattered throughout church libraries and Presbyterian historical societies. Many days had been spent sifting through a river of microfilm letters from California missionaries when I stumbled upon the nugget of Brier's signature, copied the letter, and transcribed it to assess its true value. Many times I thought it would be easier to learn a foreign language than to read Brier's handwriting.

I discovered thirty-five of Brier's letters to the American Home Missionary Society about his church planting activities. These are currently held in the Amisted Research Center at Tulane University in Baton Rouge, Louisiana. Brier descendants have provided other letters, and showed me an inscription inside the front cover of the Brier family Bible, with a more complete record of the congregations Brier had helped to organize. Each of these churches contains a fragment of the Brier story.

Churches founded or served by W. W. Brier

Indiana Churches:	*1846-1849*
Romney	1848
Wea Presbyterian	1849
West Point	1849
Hickory Cross	1849

California Churches : 1850-1887	
Marysville	1850
Grass Valley	1852
Centerville	1853
Santa Cruz	1857
Alvarado	1860
Brooklyn Oakland	1860
San Leandro	1864
Red Bluff	1860
Watsonville	1860/1864
Alameda	1864
Gilroy	1860
Milpitas	1871
Livermore	1871
Pleasanton	1871
Salinas	1872
Portersville	1872

Nevada Churches :	*1860-1865*
Carson City	1860
Virginia City	1862
Gold Hill	1862
Austin	1864
Hamilton	1869
Elko	1870
Eureka	1873
Pioche	1874

It became clear that studying the life of W.W. Brier would hold important keys to the history of the Presbyterian Church on the West Coast. He did not have a flashy personality, nor did he write a shelf full of books. But he was a faithful man with a passion for planting a Presbyterian church in every farming and mining community in California and Nevada. He would spend his entire life and his personal fortune to make the dream a reality.

I concluded that Brier was a significant but overlooked figure in the histories of the 49'er era. What follows is my journey to trace a story that began to take on additional depth as I dug through boxes of records in research libraries and churches in Indiana, Nevada, and California. I examined correspondence, the minutes of both Presbytery and the Synod of California, and the local histories of each congregation. Brought together with the history of each individual church, the sparkle of color began to reflect a picture of a man called by God with a unique gift for launching churches in the early days of California. I followed his movements from Indiana to California year-by-year, city-by-city, church-by-church and through his various career roles in the Presbyterian Church: pioneer, church planter, pastor, stated clerk of San Jose Presbytery, and Moderator of the Synod. In the last years of his life, he was working on a comprehensive history of the growth of the Presbyterian Church in California, but his manuscript was destroyed by fire.

With Brier's records destroyed, this book is an attempt to reconstruct what was lost, not as a definitive history of the Synod, but as a reconstruction of how Brier's inspiring ministry shaped church and society in an exciting period of California history.

CHAPTER 1

Scottish Stone Foundations

1821-1848

The beginning of the story deals with foundations and legacies, as William Wallace Brier is born as the fifth of eight children. He was born in Stillwater near Dayton, Ohio, November 6, 1821. It is thought that his grandfather emigrated from Scotland in the late 1760's. Brier's father, James Malcolm Brier, was married to Mary Lodge, whose father was Benjamin Lodge Jr. He served George Washington's militia as a Colonel in the 2nd Battalion of Westmoreland County, Pennsylvania, in 1776. It may have been that his gift of land from the government for military service was passed down to the family in the division of the family farm in Ohio, then later transferred to a larger farm in Indiana.

The Brier family originates in the Highlands of Scotland under the name of Mac Brayer or Mc Briar. The name "William Wallace" is taken directly from the Scottish clan leader. When he was five years old, William Brier's family moved from the Ohio valley to a farm near Rob Roy, Indiana, in the northeast corner of the state.

The History of Fountain County contains a narrative history of the Brier family farm, which focuses upon William's brother Samuel. This biography sheds some light onto William's father and their childhood on the family farm near Rob Roy, Indiana.

From this description we gain a great window into the childhood of William Brier. The family was patriotic, staunch supporters of the revolution, autonomy, and settlement of the wilderness. His father and mother were long-time Presbyterians, of Scottish and Irish Presbyterian descent. We can surmise that he came from a godly family as his oldest brother, James Welsh Brier entered the Methodist ministry. They were both frugal, and rugged individuals who were committed to the Lord.

Childhood is a tender and formative experience that often sets the themes for a lifetime—either by the magnetism of a positive experience or the repulsion of a negative aversion. In William Brier's case, the wilderness of Indiana would teach the lessons of a lifetime, which would capture his heart and set boundaries for his lifetime calling and ministry. Brier's imagination was defined by the fragrant smell of the earth, the wind and water, the visual grasp of the open sky and the land that was rolled out like a flat carpet of green earth and raw brown fields. The reliance upon earthy elements for produce and sole dependence upon the Lord for the family's livelihood create a tension of life that is not easily removed. But there is also a difficult tension: the anguish of defeat or illness, the lack of community and culture that wears away at the soul.

Prior to the construction of the Erie Canal the wilderness of Indiana was a vast woodland and swampy arena for farming. The Indian wars of 1827 were still fresh in the minds of the pioneers, and all was not secure. Farms had to be carved out of the muck and the thick forest. Much of the work entailed felling trees, removing stumps, and devising a drainage plan to keep the crops from becoming mud basins. The Brier homestead had a small log cabin, which was a temporary residence that was later used as a corncrib, but the family moved into this small one room home while logs from the farm were wagon-teamed to the sawmill on the river and returned as lumber to construct the family home.

The winters were harsh, particularly the winter of 1831, which froze the frontier of Illinois and Indiana so thoroughly that the remaining buffalo in the region froze to death. The drifting snow often reached fifteen feet, and farmers remembered it as "The great snow" and were forced to top trees to have adequate firewood to keep their families warm. Many nearly froze in hostile winters. There were lessons of struggle, surrender, and survival, which would be imprinted in William Brier's heart and soul for a lifetime. He learned perseverance in the face of impossible odds.

The Fountain County History notes, "On September 27, 1828 they arrived in Shawnee Township, and settled where Mr. Brier resides. A part of the land, the W, ½ of N. W. ¼ Sect 31, T. 21, R, 7 was bought from Wilson and Abel Claypoole, and his father received the patent in his own name".

William Brier as a young boy learned lessons about the value of working the land with his hands and the blessing of the harvest. He loved being frugal and was committed to being out of debt. The family farm was large for those times. Corn and wheat were cultivated by plows drawn by horses or oxen. Hogs needed to be tended, and fed. The Briers had crops enough to hire farm hands for some of the labor. They had income enough to provide adequate schooling for their children and hoped to save for their eventual college. The family would have taken wheat to the nearest mill in Tippecanoe County, a mill operated by Elias Beard some twenty miles away. This business relationship with Beard led to an emerging friendship.

The farm was unusually profitable. Samuel's testimony states, "when the Wabash and Erie Canal was building his father sold corn at his farm for fourteen cents per bushel, and was paid in canal scrip at sixty per cent discount. At the same time he sold dressed hogs for $2.10 per hundred, and received payment in the same paper. Good farm hands were hired for $9.00 per month."

The farming lifestyle is honorable; there is glory in hard work, and the fruit of the labor is often an abundant crop. William saw the value of having clear transportation routes to markets, which would feed the teeming metropolis of people. His experience with his father, of taking the crops to market, some 150 miles to the northwest in Chicago, taught the Brier boys the quality of perseverance and built a hearty fortitude in their souls at an early age.

The obituary continues, "Mr. Brier used to wagon his produce to Chicago, usually selling flour delivered at $4.00 per barrel. At that time he turned his oxen loose on the north side of the Chicago River to graze overnight on the prairie. It took two weeks to make the trip with horses, and nearly twice as long with oxen. The roads were generally in wretched condition the greater part of the way, and from Thorn Creek to the city, some twenty miles, nearly impassable the year round. This stretch could be traversed only by making short pulls, frequent unloading and reloading, and this usually in the water, and by doubling teams."

We can almost visualize William Brier spending his childhood from age 5-14 working on the farm. The lessons he learned from his father about the dignity of farming built important principles in his life. He faced the overwhelming odds of frontier farming, the dignity of hard work and dependence upon the sovereignty of God, and also the risk and reward of delivering flour and cattle to the market.

In his early years William worked side by side with his father in the seasons of farm life; plowing the field, sowing the wheat, weeding, and then thrashing with a team of migrant workers. The season ended with the transport of wheat wagons to Beard's flourmill in the nearby village of Attica.

A son often competes with brothers to seek their father's blessing. The lifestyle of a farmer was not for him, and there was a growing restlessness in his soul. His brother Samuel was three years younger, was more adept at farming, and had a closer bond with his father. He was stronger, showed a natural inclination with the animals, and had a knack for plowing straight. William was older and more bookish and was impatient with the crops. He excelled at his schoolwork, as the Brier children all attended the one room schoolhouse a few miles from the farm.

William Brier also learned lessons of faith, which would anchor him his whole life. Mrs. Brier home schooled the children in Bible reading, showed them a love for the Lord, and a passion to be involved in leadership in the church. He was involved in the Presbyterian Church, training for his future studies. Whether he aspired to the ministry in his childhood or not, we do not know. His brother James, seven years his senior, was already preparing for the gospel ministry in the Methodist tradition.

We can assume that he learned many lessons from the Presbyterian pastor in Rob Roy, where his father was Sunday school superintendent and director of the choir. The bright eyes of a child formed an admiration and respect for the two male figures in his life: his father, the farmer and church elder, and his pastor as the spiritual center of rural community life. Yet, in spite of this flaw there seems to be some flaw in William's relationship with males who were in authority over him. In the years to come, this anger would cause him to stumble, as he would have a passionate reaction of rage when he suspected he was not being adequately supported. There were also lessons from the challenges and values of schooling in a frontier situation that would shadow and strengthen William Brier throughout this life and ministry. Most farm families home schooled their children, or taught them in clustered schools in the villages nearby. One-room schoolhouses were effective ways to train broadly, but rarely to train with the depth needed for advanced schooling. The schooling was spotty in its effectiveness, and many farm students dropped out after eighth grade proficiency testing. The Brier family had high aspirations and made great sacrifices for their children. Of the five children, four went to college, and all these went for advanced training as well. For William Wallace Brier this included teacher training at Wabash College.

CHAPTER 2

Training for Ministry

Wabash College
Photo by author

Wabash College was located on a new campus, about sixty miles southeast of the Fountain County family farm. This medium sized town was a regional center and held the county courthouse, a brand new College campus, and little else. Although there was no direct route from the Brier farm, the six-hour buggy ride to school seemed like a short distance—in order to get the necessary schooling for future ministry.

The all-male college was located just a quarter-mile from the central business district of Crawfordsville. Three-story commercial brick buildings lined the central road that led from the riverbank. Many students boarded with local families. Students were paid twenty-five cents a cord to split wood in preparation for the winter.

The life was simple; students or townspeople enjoyed comparatively few luxuries. There were few distractions to study. The community was modest with no people of wealth in the modern sense, merely the well to do and the less well to do. To have status in the community meant you had a brick two-story house on one of the tree-lined streets in town.

William Brier began his schooling at the college prep academy attached to Wabash in 1839. The school was used as a preparatory school for three years before enrollment in the college classes. You can imagine that the students quickly learning the ropes of the school in a small school the professors became mentors and father-like figures. William quickly blended into the college and civic community, joining the Center Presbyterian Church in 1840.

He joined a small class of students. *The Catalogue of the Officers and Students of Wabash College*, dated July 19, 1843 notes twenty-two students in the college section. Among them were seven freshmen, including William Brier of Fountain County, Indiana. He is listed as renting a room at Mr. Gregory's house on College Avenue.

The terms lasted thirteen and a half weeks, with Brier's fall term beginning September 21st, 1843, and the two successive terms ending July 15th the following year. The food and lodging for the year was $55.00, and tuition and fees would reach $91.00 per term.

It was at Wabash that Brier became interested in a career in education. He sat under the teaching of Caleb Mills. Caleb became a regional leader in the public educational movement. A January 4, 1846 article by Mills titled, "One of the People," was published in the *Indiana State Journal*. It aroused much interest and comment in the state, and members of the House of Representatives were moved to pass a resolution on January 8, 1847, requesting the friends of education to call a convention for the following May for the purpose of discussing a system of common schools for the state.

A freshman like Brier would be expected to master the subjects in Rhetoric, Logic, Mental Philosophy, Natural Theology, Evidences of Christianity, Constitution of the United States, Political Economy, Moral Philosophy, and Butler's Logic and Analogy. In the definitive school history, *Wabash College, The First Hundred Years,* James Insley Osborne and Theodore Gregory Gronert described the shape and character of the college that Brier attended. On July 19, 1841, Brier joined the students, and well wishing citizens and leaders of Crawfordsville in filling his home church to the rafters. The tiny Center Presbyterian Church was packed for the midweek inauguration of the second president of Wabash College. The church chancel was packed with the faculty of the college. Trustee General Howard rose to introduce the new president of the school. In his introduction, Howard prayed that Dr. White, as the new president, would be worthy of his post by building a passion for learning and culture within the framework of this western frontier.

Dr. White rose to the platform, delivering a speech to match Howard's request, on "Religion as an Essential Part of All Education." Professor White issued an eloquent charge that captured the imagination of all present and, we may presume, William Wallace Brier.

Dr. White said, in part, "When a fine large vessel goes out of port freighted richly for the other side of the world, she is looked upon by the owners, underwriters, and men on board with intense emotion. There will be a general interest in the neighborhood. A crowd will be gathered at the wharf when she is pushed off, and, as she spreads her wings to the wind and moves proudly away, the multitude will give a most hearty hurrah to the gallant ship. Each, as he goes away, will turn to take another look, and watch with straining eye until she becomes but a speck in the horizon. All are delighted with the length and splendor of the prospective voyage. If she is a ship of scientific discovery and adventure, there is a higher and wider interest still, as also a more numerous and more literary assembly on the shore to witness the departure, and to speak of the importance and high character of the enterprise.

The scene we are witnessing now bears a striking resemblance to such an outset upon the broad ocean. A class of young men are weighing anchor and setting compass for a highly important voyage upon a wide sea. Many have gathered to witness their departure, and are already thinking of the things which may await them in their course. A few of sadder temperament find their thoughts dwelling unwillingly on the storms and shipwrecks, which they may be called to encounter. Most, however, more wisely are thinking of the beautiful lands which they may see, the gainful cargoes they may take in, the scientific researches they may pursue, the splendid discoveries and rich literary acquisitions which they may make."

The theme of Dr. White's sermon shaped and defined Brier's future at the school and beyond. Brier had been at the Wabash prep school for three years, and his experience began to test his leadership abilities. We learn of his adventures through a second story in the annals of the literary debate societies. It is a story of intrigue and division. Schools allowed secret debating societies to be formed by students in order to train the power of the orator. It was hoped at the time that the intelligent, witty, razor tongued debater would be called upon to be a leader in society. Brier was not to be left out. The second literary society at Wabash was the Western Literary Society, and from this group a number of secret literary societies were formed. The purpose of these societies was to prepare students as to become serious scholars and community leaders. This preparation involved gaining experience in debate, and constructing an essay for public address that was eloquent, persuasive, and moved people into action. One of the activities of the society was to obtain books of great scholarly value, which would form a private library for the secret society. Students believed this library would propel members of the society to academic superiority. On occasion, these societies were so competitive that their efforts to obtain a library were not always honorable.

In the Wabash context this simple schoolboy controversy about gaining control of the literary society library created a school-wide civil war. Infiltrators wanted to split the society so their society would be victorious. The discussion of the Euphronean literary society gives us clues about the conflict. The resolution by Mr. Veal on June 28, 1844 is self explanatory:

"Whereas several members of the Atlantian Society have at an unusual time of the year joined the Euphronean Society in such a manner as itself to create suspicion of their intentions. Whereas on several occasions they have voted together and in unity on questions brought by the society thus forming a society in a society. They elected their officers on the last evening in such a manner as clearly to show (their) previous concern. Whereas on the proposal of two Atlantians for membership in this Society they to a man voted for them, and after means were used to prevent their election became angry at their rejection, thus evincing that they had a secret design in their election. Whereas they endeavored to bring up a motion of the previous evening to abrogate an article of the constitution providing for a division of the Society, knowing that from the absence of some of the members they had a majority and therefore the power of settling that resolution to suit their own interests. Whereas on being accused by Mr. Brier of intending to divide the Society and take half of the Library, Mr. B. O. Deming told Mr. Brier that 'he had either listened to their proceedings or some person had told him and if he did so again he would get his neck twisted.' Whereas by the various boasts and threats they have shown that they have no regard for the Euphronian Society. Resolved—that we believe that the said Atalantians—are unfriendly to the best interest of the Euphronian Society and therefore ought to be and hereby are expelled from all connection with the Society. On July 5, 1944, the expelled students protested against the action of the Society on the grounds that the expulsion was unconstitutional, was accomplished by secret collusion, and amounted to condemnation "without evidence, trial, judge, jury, in direct opposition to the fundamental principles of common law and justice." The rebels further held that the action of the majority amounted to a legal splitting of the Society: hence they were entitled to a share of the library and the funds of the Society in proportion to the amount of the contributions made by the expelled members to the funds of the Society. The protest continued with the declaration that the resolution was "dishonest, highhanded, and tyrannical" but contrary to the fundamental rights of the citizens of the United States."[1]

Throughout this conflict, William Brier stood in a position of leadership gathering information about the conflict from both sides—as if he were standing close enough so that he would not be surprised by the movements of either. At the same time it was clear where he stood. These leadership, negotiations, and conflict brokering skills would help him in the decades to come in the divisions that would vex the Presbyterian Church.

William Wallace Brier as college student
Photo courtesy of Doug Kinney

Brier as College Student at Wabash

He was still a maturing young man. Wabash was an all-male teacher's training school, and young men had to look elsewhere to gain the eye and favor of the girls about town. William began to make visits to Eliza Duncan, the niece of Professor Hovey, who stayed near the campus with her uncle. A letter is preserved in the school archives, in which Mrs. Hovey wrote to this niece, Eliza Duncan, who was a trained schoolteacher, after she traveled to the city of Terra Haute on a visit. In the letter dated May 4, 1846, she notes:

"But I assure you we shall all be glad to see you at home when the right time comes and I shall give up the keys with a cheerful heart. I laid my pen down to receive a call from Mr. Brier, Mr. William Brier, the third or fourth one he has made since you left. How many did he make in the same length of time when that little Ross girl was here? We will see if they are continued as frequently after her return."[2]

In the months to come, Brier's expression of interest in Eliza would lead nowhere, and as we will see, a romance began to blossom with another young woman by the name of Elizabeth Naylor.

CHAPTER 3

Providential Mentors

William Brier continued as a student, growing and maturing in his schooling, and already preaching in a nearby farmland parish. Lane had less than a hundred students and seven professors, and in the three-year Biblical training program, it was expected that each student engage in a visionary evangelism and church planting. In Cincinnati the priority was to reach into frontiers and establish a growing congregation. Few seminary graduates were assigned to existing churches but would be sent to a new area. Brier heeded the call to church planting ministry, but the seeds would lie in his heart for a few years while he trained for ministry. Perhaps this is why Brier completed a two-year program, instead of the standard three. He was eager to get into the field of church planting.

It was expected at the time that anyone preparing for Presbyterian ministry be trained in the liberal arts, the English Bible, and theology. In addition they were required to have both mentoring and formal training in theology, church history, sacraments, church government, Hebrew, Greek, and Latin. The training for ministry demanded translation of a Latin treatise, an interpretation of an assigned portion of Greek scripture, a lecture on a theological subject, and a popular sermon. Brier dove into this stimulating pool of intellectual leaders, and was fortunate to be exposed to some of the leading lights of religious thought of his day.

Brier's Connection with Henry Ward Beecher

For many years, it was evident that Brier had a hunger for the blessing of a mentor, who was a father figure of the faith. For Brier this was satisfied through a friendship with Henry Ward Beecher. Brier hosted Henry Ward Beecher to speak to a gathering at the Euphronean Society, on July 18th, 1843. The *Indiana State Journal* of August 2, 1843, reported that he delivered his address "in a manner apparently very gratifying to a large and intelligent audience." However, in the remarks he made some derogatory comments about the upcoming gubernatorial race of Matthew Simpson, which led to significant conflict at the school and in the political area.

Henry Beecher was a school trustee and preached often at the school. Brier would grow closer to him through personal observation. Beecher was Brier's kind of pastor. In addition he reflected the love for gardening and farming that Brier had in his soul. Beecher launched the 1845 periodical, *The Indiana Farmer and Gardener* as a semimonthly journal devoted to the garden, orchard, and farm. Wherever he pastored, he always maintained a farm with an orchard of a number of rare fruit trees.

Beecher would ultimately link Brier with other significant leaders. After Brier completed three years at Wabash, he needed to make a critical choice between teaching or pursing seminary. Wabash College had a stated purpose to train men "as teachers and for the ministry." Now William had completed his teacher training, but had a higher calling to ministry, yet had no money to continue studies in seminary. Back home on the farm, he had four other brothers and sisters in line to continue their college education. William's resources were limited. Due to his father's failing health, his younger brother was looking after the family farm and there was little income. William's desire was to study further, but it seemed as if a mountain stood in the path of his going further.

Brier's Connection with Rev. Lyman Beecher

Circumstances led Brier beyond Wabash College, and created interesting connections from his past and linkages into his future. Henry Beecher's attention was drawn to a few of the outstanding students at the college, and he recommended him to his father, Lyman Beecher, for a scholarship to attend Lane Seminary. William Brier was one of three students recommended, and Lyman Beecher took on the young student, providing a full scholarship to Lane Seminary in Cincinnati. [3] These scholarships were awarded to the students who showed the most promise to preach in frontier communities of the west. In his autobiography, Lyman records a letter to his daughter Catherine, which portrays his passion for the Indiana/Illinois frontier and the west beyond.

"The moral destiny of our nation, and all our institutions and hopes, and the world's hopes, turns on the character of the West, and the competition now is for that preoccupancy in the education of the rising generation, in which Catholics and infidels have got the start on us."[4]

His personal passion was to train ministers for the westward expansion of Protestant Christianity. Dr. Beecher preached at a Lane Seminary chapel service about the open doors in the Far West.

"This year we have also found the Far West: which had been here, and there, and everywhere, and yet we had not been able to reach it. Before we could get to it, it was gone. Fifty years ago, it seemed to be in Central New York; forty years ago, in New Connecticut; twenty years ago, in Indiana and Illinois: and fifteen years ago, to be meditating the passage of the Upper Mississippi. But, this year, it has made its permanent settlement on the shores of the Pacific, and men are calling unto us from thence for the bread of life—the Pacific unto the Atlantic-deep calling unto deep."

Dr. Beecher, enlarged these themes in his published book titled, *A Plea for the West*. "It is equally plain that the religious and political destiny of our nation is to be decided in the West. There is the territory, and there soon will be the population, the wealth and the political power." [5] This was a consistent theme for Beecher, as he highlights later in his book. "But whatever we do, it must be done quickly; for there is a tide in the human things which waits not,—moments on which the destiny of a nation balances, when the light dust may turn the right way or the wrong. And such is the condition of our nation now."[6]

Beecher had a provocative way of portraying the urgency of the call as the epic struggle for the soul of the country. The context for this call to the frontiers of mission was often done within the context of a difficult mission work in frontier farmland of Ohio and Indiana. Indiana was mostly woodland in 1831, but by the 1840's there were intensive efforts to log and clear the rich land and get it under cultivation.

Brier's Years at Lane Theological Seminary

In order to further his training in theology, Brier would have to surmount new challenges and tests to his faith. But faith moved the mountains. Through the good references of Brier's mentors, Presidents Dr. White and Henry Beecher, he was offered a full scholarship to Lane Seminary, where he joined a class of 17 students to enter in the fall of 1846. After spending the summer helping on the family farm, Brier arrived at the booming Cincinnati town of 30,000, a factory town with significant foundry, factory, and mill. It was a cultured town, often referred to in conversation and publication as the "Queen City of the West."

Ohio was proud to be "a slave free state". This attracted many Presbyterian and Congregationalist settlers, including pastors and business leaders interested in theological education. Lane Seminary was established in Cincinnati in 1829 in honor of Ebenezer and William Lane, who had pledged $4,000 for the new school. This pledge was joined with a generous gift by the Kemper family of 60 acres in the Walnut Hills section of the city.

Opening in 1832, Lane Seminary was viewed as a forward outpost of civilization in the western territories. The Lane trustees made a bold move when they called Lyman Beecher as the first president of the seminary. As a strong teacher he was controversial on a number of social issues. The conflicts at Lane reflected the broader social and theological conflicts of the era. Indeed, many looked to Lane as the key to success of either the "Old School" or the "New School" view of tradition, denominationalism, doctrine, and public engagement in contemporary politics. Lyman Beecher's social activism was merged with a conservative impulse toward moderation. Beecher and his colleagues pursued a New School agenda: they were dedicated to cooperating with Congregationalists and others in mission and education efforts: they were involved in social reform movements like abolition, temperance, and Sabbath legislation; and they tended to consider (Protestant) denominational distinctions to be less significant than joining in the educational and evangelistic tasks facing the churches in the West.

True to his conservative moral and theological roots, Lane was passionately anti-slavery. It is no secret the Beecher family were leaders in the school in its anti—slavery positions, and practical action. Beecher's daughter Harriett (later, Beecher—Stowe), was still living with her father during his Lane presidency. It is likely that William Brier met her during the monthly student gatherings at the Beecher home.

Beecher insisted the seminary teach about ministry that was militant in action on behalf of the Kingdom of God. Pastors who longed to see the "Kingdom City of Zion" established on earth, would need to stand up against the injustice of society. Students who graduated and became pastors were now pulled into a national debate on social issues firsthand alongside gifted orators and social commentators of the day. The role of many pastors in the congregation and community was not simply as a Bible teacher, but also as a prophet focusing the searchlight of scriptures upon the needs of society. These pastors saw the purpose of the Church to transform society, until it grew up into "a perfect Zion", as the religious image of a perfect city of God.

Lane Seminary reflected diverse training. The first major area of study was outlined in the school handbook. "There were four major departments: Biblical Literature, Church History and Polity, Systematic Theology, and Sacred Rhetoric. Students took courses in all four departments, each of their years. The Biblical students read the Bible and commentaries, both ancient and modern."

A second area of study expanded their breadth of church history. They used Stowe's texts and those of other professors and then compared them to the commentaries of Calvin and other reformers. Church History, which seemed to receive the least emphasis, combined an overview of major theologians both ancient and modern with a study of the polity of the Congregational and Presbyterian churches. A third area of study included reading major philosophers, including Hume, Locke, and Berkeley, as well as theologians such as Augustine and Calvin, and American interpreters such as Dwight and Edwards. Finally, in rhetoric the students began by presenting Biblical studies for criticism, which were developed into sermons and other lectures to be presented for class discussion and criticism. All in all, it resembled a curriculum very familiar to a modern student, with perhaps a little more emphasis on philosophy and theology that of the average seminary in the twentieth century.[7]

Brier meets Horace Bushnell

Brier met the New Englander legend, The Rev. Horace Bushnell, when he lectured as a visiting professor at Lane. Bushnell was a leading light in New England Liberalism, and served as the pastor of the North Church in Hartford, Connecticut. During the 19th Century he was a prince of the American pulpit, with his sermons commonly printed in newspaper columns around the country. Author of twelve books about theology, education, and civil society, he had a unique voice to speak to the social issues of the nation. Bushnell would be known for his voice as a trumpet for Liberal Protestantism. A complex man, with a magnetic personality, he attracted and repelled many leaders of the day. He excelled as a preacher, scholar, lawyer, sportsman, and adventurer. Never content to be idle, he had a wide variety of interests and agendas. Brier was captured by Bushnell's robust energy, his love for the rugged wild of the west, and his civil order. Bushnell was also pragmatic in his passion for education and reaching a generation with the Gospel.

Bushnell was an advocate for city parks and was instrumental in the establishment of Hartford's Bushnell Park and New York City's Central Park. He had a knack for civil engineering, and held two United States patents on home heating devices; he also drafted routes for railroads and canals to speed regional transportation toward the frontiers. He was an advocate of education, and worked for the countywide support for local educational systems and standards. As we will see later, his connection with Brier helped him be an instrumental figure in the establishment of what is now the University of California at Berkeley.

We know there was a personal chemistry between Brier and Bushnell that created an endearing relationship—as evidenced by their correspondence a few years later. Brier continued his studies, readying to graduate and then return to save the Western frontier.

CHAPTER 4

Chosen to Plant Churches

His appearance hid his potential. At this time, Brier stood at medium height, 5 foot ten. He was slender, had a purposed stride, as if he were walking in from the farm field. His hair was brown with a streak of sun-bleached blond. When he smiled it was as though a beam of sunlight had burst through the fog of a spring day. Yet clouds often obscured the comeliness of his face; he was known at times to be shy, retiring, even aloof and arrogant. At other times he seemed forceful, brash, and overly confident. But most of all, he was known for his diligence and stubborn fortitude, the persistence of a farmer who continued rain or shine, never willing to give up on a crop until the harvest was fully brought in, and he caught the eye of those who had their eye on the harvest.

Brier was the kind of leader they needed. Agents for the American Home Mission Society recruited him to church planting ministry. They promised a yearly salary of $500.00, with a promise of two years' support until he could get salary pledges from the congregation he founded. It was a difficult calling, but one, which seemed to captivate the imagination, and water the missionary seeds planted deep in his heart. Following his graduation from Lane, it was time for Brier to get involved full-time in the church preaching and planting ministry.

Romney, Indiana lies in a fertile farmland that had been carved out of the swampy forest, some twenty miles from the place of Brier's college training and twenty miles from his boyhood farm near Attica. It was the perfect context for his continued contact with his family, friends, and mentors at Crawfordsville. In March of that year Brier began exploring the villages surrounding Romney and was commissioned into the ministry by the AHMS on April 23, 1848. The Logansport Presbytery (Indiana) ordained him in the same month to a tough assignment.

He was sent by AHMS to take over an abandoned post some miles in the interior. It was a rural farming community at the crossroads of two small roadways. The village had been a preaching post of another pastor who was "starved out" by the lack of adequate financial support for his salary. About five hundred people created a church community with two other denominations already working the fertile soil of the Indiana woodlands—but he would be the first minister to stay and build the church on a solid foundation.

In the Tippecanoe County Historical Museum, is a small leather covered account book on file which has the title written in ink on the front cover, "*Session Book of the 1st Pres. Church of Romney*". The first entry dated October 15, 1843, states that *William Throckmorton had been elected an elder; it was signed by the Rev. G. A. Milben, clerk*. The next entry in 1845 tells of the election of two more elders, David Todd and Samuel Franklin.

The church group had been served by traveling ministers, and was struggling and small. They had no house of worship. The Methodists and the Presbyterians alternated for their services using a large structure called "The Red Barn," a familiar landmark in the early days, on the corner of the junctions between roads 43 and 28. Meetings were held at irregular intervals in the winter. In the 1830's many groups of families moved from Virginia and Pennsylvania to the area, and came together to form a church fellowship: Throckmortons, Inskeeps, Oglebays, Foxes, and Huttons. These two groups felt the need of a good church in the new country. It is interesting that church members debated whether the new church should be Presbyterian or Episcopal. The Presbyterians won.

On May 1, 1848, W.W. Brier was called as the first regular minister by a vote of the congregation who promised $119.00 toward his salary. The minutes of Session for November 18, 1849, declared, "On this day was dedicated our House of worship which cost $840.00 'Blessed be the name of the Lord'." Signed W. W. Brier, Moderator.

In the list of supporting church members, it is curious that a number of doctors were listed in this rural area, until you link it with the proximity to Wabash College. It appears that teachers of the school were establishing family farms in the area surrounding the water of the Wea Creek. The Session records of July 20, 1848 include a note by Rev. W. W. Brier that "the Rev. Prof. Thompson administered the sacraments of the Lord's Supper." The next entry is that of November 4th, 1848, where, "received by letter of transfer, Dr. Leaming and Mrs. Mary Leaming in to the church and fellowship from the 10th Presbyterian Church of Philadelphia." During Brier's pastorate, the first Church building was erected, a simple one-room frame building in town. Across the front was a Doric porch supported by large square columns. This was an impressive site in the newly formed village.

Working at Romney, Brier was able to make frequent trips to Crawfordsville to complete a Master's Degree from Wabash College. In those days a college student verified that he was building a personal library, working at the disciplines of reading, teaching, and writing. After certifying his ongoing research he was granted his Masters diploma.

Brier's Quarterly Reports to the AHMS

His first letter comes just three months after his arrival in the field. It is his second report to the AHMS board, but the first quarterly report we have in existence. These reports through letters would continue for decades with the AHMS. Brier was twenty-seven years old. This was his first experience both in rural churches and in sharing his pastoral leadership between two small struggling congregations. This tough challenge would imprint the skills and calling for a lifetime work within the Presbyterian Church in difficult communities.

In the spring of 1848, the Logansport Presbytery ordained Brier, and he began attending the quarterly meetings of Presbytery. But his real heart support was through the staff and New School Pastors associated with the AHMS. The first letter we have dates from his assignment in this farming community amidst the scrub and swampy forests of the Indiana wilderness. Missionaries had little support or structure of accountability in those days. They often worked solo, cooperated broadly with other denominations, and yet had only the society to report to. Perhaps this explains W. W. Brier's interest in going to California after 17 months of ministry in Indiana.

Brier Letter #1

Romney, Tippecanoe County, Indiana April 23, 1848
To: Rev. Milton Badger D.D. and Rev. Charles Hall D.D.

It is with gratitude to God and sincere thanks to your society that I sit down to make my first quarterly report. My labors have been uninterrupted. I have preached on the average of four times each week to good congregations throughout this country. My health has not been very good: for circumstances call for more labor than I ought to perform. I have received into the church (on examination) eight persons. The Sabbath schools are growing in interest. The attendance on the preaching of the word is increasing. I have frequent calls to preach at new places from five to twenty miles distant. Since my last report we have lost one of the principle supporters of our church. He had united with the church but a few weeks before his death. He departed triumphantly in Christ. Two of the trustees of the church, which we are building, have fallen (dead) within the last three months. Yet I feel strong in my faith in my God, which he will build up his Zion here.

There is due $50.00 in my last installment.

Yours truly,
William Wallace Brier.[8]

The Presbyterian Church Split and the Role of the American Home Mission Society.

In order to follow the rest of Brier's career, we must understand the issues that caught him in the middle of powerful movements of the nation, the church, and the spirit of God. The largest issue was the split of the Presbyterian Church into The Old School, and The New School Presbyterian Church. In Stewart Memorial Chapel at San Francisco Theological Seminary, there is a series of stained glass windows that reflect events and leaders that have been significant in Presbyterian Church history. One of those windows commemorates the split between New School Presbyterians and Old School Presbyterians.

Old and New School church
stained glass windows.
Stewart Chapel STFS Seminary

The seminary narrative booklet explains the symbols in the window. *"Here enlightening with the dates 1837 on the left and 1861 on the right is splitting a church. The split church represents the two major divisions of American Presbyterianism—the first into the New and Old Schools and the second into the North and South. The top triangle depicts the firing of Fort Sumner in 1861: the Civil War divided the Presbyterian Church into north and south. The bottom triangle portrays the discovery of gold in California and the date, 1848: it was this discovery that brought Protestant people to California in large numbers. The four medallions are: (top left) cross, gavel, and chains to represent the chief causes of the divisions—theology, polity, and slavery: (top right) a covered wagon to represent westward expansion: (bottom left) a Confederate flag and the lettering, "CPC 1863" to represent the founding of the Confederate Presbyterian Church, later to become the Presbyterian Church in the U.S."*

In addition of the issues of slavery and the rights of states to determine their own laws, a deeper division between Old School and New School Presbyterians over the centralized planning of the mission strategy. Old School advocates wanted a centrally planned and funded Mission strategy, while New School advocates wanted more freedom to cooperate with other denominations. New School advocates joined the Mission network of the American Home Mission Society. Old School pastors were slightly more conservative in doctrine, but this was not the main obstacle.

Milton Badger and Charles Hall

Most of the letters we have from Brier were sent to the Rev. Dr. Milton Badger and Rev. Dr. Hall. These served for decades both as corresponding secretaries and directors of the AHMS in New York City. They were known for many things but were legendary in their passion for supporting the work of planting churches.

Dr. Milton Badger was a forceful administrator and held beliefs deeply rooted in puritanical attitudes. He was known to be shy, at times bombastic, and always frugal. He held the intellectual portfolio of the team and poured over letters and reports from the mission field with an eye for detail, demographics, and geography.

Dr. Charles Hall was cut out of a different cloth. He was known as a pastor to pastors, and prone to believe both sides of an argument at the risk of diminishing his own power. He was the easy touch with a financial request, and had to have the accountability of Dr. Badger and the society's treasurer to keep his kindness from exhausting the treasury.

Every day, Badger and Hall would receive a sack of letters from missionaries around the country and the world. They would labor each day to read the letters, editing them for the society newsletter, responding to both donors and missionaries for the next day's mail, and enclosing the drafts of financial support for each mission staff. Over the years of leadership, thousands of letters were filed by name, state of service, and month of correspondence. It is from microfilm pictures of these files at Tulane University that we have retrieved the Brier letters.

Through the course of their letters we notice that Brier's friendship with Dr. Badger and Dr. Hall would run hot and cold. At times he would write to Charles Hall thinking he would get a fair hearing for his concern. Yet the letter he receives back is from Dr. Badger.

Brier now writes his second letter. In this letter to the society, he attempted to wrestle with his call to ministry, wondering what type of city he had been assigned to. He established himself as an educated man in a swirl of uneducated preachers. In these lines, he suggested that people prefer a Presbyterian pastor, because they appreciate a studied pastor.

Brier Letter # 2

July 25, 1848
Romney, Tippecanoe County, Indiana

Dear Brethren,

I have been looking over some old Home Missionary journals to find a form for a report, but finding none, have concluded to adapt the true Hoosier plan of telling my story just as if no other missionary had ever reported: I hope it will meet your requirements.

First, I will give you some idea of my field of labor and what I have been doing. I am boarding at Romney, the place where Brother Miller has labored for several years. He left last December having been "starved out", as he expressed it. The church here has dwindled down to 8 females and 3 male members, and these are very much scattered, and possess very little of this world's good's—This was the only Presbyterian church within my field when I commenced preaching April last. Rather a dark prospect you think— But what is your society for but to cast light upon such darkness. It is not so dark: there are many sinners here for who Christ has died.

Then I came to this place in the middle of April. I preached three times and then told the people what was the least sum that would procure my services. Principally those who are not professors of religion subscribed more than the required sum in less than a week. Here I have preached to full and attentive congregations, twice every week on the Sabbath and sometimes on weekdays; and I have reason to hope that the Lord will soon visit us with Salvation. The Sabbath school conducted by our church meets at a private house, the Methodist society is occupying the schoolhouse, which was built for a "union meeting house", as well as for school purposes; but they are building a new meetinghouse, so that we will have the old school room.

I think the people will build a house for me to preach in during the coming year. I say "the people" because if the men of the church should give all their property it would not be sufficient to build a house of worship. The Methodist minister preached only once in four weeks. Still we do not expect permission to preach in their house. I regret that there is so little Christian fellowship.

On every other Sabbath I preach at Hickory Grove, eight miles from this place. The people there have built a very comfortable "union church" and a Lutheran minister has organized a church of eight or ten members, which is the only church organization in that region. The people generally like the Presbyterian Church. This Lutheran minister and I preach on different days, so that the people have services every other Sabbath. After Superintending the Sabbath school and preaching, I ride seven miles to West Point, and preach in the afternoon. West Point is a small village situated in the midst of a country, in point of beauty and richness of soil unsurpassed by any in the world. On one side of it is a prairie about 6 by 8 miles in extent, all under cultivation. It is nearly all in corn this year and will average at least eighty bushels per acre. The people give their land no rest; still it does not fail. Through this passes the Wabash and Erie Canal connecting the Lakes of the North with the Ohio River which when finished will be the longest canals in the world. In this region, destined to be so great in wealth, society is without form. Infidelity has here exerted a baneful influence. Twenty-five or thirty copies of the Boston blasphemy-breathing investigator are taken; and a great number of infidel books and tracts are received and scattered through the country—which, like locusts from the bottomless pit, have threatened to devour every green thing. Old exploded objections to the Bible, drawn from astronomy and geology, gotten up in the form of dog-eared pamphlets are palmed off for the truths of science. But I thank my God there are some there who have not bowed the knee to Baal. On the 2nd Sabbath of June, Brother Wilson of Lafayette and I organized a church of ten members." On last Sabbath four other individuals connected themselves with the church.

All but one of the members, are heads of families, and all are of the most respectable class in the community. This church, which is so promising, was organized amid the strongest opposition, opposition of which I would not speak, were it not enjoined in your instructions. It was not from the infidels or universalistic; it was not from the inn keeper or retailers of intoxicating liquors; most of these assisted in procuring my labors at that point; but it was from a man who professed to be a minister of the Gospel. I will not give the particulars. The first boasted that he would crush the "Presbyterian church" movement in the beginning, and then with demonic energy endeavored to carry out his threat.

He went to those who had manifested an interest in having the church organized and endeavored to prejudice them against Presbyterianism; but all his labor was in vain, it was the will of God that this little vine should be planted. At this place my congregation has increased regularly in numbers and in their attention to the word. Last

Sabbath the church was crowded. I preached in a large building erected by a society known by the name of the Christian Church. They are a liberal people and are favorable to all my movements. They have preaching only once in the month and are glad to have me preach in their house. From these facts you see that my field is not devoid of interest. There is a great deal of work to do here—The people are dissatisfied with an uneducated ministry. Often is said, "How can we listen to me speak, who know less than we do ourselves." The people in my field belong to a race of the giants in energy and enterprise. They are becoming intelligent as well as wealthy. But they have no fixed habits of attending church, or listening when they are there. If the preaching is not "eloquent" many of them will stay at home, as they do not feel that it is a duty to go to church when they do not like the preacher. Around such people, if a minister is to accomplish anything, he must have considerable pressure of a high steam locomotive.

I rejoice that I am permitted to sustain the attack on a small portion of this field, but who will stand up for God in this vast region round me? If I could multiply myself by ten, I could then supply this country. I am often led to exclaim, "Who is sufficient for these things? It is not the labor that I regard for I have always labored, and glory in it, but to one just commencing to preach, this field has much to cause trembling.

I wish the treasurer of the Home Mission Society to pay to the order of Mark Newman of the bookseller of NY City the fifty dollars, which was due me on the 23rd of this month. Your society enables me to get books, which we western men need very much there being but few libraries.

Yours,
William Wallace Brier [9]

In this lengthy letter Brier brought news of the frontier and his growing sense of despair over the lack of resources. He was not content with the salary they offered. He revealed passion, vision, and a gracious insight into the nation; the epic struggle of infidels and the gospel. There are themes of hard work, prosperity, a great land of epic proportions and potential for growth. He modeled a cooperative spirit with other churches and denominations, the theme to challenge to the darkness, and the need for new laborers.

He also showed an inner restlessness that would mark his ministry life-long. Not content to settle in one town, he established a base camp as a home, and began to travel like a circuit rider from there. Six months pass, filled with hard work and a growing church and Brier had started additional churches in the town of Wea and West Point, 25 miles to the northwest. In his third letter he provided extensive detail about the struggles of ministry in that barren land.

Brier Letter # 3

"It is a wicked place but God is able to save."

October 25, 1848
Romney, Tippecanoe County, Indiana

Dear Brethren,

This day completed my second quarter of Missionary labor in Tippecanoe County, God has dealt kindly with me. The sickly season is now past, and although I have been much exposed, and have been slightly afflicted with the chills, yet I have preached every Sabbath, and sometimes during the week. I preach half my time in this place. My congregation here continues to be full and attentive. Two persons have united with the church within the last three months.

Every other Sabbath I preach at three different places—two of these I described in my last report. The third place is Granville on the Wabash and Erie Canal. It is a small town on the verge of a rich tract of country under a high state of cultivation. I hesitated whether to make this a preaching point; but it is destined soon to be a place of importance, and the people have had little or no preaching of any kind. I could not forbear going down to Granville, also to preach the Gospel of Christ. I found that the people were very willing to hear preaching, but a part of them knew not how to conduct themselves during services. They would talk and laugh and walk out as if there was no inconsistency in such conduct. They had always been permitted thus to act, and were very much astonished when I gave them a regular lecture of the subject. I think this is brought to an end. It is a wicked place but God is able to save. The people crowd out to hear the words and although I have to ride nineteen miles and preach three times the same day, yet I am constrained to continue. Especially do I feel so now, as a few days since Brother Hoit— a Lutheran Minster, who labored with me in a part of my field, has finished his work and gone to his rest, and left me alone. Perhaps I preach more than I ought, but how can I help it, if I should hold my peace the stones would cry out. The health of this country has been remarkably good this year and God has blessed the people with abundant crops, and I hope and trust that he will add the richer blessing and outpouring of his Spirit.

I suppose you received my last report. I need the money, for unless one is warmly clothed there is danger of freezing to death while riding over these large prairies.

I should like copies of the Home Missionary and all other communications to me would be sent to Romney, Indiana, instead of Lafayette

Yours Truly,
William Wallace Brier.[10]

Through this letter we gather he was hardworking; but the isolation and difficult work was beginning to wear upon his soul. Frontier Indiana was depressing for any pastor, but it was particularly hard upon Presbyterian missionaries. The seminary had instilled in them a passion for intellectual stimulation and taught a high standard of preaching polished sermons that appealed to the intellect. These sermons were difficult to create, and more difficult to deliver in the rough and tumble woodlands. There were few books to read, and many of the settlers were not interested in deep intellectual thought.

It is easy to see that, like other Presbyterian missionaries, Brier regarded the frontier of Indiana as a destitute sea of lost men and women—lost in their passion for success through farming, and lost through apathy toward spiritual growth. Ministers wrestled with the backwoods shunning of "uppity preachers" from the east, and found that as they attempted to preach and instruct in the classic doctrines of the faith they were ignored because they seemed high-minded.

Although the AHMS Society was active in farming the wilderness of Ohio and Indiana, there was a broader wilderness—the emerging opportunity in the news of gold being discovered at Sutter's Creek, California. The following small paragraph appeared at the bottom of page two.

"The *Alta Californian* newspaper, March 15, 1848
Gold Mine Found

In the new water raceway of the Saw Mill erected by Captain Sutter, on the American Fork, gold has been found in considerable quantities. One person brought thirty dollars worth to New Helvetia, gathered there in a short time. California, no doubt, is rich in mineral wealth. Great chances here for scientific capitalist. Gold has been found in almost every part of the country."

This singular newspaper column in The *Alta California* kicked off the rush that would change the entire landscape and population of California. The news was widely copied and included in papers throughout the east coast. News took some months to reach Indiana, which reached Brier as a restless pastor in the dead of winter. The winter of 1848 was unusually harsh and lonely, forcing him to spend weeks confined in his cabin. During those weeks of isolation, he read with great interest the *Home Missionary Magazine*, the following report regarding the growing need in California.

AHMS Home Missionary Magazine
November 1848
Mission to California.

. . . *The American Home Missionary Society has determined that "the time has come when a Mission should be attempted in California." The necessary steps have been taken for sending out immediately one or more missionaries, to commence the enterprise on such a scale as the openings seem to demand, and as the liberality of the Christian public may allow.*

The permanent population of that part of the country west of the Sierra Nevada was estimated, in 1847, at 25,000. Of these 8,000 were Californians, of Spanish descent; 5,000 foreigners, principally from the United States; and 12,000 Indians, who had been brought into connection with the missions of the Jesuits. The rapid increase of commercial enterprise on the coast; the discovery and working of the most valuable quicksilver mines, perhaps, in the world; with the numerous emigrant settlements in the interior valleys, around the bay of San Francisco, and North of it, in the Sonoma districts, and along the Sacramento for 150 to 200 miles—already furnishes abundant occasion for a vigorous mission. And as no such opening is ever left long unfilled by the great enemy, the friends of evangelical religion ought not to give him time to forestall the opportunity of scattering widely over the valleys of California the good seed of the word. Acting in their name, and sustained by their prayers and their liberality, the American Home Missionary Society hopes during the coming winter, to have upon those mountains "the feet of him that publishes peace, that publishes salvation, saith unto Zion, Thy God reigneth."

Brier's heart burned with the desire of this California golden adventure. It was a new calling in life and ministry. He dreamed this could be his chance to build up Zion in a new land. Indiana was covered with westward migrants who were set in their ways. His Romney church had not grown as he expected. Brier had not been well connected with the pastors in Logansport Presbytery, although he had made attempts to do so. The "California promise" offered a way for him to escape and serve God in a new land.

The winters of Indiana were harsh, and disease was widespread. It was easy to daydream of a better life in a better land as waves of influenza and cholera wiped out many settlers in the swampy farmlands.

While the secular press was filled with frequent news of the rush to California, the May 1849 issue of the *Home Mission Magazine* was apologetic for having so little hard news to report regarding the recruits' efforts in California.

Update on California

We are disappointed in not being able to give intelligence respecting the missionaries sent out to California, later than to Feb. 14th. At that time they were at Mazatlan, on the Pacific coast of Mexico, having touched there for a few hours in the mail steamer California. The vessel was exceedingly crowded, having three times as many passengers as she was intended to accommodate. One of the missionaries, Rev. J. W. Douglas, was suffering from indisposition, brought on by fatigue in crossing the Isthmus on foot, some four weeks previously. It was expected that his illness would yield to the improved attention, which could be given him on reaching San Francisco. Apprehensions were felt that the steamer would not receive her expected supply of coal at San Francisco; and that her crew would desert to go to the gold diggings. In either case, her return to Panama would necessarily be delayed. This will account for the non-arrival of letters from the missionaries, up to the time of putting this number to press.

It was now nine months into his ministry at Romney, and things were getting more difficult for Brier. Brier followed the heartbeat of excitement with a new letter to the board.

Brier Letter #4

Romney, Indiana

January 23, 1849

> *"O that the Lord would send reapers,*
> *strong men to gather in this worthy harvest of souls!"*

Dear Brethren,

This day completes my third quarter of missionary labor in Tippecanoe Co. Indiana. My labors have been abundant. I have preached four times per week on an average at my four stations, besides much visiting as a pastor. I have received four persons into this church during the last quarter. The attendance at the house of God has been good and I humbly hope, that there has been good done in the name of the Lord Jesus.

There is a decided change in the moral aspect of our communities; intemperance, infidelity, and vice of every description are commencing to hide their heads. Your missionary, with fear and trembling, entered the field, which nine months ago lay scathed and desolate as a prairie over which a fire hath passed. Our work here is commencing to show signs that springtime and summer are at hand; and call loudly for another laborer. O that the Lord would send reapers, strong men to gather in this worthy harvest of souls! The Home Mission Society is doing a great work in this wide valley.

I received a few days ago your (financial) draft for last quarter and must request another "quarterly" payment ($50.00 now due.) Pardon this brief report, as I am pressed. Send us aid. Are there no men?

Yours,
W. W. Brier[11]

In this letter, Brier pointed to the transformation in society that was affecting his ministry. In the late nineteenth century pastors were esteemed by community members as the high priests of social order in society. Many people believed that as pastors imposed decency and order on a community, there would be a renewed hope of social transformation in society. And he points to this in his letter, "There is a decided change in the moral aspect of our communities; intemperance infidelity and vice of every description are commencing to hide their head." Every pastor was called upon to transform communities for the sake of the Kingdom of God, and to influence the behavior of all citizens.

CHAPTER 5

A Calling to Build Up Zion!

When the AHMS Office received a missionary letter, they would send a return letter the next day with a financial draft. The draft was a crude handwritten check, to be given to the local bank, and mailed to general delivery in the city where the missionary was working. Badger and Hall would also reply with thank you letters to the donors who had made financial contributions to the society.

Badger and Hall must have been interested in Brier's letters, as he had a way of creating a poetic image of his work in epic proportions. His letters were edited by Dr. Hall, and included regularly in the *Home Missionary Magazine*. In the following report, he mentions for the first time his concept of Zion, in the context of "the Lord has been laying the foundations upon which to build His Zion in these ends of the earth." The image of Zion, the city of God, was a powerful motivation to New School ministers. It is a portrait of the New Jerusalem, Heaven on Earth, and God come down. Zion was a hallmark of revivalist preaching in the Presbyterian tradition, and often motivated pastors to envision the transformation of society. By doing so, he shares his spiritual vision and with his AHMS supervisor, suggesting that the church is in a building phase, and that "my labors have been abundant."

His report at the end of his first year follows:

Brier Letter # 5

> *"Spiritual graves have commenced to open, and the breath of the Almighty weeps upon the slain in Zion, for her desolations have been very great."*

Romney, Tippecanoe County, Indiana
Rev. Milton Badger, D. D.
Rev. Charles Hall

March 1st, 1849

Dear Brethren,

I herewith communicate the statistical report required. But it will present an imperfect view of what has been accomplished in the name of the Lord, under the patronage of your excellent society. It seems to me that during the eight months which I have spent in this wide-spread field, the Lord has been laying the foundations upon which to build His Zion in these ends of the earth.

At this place we have raised funds to build a church. A deep religious interest now pervades the community. Spiritual graves have commenced to open, and the breath of the Almighty weeps upon the slain in Zion, for her desolations have been very great.

The number of the members in the little church has been doubled within the last six months. You will observe a deficiency in contributions to benevolent societies. I have not asked the people to contribute to these great and good objects because of the peculiar state of affairs. They have subscribed $630.00 to our colleges, $400.00 to build a church, and $200.00 toward my support, also some small sums for other purposes. I expect soon to establish a system of contributing. With these things promised I submit the following statistical report.

The Lord has blessed me with health to fill all my appointments, except one, during the year but the labor is severe; and we can only look for that rest which remaineth for the people of God.

Yours Truly,
W. W. Brier.

P.S. I am at a loss to know how to make application for more aid from your society. Unless I receive more than the sum, which you granted last year, I cannot remain in the field. I *have only as yet, received $119.00 from the people to whom I preach. I will probably receive more but there is no certainty, as the subscriptions were principally by persons not professors of religion. For the coming year the Romney Church (or Wea) propose to raise $150.00. It contains 22 members. Attendance at preaching is about 100, or the house is full. There is a Methodist Church here of about 30 or 60 members. The nearest church of any other denomination is 8 miles distant—maybe 12 miles.*

The West Point church, which I organized last June, refuses to be considered a Presbyterian Church. The elders say they will pay me for the time that I preach there, and are making arrangements so to do. There is no certainty about what will be raised at the other place where I preach. If you grant $200.00, my salary will probably amount to $400.00. The church here has spoken of giving me a call to be the pastor, but I am not willing to be settled and would prefer to be a missionary in Tippecanoe County.[12]

In this report, Brier offers them what they want: statistics and stirring commentary on his experience in Indiana. The statistics reported in this letter would be packaged with other churches, and listed in the annual mission report for the American Home Mission Society. The attendance of 24 in his Romney church must have gratified the AHMS. The library of 400 books for the Sabbath school must have been extraordinary for such a farming community and is reflective of the clustering of teachers and professors from Crawfordsville. Brier was deeply influenced by their model of teaching, preaching, and farming in an area near the school.

In this letter, Brier talks of the transformation of society, and of the hard work involved in the planting of churches. " . . . It seems to me that during the eight months which I have spent in this wide spread field, the Lord has been laying the foundations upon which to build His Zion in these ends of the earth."

It was a difficult work that called deep within his soul. Yet he was revealing the ongoing struggle of making ends meet on the salary they offered him. His plan was not to accept the call as pastor of the church in order to be a traveling evangelist. On one level, this role would assure that the society would continue to support him at the $400.00 level. On another level, it would free him to be a touring evangelist, not attached to any congregation. There is a common personality style in the life of evangelists. They are often effective communicators, and great storytellers with an occasional tendency to exaggerate. Evangelists show a driven restlessness, a passion for souls, and a desire to reach out to new towns and peoples. Yet, there is also a downside to the personality style. The task is so vast they easily get overworked and overwhelmed. Brier writes, "The Lord has blessed me with health to fill all my appointments, except one, during the year but the labor is severe; and we can only look for that rest which remaineth for the people of God."

Evangelists also often show a brusque impatient with themselves, and those they work with, and there is also a tendency toward paranoia of those in authority above them. Men and women with this personality structure need constant reassurance that they are in good favor with God and their earthly boss.

CHAPTER 6

1848-1849: Gold Rush Fever

There is great fruit and prosperity in Brier's ministry, but a fever that began to afflict him was not a medical virus, but Gold Fever! The society marveled at the promise of mineral and agricultural resources in the area, and the assured flood of pioneers who would go to be a part of it. This created a growing vision for the AHMS society to recruit church planters.

As the mission society's appeal for missionaries fell into Brier's hands it pulled at the strings of his heart. He claimed it as his own call, but he was clearly torn already by his separation from his family in Attica, Indiana. Now he was longing to move across the continent, and wondering if he could minister alone.

His resolution came, and he volunteered for service. He became one of five missionaries who responded to the call and initiated correspondence with the AHMS. Brier's letter is clear that he is eager to get to work.

Brier Letter # 6

"I have long had a desire to plant my feet upon the western shores of our continent."

Romney, Indiana

August 22nd, 1849

Dear Brethren

I wish to make an inquiry in respect to the California Mission. I have long had a desire to plant my feet upon the western shores of our continent. And now I feel the time has come: circumstances have brought it sooner than I expected. I wish to go but have not the means.

Please let me know whether you design sending more men soon. Also, what is the probability of my receiving an appointment? Brother Wilson of Lafayette thinks I can appear before your board as well recommended as any other man for that kind of work.

I have a strong indescribable desire to preach the gospel to the thousands who are rushing to that far off land. Multitudes have gone from this state with their families. I would not be a stranger there. I know not why I desire so much to leave home and friends to go, but so it is. Will you send me a line soon?

Yours truly,
William Wallace Brier

Brier was hard at work networking his colleagues for personal recommendations for the AHMS society to select and support him. He showed a passion beyond the shadow of a doubt. He emphasized his connection and fit for the frontier work. But he was not alone. It seemed as if the whole social structure of Indiana was being emptied of anyone who had an entrepreneurial bone in his or her body. Farmers, contractors, merchants, bankers, teachers, laborers, and now even preachers dreamed of a new society based upon gold. As Brier noted, "I know not why I desired so much to leave home and friends to go, but so it is." Perhaps it was the harsh winter of 1848/49 combined with the devastating turmoil of cholera that made the people of Indiana open to gold fever. Here is how his seventh letter reads:

Brier Letter # 7

"I believe that our God, who feeds the fowls of the air,
will not permit his servants to suffer if they labor faithfully."

Also dated August 22, 1849

Rev. John Hall, D.D.
Rev. Milton Badger, D.D.

Reverend Brothers,

The first quarter of my second year's labor as your missionary in Tippecanoe ended on July 23rd. The reason I have not reported sooner is that I mistook the date of your letter for the date of my commission and did not notice but that they were the same until today. During this quarter, I have preached regularly at the places formerly described three times per week. There is nothing of special interest to report. I see a constant advancement in the affairs of Zion.

The improvement in singing at this place is astonishing. Last year it grated on the ear like the sound of a nail factory; now we have a choir, which would not suffer in comparison with the way in which it performs like a city church.

The subscriptions towards my support were not as great as I expected. Last year the people of the world raised the principle part this year they depend on the church to retain me. Yet I hope to be able to live and labor. In these large Western fields we have no time to look after temporal matters.

As ministers, we all have more work to do than we can do. I believe that our God, who feeds the fowls of the air, will not permit his servants to suffer if they labor faithfully. We have been severely scourged by the Cholera here, but it is abating. In the winter, I expect to raise collections for the A.H.M.S. It is the best time and I think your society is doing more according to your means than any other in the world, and deserves a great part of the contributions of American Christians at this convenience for the amount due.

Yours truly,
William Wallace Brier

Although he was eager, he was clearly distressed by his field of labor. The workload of the church planter was stressful. The Sunday expectations upon a minister were overwhelming. Most frontier pastors preached three times, at three different churches or preaching points, often with significant mileage in-between.

Sickness was a major uncertainty in missionary life. Reflective of the medical expertise of the time, and unusually susceptible to the waves of disease that would sweep through the frontier, a missionary lived on the edge of life and death. This was a calculated part of the call to missionary service but often a painful part when the life demanded was not your own, but your family and children. Brier wrote in his second year of ministry that three of the elders of the church died from the cholera epidemic.

He was not ready to give up. Brier believed in the Biblical admonition to ask, seek, and knock. He asked for release to California, and would not stop until he got it. His gold fever continued, and in four months he had not heard a response from the AHMS. He felt trapped by the wheat fields and the swampy riverbanks that flowed through his area. The summer mosquitoes must have been dreadful.

In his eighth letter to the Missionary Board, William Brier revealed that he was thoroughly bitten by Californian Gold fever. He must have been anguished by not receiving a response to his request, so he brought it up again.

Brier Letter # 8

> *"Those who sow in tears shall reap in joy."*
> *"I am much interested . . . the California Mission."*

Romney Indiana

October 30ᵗʰ, 1849

Dear Brothers,

My second quarter of the second year of Missionary labor ended on the 23ʳᵈ of October. My report has been delayed a few days on account of my absence at Synod. I have preached regularly at three places, and irregularly at some other places. My congregations are increasing in numbers and seriousness. I have received but one person to the church on examination since my last report.

The Lord has withdrawn his afflicting hand from the people and they are commencing to rejoice in health. It will be necessary for me to receive a draft for the 43.75 due as soon as it will be convenient for you to send it: winter calls for additional expenses on these cold prairies. I trust that the Lord will permit me to report at the end of the next quarter greater success. "For those who sow in tears shall reap in joy."

There is a subject to which I alluded in a communication sent with my last report, about which I am much interested . . . the California Mission. I have not received an answer to my letter, why I know not. If you hesitate lest you might commit yourselves to a person unworthy, be assured that I will not feel that you are under the least obligations, to send me, by answering my inquiries, that is whether you intend sending more missionaries? And whether it would be worthwhile for me to send recommendations.

I refer you to Rev. Charles White, D.D. of Crawfordsville and Rev. J. G. Wilson of Lafayette with whom I exchange pulpits, who will speak of my qualifications. I should like to hear from you soon as I have the offer of a field second in my desire, and I desire to be where I may do most to glorify God and build up the Kingdom.

Yours Truly,
W. W. Brier. [13]

Brier's letter is placed in the file with two postcards sent separately to the society. The first is a letter of reference from Professor White, president of Wabash College, who is both glowing in praise and chilling in honesty about Brier's weaknesses.

Letter of Reference

25 November 1849

Crawfordsville, Indiana

In reference to Rev. Mr. Brier of Tippecanoe County Indiana: If you inquire, my account is a good one of him. I have known him intimately eight years. He is a good scholar, of strong intellectual powers, of sincere piety, of great religious influence and energy, and quite forceful and prophetic in the pulpit.

Every man has some fault. He has a liability to become stubborn and dictatorial when strangely excited. And yet I have not known him in all the aspects, though from his warm temperament and resolute character I have predicted that he probably would do a fine job in the frontier.

He had proved himself a man of much efficiency at Romney. He is one of our favorite graduates, and we can't spare him from Indiana. And I hope he will not leave us. But if he must, I must say there is not a man, in my judgment, in Indiana of more fitting qualifications for California.

But if he goes, what shall we do for a Minister at Romney and West Point, or Hickory Cross where Mr. Brier ministers? That field ought to have two ministers. I was at Romney last Sabbath to dedicate a beautiful little church. We shall in a few weeks, lose other ministers in the neighborhood—one at Dayton, another at Hoobray. We must have more ministers.

Yours respectfully,
Professor White.

This is a most interesting and honest letter. It is incredible that Professor White refers to William Brier's hotheaded anger and stubbornness—a quality which would both energize and humble him over the next decades. Brier's determination and vision would mark his ministry, yet conflict would also mark him as he struggled with his supervisors authority over his life and his authority over others. White's letter also tips off the New York office that there is a pattern of passion and inflexibility.

Meanwhile, he was making plans not only to go to California and also to marry before the sailing. This is quite remarkable, as he has not previously mentioned his romance to the AHMS Board, and he writes of it just five days before the wedding. Brier's next letter is penned just six weeks later.

Brier Letter #9

> *"The throbs of my heart for the salvation of the Anglo-Saxon*
> *nation in California . . . cannot be measured."*

Romney, December 14th, 1849
Rev. Milton Badger
Dr. Charles Hall

Dear Brothers,

I received yesterday your kind letter of the 6th and was much gratified by the information it contained. I have for some years looked upon the western coast of our continent as a field for Christian labor of vast importance, and one which would fill my desires for activity.

The effects of the throbs of my heart for the salvation of the Anglo-Saxon nation in California, upon islands of the Pacific, and upon the millions of China cannot be measured. I rejoice in the prospect of a way being opened for me to labor amid scenes so exciting and so full of promises of assisting in the construction of fortress, and in the elevation of a standard for Jesus Christ, so near to the strong hold of the enemy. You ask to know my plans. I have thought of many things, but have no fixed plans.

I have almost given up the expectation of receiving an appointment; hence have made no arrangements for going out. Any plan, which you, in your wisdom may adapt, will suit me.

I would like to see something of the East before leaving, as I have never been nearer you than Cleveland Ohio. I should like also to visit or go past New York in order to increase my library, if I can procure the means for so doing. I had also thought that it would be advisable to send a house, possibly a church building of light and cheap construction around the cape. What think you of such a design? What would be the probable cost? And what would be the prospect of location near the coast?

I have a little property, which I received in appointment. I will endeavor to convert into money in this I may not succeed and then I will have no funds for any purpose. You inquire whether or not I could go out this winter. This question I cannot decide at present—I had not thought of going before spring. I have engaged to preach here until the first of May, and I fear my people, will be unwilling to give me up even if I should be able to procure a substitute, which is doubtful. I am to be married on the 19th of this month. I leave you to decide the questions as to the route to California.

Will you let me know what you think best about this and other matters? I will
investigate the subject, and see if I can make arrangements for starting before spring.

Yours in Christian bonds,
William Wallace Brier

We notice that Brier was prone to stretching the truth in order to get his way. For example, his comments: "I have almost given up the expectation of receiving an appointment, hence have made no arrangements for going out." In reality, he has been making plans to depart, even in his arrangements to propose marriage with the idea he would go to California. Perhaps he was simply trying to appear humble in the face of his supervisors and funding agency. Brier commented that he owned some property he received "in appointment." It was common practice in those days to provide a plot of land for the pastor, which became their property. In this case, Brier would sell the property and take the money with him to California. This would form a pattern for the future.

He was in line to go to California, but there were a few who had arrived before him. Brier would be the only volunteer to respond out of the 5,000 subscribers to the *Home Missionary Magazine*. And what it more, he had the training of college, seminary, and church planting experience. But the society is not thinking about such problems. It is overwhelmed with the vastness of the calling to California and is in hot competition with other denominations to cover the territory to save souls. Already the Presbyterians are strongly represented on the fields of California. Hunt, Willey, and Douglas organized the San Francisco Presbytery at Monterey on September 21st, 1849. This was the first Presbytery to be established on the whole Pacific Coast. On February 20, 1850, three Old School Presbyterian ministers—Sylvester Woodbridge of Benicia, Albert Williams of San Francisco and James Woods of Stockton—met and organized the Presbytery of California. Within both the Old and New School Presbyterian denomination, five of the first six Protestant missionaries landing in California after the Gold Rush began were Presbyterians.

In this letter he revealed a creative spirit that would drive him to succeed when the odds seemed stacked against him. He suggested the idea of manufacturing a church in New York, disassembling it and sending it by boat around the horn of South America to California. We don't know if the idea he offered of shipping the church building to California was his idea originally or not, but it was put into use in four or five churches over the next decade. This strategy proved workable. Months later, a disassembled prefabricated church structure was shipped to San Francisco and became the Greenwich Presbyterian Church that was led by Rev. Pond.

CHAPTER 7

Marriage on the Eve of Departure

The growing city of Crawfordsville lay some thirty miles to the northeast of his preaching post. Brier returned to this city, which he knew well from his college years. In that familiarity, he found a strange newness to his calling. He further acquainted himself with the Naylor family, as an interested suitor for their daughter. But the acquaintance comes through a connection, and a strategic introduction. Sam Merrill was the brother of Mary Naylor, and made the introductions for Brier. Samuel Merrill was a banker and a promoter of schools in the area surrounding Indianapolis. A passionate Christian, and an elder, he was connected to both Wabash College at Crawfordsville and Second Presbyterian Church in Indianapolis.

There may be connections he made for Brier. Merrill operated a widely respected private school for his children and those of friends. As the leading advocate for State financed education for children throughout Indiana, he called for a state-wide convocation to discuss bringing education to every child. Sam Merrill singlehandedly recruited Henry Ward Beecher to Indianapolis as pastor of Second Presbyterian Church. [14] In that role, he was able to meet the young William Wallace Brier who was one of the promising students. [15] He may have also linked him with his pastor, Henry Ward Beecher.

Brier already knew the Naylor family, but it was inappropriate to move ahead without an introduction. In his second year at Wabash, William Brier met Elizabeth Naylor at the Center Presbyterian Church of Crawfordsville, which was only a half-mile from the Wabash Campus. Elizabeth was the daughter of Judge and Mrs. Naylor of Crawfordsville. She had been born on August 20, 1830, so was only 19 years old at the time. It could have been William Brier's graduation from Seminary, or the remote assignment in church planting that made his heart grow fonder of Elizabeth, but he would need to secure the approval of her parents for their relationship to move toward marriage.

Through Merrill's introduction, Brier went to meet Isaac and Mary Naylor, well-known pillars of the Crawfordsville community. Isaac served at the courthouse as County Circuit Judge. *The County Courts and Lawyers of Indiana* journal of 1917 records that, "Isaac Naylor, of Crawfordsville, who succeeded Judge Porter in 1838, was a native of Rockingham County, Virginia, born July 30, 1790. His parents immigrated to Kentucky in 1793 and to Indiana in 1805, settling in Clark County near Charleston. Judge Naylor was largely self-educated, though he had carried forward his education, studied law and was admitted into practice by the Supreme Court of Indiana in 1818. He married Mary Anderson in 1826 and settled in Crawfordsville in 1833, where he resided until his death. April 26,1873. Judge Naylor served as a volunteer at the battle of Tippecanoe and was justly proud of his record. In fact, he used to claim that if a favor was wanted of him, the way to get it was to start the subject of Tippecanoe. Judge Naylor served as Circuit Judge from 1838 to 1852."

A tintype photo of Elizabeth at engagement.
Photo Courtesy of Doug Kinney

Isaac was known as a wise man, not simply because of his title and role, but because he was a self-educated man. In his actions he revealed he had keen powers of observation and insight into human character and motivation. There was a rugged quality to him; honest, forthright, and centered upon the church.

Mary Naylor was heavily involved in the church, as well as in community social work. Years latter, she was active in the women's suffrage movements. Mary Naylor had a love for leadership in the face of difficulty. Her father served in George Washington's

Army in the conflict at Valley Forge. In a funeral sermon some fifty years later, her pastor, Rev. R. J. Cunningham recounted her strength of character in leadership. "She was a strong, remarkable woman. It is clear that she herself is the source of such bravery tales that she learned at her father's knee, and perhaps she passed on to her young daughter. "[16]

This love for courage and difficult struggles would help her become enamored with her husband, the veteran Isaac Naylor. His first person narrative of the battle of Tippecanoe with the tribes of Indian chief Tecumseh is the lone authentic description from the northern Indiana battlefield.

Mary Naylor was a pioneer in her own right, having organized and taught the first Sunday School in the state of Indiana when she was 16 years old. Known by her friends as both gracious and firm, she provided poise and strength for her husband and her children. At her funeral, a friend recalled that "to the last, her words were seasoned with salt, always in grace, and at last, 'salted with fire' of a heart at whose center glowed in a consuming flame the love of Christ."[17]

Imagine Mary and Isaac Naylor welcoming their daughter's suitor, William Wallace Brier to their expansive brick home on East College Street. At the end of the evening, their agreement to give Elizabeth's hand in marriage to W.W. Brier was in part due to his devotion to the Presbyterian Church they loved, and in part due to the pioneer spirit within him.

It is no small wonder why that daughter, Elizabeth Naylor had a similar attraction to William Brier, the rough-hewn stump preacher who would be drawn to the swampy frontier just 20 miles north of Crawfordsville. She had a love for the Lord, and a passion to see the influence of the church spread.

Yet the young couple would not stay close to home. Newspapers printed front-page stories about the gold mines discovered at Sutter's Creek in California. Many a man and minister hastened to answer the call of the West. Some ministers, serving poor rural parishes took this economic opportunity to exit the mission field and enter the gold field.

The Naylor family could easily read the signals of the pioneer spirit in W.W. Brier. Perhaps they were drawn to the strong, quiet, sometimes brusque farm boy from Rob Roy now turned preacher. They would have to trust their daughter to Brier's care in the wild frontier. We do not know what promises William made to the Naylor family, but we can see from the events that follow, Brier was under extreme obligation to make certain his wife was well taken care of.

Frontier exploration is deeply rooted in the Naylor family—it seemed to be a respectable, even welcomed vocation of risk for the sake of the gospel. They added their blessing to the marriage. Isaac Naylor was a single man when he fought off invaders in the Indian wars, and Mary Naylor's father engaged the enemy on the battlefield. The Naylor's would be uncomfortable with William Brier taking Elizabeth into harm's way but they understood the call of mission to the miners in California. In the end they consented to bless the marriage.

William Brier was happy beyond belief. The wedding took place on December 19th at the Center Presbyterian Church in Crawfordsville. There was no honeymoon, other than the return to the village of Romney, as the couple eagerly packed for departure to California.

Yet all was not sunny with the newlyweds. It seems Elizabeth began to have her doubts about going to California, and William began to open the door to discussions with the Society that they may need to send someone else.

Brier Letter #10

Romney, January 13, 1850
Rev. Dr. Badger

Dear Brother,

I have just received your letter of the 5th (January) and I would have responded to it sooner had I not been absent. In answer (to your question) I will say that if possible, I will be in your city on the first of March. But I wish before starting (my journey to California) from this place to know a few things.

1st. What length of time you will require me to labor in California provided (that once there) I wish to return, which is not probable?

2nd. Will you provide a support in case the people will not? Will you pay all expenses of our outfitting for the journey?

I have no available means of personal support whatever, and all my friends oppose me in my designs (to move to California). My wife shrinks from the design, but I hope the Lord will strengthen her brow. I will proceed in respects to (the purchase and packing of) goods. Would it be best only to take my books to New York? I must have an addition of books to my library. Can books be sent round (the horn) in safety?

I will endeavor to have my pulpits supplied by brethren in the neighborhood (Professor's of the College) for the rest of the year, on the condition the people will release me but very reluctantly.

It will be necessary for the society to pay my last installment, to be divided among those whose (preaching) labors I secure to cover the church. Can you do this?

In conclusion permit me to say that if you have applicants in whom you have as much confidence as in myself, you may feel yourself at full liberty to send one of them in my place. All my friends, and all the ministers say, "Send them, send other men from the

East". It makes but little difference to me as I labor in the service of Christ. I have the same desires as formerly (to go to California) but am at your pleasure.

Write soon. I will wait here until I receive an answer but will endeavor to be ready to start (toward California).

In haste,
W.W. Brier

This created quite a stir in the AHMS society, as his letter sends some mixed messages about his ability to follow through on the call. His first question raises the possibility that he may return to Indiana after a short assignment in California. This must have raised a number of questions in the mind of Dr. Badger and Dr. Hall. Was he fit for the call? Was his wife the one who was placing doubts into his mind?

Yet they gave him the benefit of the doubt, and responded to him with answers to his questions.

Letters often crossed in the mail, and pioneers would use personal couriers to get a letter closer to its destination before mailing it. So there is a flurry of letters back and forth between Brier and the directors. This letter of the 15th of January confirms the call, and asks him to hasten his departure. The board was eager to get him on the road, as he would be the fourth and final appointee they would send to California. The question remains as to what would happen to his current Indiana congregation and preaching points. A second letter, this time signed by both of the directors, answered more of Brier's questions. It gives us a window into the Society representatives who recruited him to help in California.

AHMS Administrative letter #1456

Dated Jan 15th, 1850

I respond to your letter of 14th December that I just received. We think you had better leave for California from your post, as early as is possible. Another Missionary, Mr. Douglas, recently of the Yale Theological Seminary in New York City, is most amiable, excellent young man is going, and intends to leave in the steamer the first of May. If it were possible for you to leave you would go as companion with him, it would be very desirable that you should. The call there was urgent, and the forming period so important, that the least possible delay seems indispensable. Besides, the months of April and May are much cooler and we hear that it is hardly possible for us to do anything toward setting off on such a mission.

The work you have been called to is so important that your people, I suppose would release you at once from your engagements with them and allow you to give yourself immediately to the work of preparation.

But if you must remain with your church till the first of June, then we will make do. We inform you that your contents will be shipped at $24—$36 a ton.

We shall hope to hear from you soon and await your information regarding your departure to California.

If you will give me your arrival date, I shall hope to make your bride's acquaintance.

Yours in Christian Bonds,
Milton Badger, Charles Hall

Yet once the directors received Brier's letter of January 13th, they spell out a detailed response to his questions, by issuing a confirmation letter.

AHMS File letter # 1631

January 30, 1850
Rev. W. W. Brier Romney, Indiana

Dear Brother,

You letter of the 23rd is in hand and was received this morning. We offer these answers in reply to your questions.

1.   *We are not to limit the term of a missionary in California. We will not prevent his continuance, as there may be reasons not to decide what may happen there. A missionary is looked at deliberately and we believe that God has called him to labor in the fields of his vineyard, and that he will go out faithfully to make that the field of his best efforts for the cause of the Kingdom of Christ. Providence prevailing with him, we will not test his conscience once again to go on with the work of his ministry and resources and rewards. If his health fails, or there are other complications or providence—then he should return. We realized of course that if proper concerns arise he should indeed return, then such a case is plainly made. If the cost of getting another missionary upon the ground is too great then we should not think of encouraging him to go with another and settled purpose.*

2.   *We shall expect to hear from you regarding your intentions as to your traveling from Indiana to here. We designate a sum of two hundred dollars or more, with more to follow to assist the purchase of things that you would need to pack and ready for a trip and arrival in California.*

3.   *The Society will expect to give you some assistance while you are then laboring in California, as well, then together with what your receive from your people, you may give us a complete report. We will deduct what you receive from your supporters in the eastern churches once you are out in the west. You may not receive the assistance of the society at all, after you quit the territory, as it will be our desire to have you sustained by a congregation, independently as one and as soon as may be.*

4.   *If the Steamer by which Mr. Brayton is also going out as one missionary is about to depart on March 15ᵗʰ. But to labor side by side with him is a convenient desire. On the other hand, it maybe is necessary to make the congregation advance the money for the tickets, as we have done an advance of $100 each for you and Mrs. Brier to the Isthmus, and $300 each in the Pacific steamer to California. This secures to you a room in third class and your personal effects across the Isthmus will be gained for us for an additional charge. If you should be here by the first of March, you will have sufficient time I think to make your arrangements here, and be ready by the time the steamer leaves. We know this is tight, and you must send us your plans and hope you have done much. We pray the Lord would give you more light and give you strength for this undertaking. If you decide otherwise, you will please give us proper notice within two or three weeks time, so we could sell the ticket to someone else.*

5.   *In relation to your question regarding baggage. The most you can carry with you over the Isthmus, with the enormous cost of transportation will be about 300 pounds for each person. Put it in strong trunks or boxes shaped like them, containing no more than 150 pounds each. All other baggage, goods, and supplies have to be sent round the Cape. You will judge better, perhaps, than me, when you have enough. If it is not with you, or is to be sent there later, they had better be shipped as books, as the freight to many destinations can be sent around the horn with a good degree of safety. The rates I mentioned in a previous letter. I will send you again a check for the amount due you.*

I believe I have now answered all your questions, and given you all the information that is expected before you shall come here. We pray that you may have divine guidance, and may be prepared to tutor many in righteousness.

Yours in Christian bonds,
Milton Badger [18]

You can imagine how this confirmation letter stirred his heart to leave for California. There is some nuance in the letter that leads us to wonder if Brier was testing whether he would be financially supported, should he begin part-time farming or commerce. The board clarifies their intention that as the church is planted, the congregation would fully assume responsibility to pay the pastor's salary.

An inherent conflict of their strategy would quickly emerge. City churches could easily be expected to support a pastor. But churches that were found in rural areas would struggle with their ability to support a pastor, and churches set in the explosive growth of California would have further complications. The percentage of his salary needed to secure housing would either bankrupt the pastor, or lead him into other ministries.

Having married Elizabeth Naylor, Brier writes back a response to confirm that he was ready to go. He has been married for one month, and he took his young bride to his cabin in Romney as he continued his missionary work on behalf of the AHMS until the details of their trip would be confirmed. It was not an easy transition for Elizabeth Naylor Brier, as she left her parents in the city and moved to the cold, wind-swept farmland near Romney.

The Missionary Candidate, William Wallace Brier 1949
Photo courtesy of Doug Kinney

Brier Letter # 11

Romney, Indiana.   February 8th, 1850
Rev. Dr. Badger

Dear Brother,

I have just received your letter of January 3rd, and am gratified by its contents. I have procured the promise of release (from the Romney congregation), which did my church refused, at first. When they voted on my release, they had the impression that if they could prevent me from going at this time I would stay with them another year. But since they have found that I will go in May they have agreed to release me now. I will be in New York about the first of March. I had intended to start next Monday; but it will not be necessary to start so soon.

I have procured an excellent Brother to preach for me the rest of the present quarter at two of my places: and Dr. White and the professors of Wabash College will supply my pulpit here. I will get Rev. Mr. Wilson of Lafayette to make out the report for you and you may send to draft to him to be signed and handled to the brother in Lafayette with whom I will leave orders to pay my supplies.

I thank you for your kind and frank letter. It contained all that I wished to know.

Yours in Christian bonds,
W. W. Brier

There was an interesting Brier family drama that takes place during these months. William Wallace Brier's older brother, James Brier was a trained pastor in the Methodist tradition. He and his wife, Juliet W. Brier were called to the West Coast at the same time, and chose to travel overland in the covered wagon trains.

Writing a letter to a friend on Christmas morning, 1949, James wrote, "Yesterday, I received a letter from my brother, William. He is planning to go to the gold fields to minister to the miners. They will leave Crawfordsville in February, go east, and take a ship from New York. When, and if, he has a church, the American Board of Missions will pay him $600.00 a year. His bride Elizabeth welcomes the adventure, he says."

James and Juliet Brier followed the example of his Brother William and Elizabeth Brier in going to California, but they signed up for a wagon train west because he thought it would be quicker. Their overland route was just months after the winter tragedy of the Donner Party, which perished in the northern high mountains near Lake Tahoe.

The James Brier family joined the Jayhawker party in seeking a shortcut through the southern mountains. The trail was lost, and the party divided and nearly died lost crossing the great desert. They would languish on the trail for 20 weeks, and four of the members of the party would die in the Mojave Desert before the survivors arrived in southern California. Juliet Briers diary names the vast wasteland they were trapped in, "The Death Valley"—a name that lasted.

Brier' Supervisor Sam Hopkins Willey

By the time Brier met him, Sam Hopkins Willey had been in California a year and a half. The tall and lanky, New Englander, was said to have a stature beyond his years. His accent and demeanor was firmly rooted in the East coast of his upbringing, and Dartmouth education. What he exhibited in the coolness of a crisp and precise speech pattern, he more than made up for in his personal warmth and passion for the gospel and for the people of the frontier of California.

While in Dartmouth he volunteered to go to California with his classmate Isaac Brayton. Willey was a scholar the one who wrote prolific letters back home, often calling upon East Coast sensibilities and resources to meet the frontier needs of California. He would later be recognized as a visionary, a seer who would fight to see the spreading influence of Education. His friends saw him as cordial and fair, a warm pastor who treated the ministers under his care and his flock. He was an encourager, not a particular visionary or strategist, but was involved in his church and in the pastoral networks.

The window on Sam Hopkins Willey
From Stewart Chapel at SFTS

"Samuel Willey is standing is front of his desk with a pointer in his hand. Behind him on the left is the Campanile tower of the University of California, which he was instrumental in founding, serving as acting president from 1862 to 1868.

The top triangle shows the pipe organ he brought around the horn for the Howard Street Church of San Francisco.

When Willey first arrived in California, he served as chaplain to the to the United States troops at Monterey, symbolized in the bottom triangle by the cross, gun, and saber. He was the first commissioned missionary of any Protestant denomination in California as depicted by the scroll with the missionary cross in the top left medallion. The Seal of the University of California, in the top right medallion, along with the lamp of knowledge and a library of books in the two bottom medallions represent his scholarship. The books also represent the first public library in the State, which he started in Monterey."

The AHMS Board wrote to Rev. Sam Hopkins Willey, one of the three Presbyterian pastors already in California, with news of Brier's appointment, and a sense of urgency about his departure date.

The letter from Dr. Hall, AHMS dated February 16, 1850 to Rev. Willey, raises this hopeful observation:

"The other missionary under appointment is W.W. Brier, of Indiana. He is a graduate of the College in Crawfordsville, a student of Lane Seminary, and has been home in the ministries. Dr. White of Crawfordsville, his professors at Lane, and many others send him the highest regards, and he is ready to go into the field that we send him. We hear from his people that he is more than ordinary and we are sending him to you may please you in this regard. He has lately been married and we suppose this will help him. Their passage is not engaged, and might be on the first steamer, if he could come as soon as he is available."

The appointment of Brier was welcome news to Rev. Willey, who would emerge as California supervisor for AHMS, and Brier's direct supervisor. Brier would have to wait for over six months before he would meet him face to face, but he was joining a small circle of Presbyterian pastors struggling to preach the gospel in California. As we will see, Brier's name and reputation would precede him.

1850
The Departure to New York

In 1897, in the last years of her life, Elizabeth Naylor Brier wrote a three page *Reminiscence of the Trip to California*, which was passed on by the family to historian Clifford Drury at San Francisco Theological Seminary. In it, we learn a great deal of detail about their journey. She records that in the early weeks of February, William Brier packed a small melodeon, some books, and silverware, some pieces from colonial days in Pennsylvania, quilts and other necessary articles. Elizabeth notes that she was newly pregnant, and debated whether she should travel to California. While they packed, and he was closing the house in Romney, she was living with her three sisters and her parents in Crawfordsville and considered staying there and bringing her to California after the baby was born. In the end, she decided to make the arduous journey with her husband via sailing sloop, instead of joining an overland wagon train. The trip by sea proved to be equally difficult and fraught with danger and delay.

On February 16th, 1850, Mr. and Mrs. William Wallace Brier left Crawfordsville Indiana, in a horse drawn snow sleigh to travel to Indianapolis. Elizabeth's narrative of the journey recalls, "We were in a sleigh. The snow was melting fast so we felt the Jackson roads perceptibly." This was the first leg of a journey, which would change their plans, and their lives along the way.

While in Indianapolis, the Briers' were the guests of Elizabeth's uncle Merrill. She notes that one of the most pleasant memories of her life was the kindness of the ladies of the Second Presbyterian Church who made many additions to her wardrobe. She also remembers an Album style Quilt, which was made and given to her by Miss Ellen Douglas' pupils. Elizabeth wrote, "On the 19th we left Indianapolis by Rail Road—the only one in the State for Madison. We were nearly the whole day. That night we went to Cincinnati by boat. Started for Pittsburgh on the 20th, which we reached on the 23rd. The trip on the river was delightful. We then went up the Monongahela (river) to Brownsville. Thence 73 miles by stage (coach) to Cumberland, Maryland, where we spent the Sabbath. Called on President Taylor, who received us very graciously. Reached New York on the 28th."

This is an astounding statement. The first stop after church on Sunday was a visit to the White House! Elizabeth Naylor may have had connections, either through her Uncle Sam Merrill, or through Jane Beard who was traveling with them at that time. A national focus on the Gold Rush made President Taylor interested in visiting with any departing Missionary to California. President Taylor was viewed as an ineffective leader, but one who was very excited about the prospect of California and the Western Nevada. As such, he wants to meet the Church workers who would Christianize this barbaric part of the continent.

The rush for Gold was in full swing, and no room was available for their immediate boat departure. The Brier's passed the time by making connections with family and friends in New York City, Brooklyn, and New Jersey while waiting for passage. They attended Mr. Beecher's church several times and greatly enjoyed his preaching. They return to Washington D.C. to where they had a lengthy visit with Jessie Fremont, who had just returned from visiting her husband, Charles C. Fremont in California.

Meanwhile, word spread from the New York Office related to Brier. On February 16th, 1850, Charles Hall sent a letter from the AHMS office, to Rev. John Douglas in California. He informs him "Rev. Brier of Romney, Indiana is coming. Rev. Brayton appears to have fineness of character, to be deliberate and somewhat nice in his tastes, but is certified to us by all to be a sterling man. Brier is represented as having great decision and independence—has been in the ministry some three or four years and is a long-term man. He takes his wife. With them will probably go Mrs. Beard, who we understand is your neighbor. A man by the name of N.T. Jones goes out with her, as a laborer, I believe. They wrote us to engage their passage, but we have not been able to obtain them—though we hope to do so. There is a great rush for the steamer." [19]

There are some wonderful compliments to Brier here, in that he has the reputation of being a great decision-maker and is independent. He is not a quitter, and is known as a long-term man. He is married. And they will travel with the wife of a well-known farmer in the southeast bay of San Francisco—Mrs. Jane Beard.

It is hard to think the contact between the Briers and the Beards are coincidental. Elias Beard owned the flour Mill in Attica, near the Brier family farm, and his family was the industrial contractor who built the Erie Canal segment through northern Indiana. E. L. Beard had already migrated to California a year and a half earlier, and now sent for his wife and children. Mrs. Jane Beard, her seventeen-year-old son from previous marriage, Henry Ellsworth, and a five year-old son, John Beard traveled to New York, and boarded the Steamer with the Brier family. Whether this was the first meeting, or a continuation of a casual friendship, this trip would forge their friendship through the trials both families' face in the years to come.

From February 28th, the transportation problems emerge. Elizabeth Brier wrote of these weeks. "There we found that there had been a change in the program, and that we could not get a steamer for the Isthmus until May 2nd. It was a disappointment for we were desirous of reaching Panama before the rainy season. Tickets were sold months in advance of the time of sailing. There were not enough vessels to carry the throngs of gold seekers. Steamers and sailing vessels were brought in to use that were un-seaworthy. Large prices were paid for passage 'to California around the Horn."

A Change in Travel Plans

Elizabeth notes that there was a change in program. This was not an incidental item mentioned in her narrative, written forty years later. As far as William and Elizabeth knew, they were to arrive in New York and depart on a steamer to California, around the Horn of South America.

After a four-month wait, they had tickets for boat passage. There were two clear options, as the Gold Rush was full swing, and gold seekers were crowding the docks for passage to the dream like fortunes of California. The first option, taken by their partner Rev. Brayton, was the singular passage on a sailing sloop around the horn of South America. This was considered a three-month passage, but passengers stayed aboard for the duration. Brayton outfitted himself with a collection of books in a small library for the journey.

The faster option was a three-pronged route to Panama. The Briers and the Beards would take this route, as it was promised to be quicker. It would entail separate boat passage, first to Panama, which would be followed by travel by canoe and donkey across the Isthmus of Panama, and then connecting in Panama City with a separate steamer up the coast to California. What they did not realize at the time was crowds of miners had already overrun Panama City and were waiting for boats that would not materialize to take them to California. The true nature of the adventure awaiting them ahead was still hidden to them.

The society had sold the tickets round the Horn, and had instead secured them on a trip through Panama. William Brier boiled with anger. This new plan would mean that they would have to depart the first boat in Panama, and go by canoe and mule train over the mountains of Panama. He was newly married, and had promised the Naylor's that he would take care of their daughter and now the Mission Society was exposing his young bride to the most dangerous route of travel.

Perhaps his anger was magnified by the confinement of some weeks of travel, the adjustment to the early months of marriage, or the frustration of the delays in the departure to California. Whatever the reason, within the early hours of his face-to-face meeting with Dr. Milton Badger, William Brier locks into a combative disagreement with him. Dr. Badger is clearly not impressed, as is evidenced by the letter they send to Rev. Willey in California.

AHMS Administrative Letter, #2113

"He appears well, has a bright face, and his expressions of courage and energy; but the point in which he does not equal the recommendations is the capacity to impress his hearers with the conviction of his intellectual power."

To: The Rev. Sam Hopkins Willey

March 28th, 1850

Rev. I. H. Brayton was to sail this day by the steamer for California, but early in the month he changed his mind in reference to the mode of conveyance, and chose to go around the "Horn" by ship. We could not agree with him as to the wisdom of this, but did not wish to overrule him by a positive decision:—so we let him have his choice. He sailed from New York in the "Hasquera", a fast sloop and first-rate ship. March 14th expecting to make the voyage in 4 months. He is well provided with library and other facilities. Now what I wish to say about him is this, the longer I knew brother Brayton, the more I felt apprehensive that there is a softness and delicateness of character, not the least of stamina which will be a loss now—and cautions for the rush and impulse of California. If there is a place, therefore, which more than others are suitable for a polished and delicate man let him be placed there.

Now about Mr. W. W. Brier. He and his wife are waiting for the Steamer of April 15th. This brother was praise to the AHMS by the correspondents President White of Crawfordsville, Indiana and Rev. Peer and others. We suppose him to be of power and force; and yet in our interviews here he has shown not to be the superior man we took him to be. He has preached here in Dr. Adams and Rev. Hatfield's Church, I failed in both cases to be much impressed. Still, my opinion is that he is in this great city something of a "cat in a steel barrel" and when out where there is mud and trees enough, he will find his native powers revived. He appears well, has a bright face, and his expressions of courage and energy; but the point in which he does not equal the recommendations is the capacity to impress his hearers with the conviction of his intellectual power. Western men say of a favorite preacher, "he is a smart man"; my fear is that they won't say this of Brother Brier. Again, I have my suspicions that his wife is almost homesick already. She is young, sprightly, and sufficiently cultivated. I should not judge, for her husband, but she has seen Mrs. Fremont and others who have come back with terrible stories of the discomforts of a voyage and of the Pacific coast, and she evidently shrinks from them.

Still, she has so much sense of what is required of her (due to consistency) that she does not intentionally let slip any morsel of regret. Now, the prospect is that they may be detained on the Isthmus: for this passage from Panama is engaged on "The Sarah Sands" steamer for the 2nd trip up to San Francisco: but in the first instance the Sarah Sands had not yet arrived at Panama to make her first trip. If Mrs. Brier should not have perfect health, the discomforts of the Isthmus in May might be trying to her spirits. The amount of all this is, that I wish, if they should be at Monterey, or any where within the kind influence of Mrs. Willey, she would infuse some sisterly hopes into the feelings and prospects of Mrs. Brier. And, if possible, we wish to have a place offered to Brother Brier where he will find work of a strong, coarse rather than refined and intellectual order, and plenty of it, to be done. We tell the brethren, that their location is to be subject to the advice of yourself and Douglas, and if it were needful for you to make journey to settle these locations, the committee will meet the cost of the same.

Dr. Charles Hall[20]

A change in Perception

The glowing compliments given to Brier would soon be challenged by these awkward exchanges with Dr. Charles Hall. This letter registers comments that will confuse and damage the perception of the Briers' for some years to come. First, they conclude that he is not considered an eloquent preacher. "Still, my opinion is that he is in this great city something of a "cat in a steel barrel." The conclusion that he is a "Cat in a steel barrel" suggests that he is out of his element in the city. This is contrasted by their description of his physical presence. "He appears well, has a bright face, and his expressions of courage and energy."

Clearly, Brier has shown them he has some rough edges. In this letter Dr. Hall connects William Wallace Brier's feisty nature with a desire to please his wife. It may be that the society has not yet sent a young bride to California. Elizabeth Brier had some news that was not widely known. She was pregnant, and already struggling with morning sickness, and William Wallace was struggling with providing a safe way for his wife to accompany him. But perhaps there are circumstances that changed his demeanor. He is not intellectual enough for the society. They talk down to him, and talk down about him. Brier may have been struggling with exhaustion or depression, as they allude to "when out where there is mud and trees enough, he will find his native powers revived. "

It must have been a fearful thing for him to embark on the Panama route with a young pregnant bride, but perhaps that was the only route available to him. Rev. Brayton took the longer, more leisurely ship route around the horn of South America. Although he left three months earlier, in the long run it landed him in San Francisco just a month ahead of the Briers.

The Panama Isthmus route promised to be quicker, and it was the only ticket available for William and Elizabeth. Quick is a relative term. The newspapers were already reporting that the Panama route was fraught with dangers and delays. It is curious that Dr. Hall knows already of the troubles that await them once they cross the mountains of Panama—that the second booking ship of their passage on the Pacific Ocean side of the journey is already delayed by many months.

Another admission by Dr. Hall letter is that Mrs. Brier has already been to see Jessie Fremont, who has made one trip to California. Mrs. Fremont painted a dismal picture of her trip to California and the lack of civilization and culture, which seems to have affected Elizabeth Brier.

It may have been attributed to bad chemistry, or it could have been the immaturity of a young recruit. In the correspondence to the agent Rev. S. H.

Willey, Milton Badger conveys a number of concerns about his initial encounter with Brier. This note points out the hostility Brier shows toward the society. This forceful behavior is evident in the questions he posed in the letters just months before. One possible explanation is that perhaps Brier was nervous about the arrangements made for the journey for his new bride. Perhaps he was trying to be the valiant provider for her every need. From his letter with detailed questions to the New York office, it seemed he wanted detailed definition of what the agency would provide for the family, and what arrangements they had already made for him. Combine this speculation with the comment of Dr. White, that "he has a liability to become stubborn and dictatorial when strangely excited" and you have a portrait of a forceful, stubborn man.

This fits. It seems that he is a serious Scotsman, who is awkward in social relationships, but has inordinate integrity and perseverance. It is also clear that he is so concerned with the support level, that he lays on the table the possibility of combining his preaching and church planting ministry with the opportunity to farm or search for gold. This frightens both Badger and Hall, and creates a cloud of suspicion over Brier's motives for years to come.

Dr. Hall, always the more pastoral of the two, responds to Rev. Willey, with some compassion, and curiosity. He gives insight into the delay of the Brier's arrival. It is also confirms that Brier had a poor connection with Badger when he was in New York. It is curious that he came across as difficult to please.

AHMS Administrative Letter

To Rev. Sam Hopkins Willey, in Monterey

Letter from Milton Badger February 16, 1850

". . . . We took brother Brier from the train and met with him here. We were surprised that he is such a bother to us, since he is referred (to you) by relatives and friends. We think he may have other motives than to the (preach the) gospel. He is in this city and is gone out on his own hook, by the route of the Isthmus about the middle of next month.

He feels hostile toward us, and we have always found him a difficult man to please: but have the kindest feelings towards him. We have not done anything or failed to do anything, which would cause this reaction. Perhaps he will not be pleasing to you when he arrives. I hope he may prove to be most compatible and useful worker in that field. You would not be obligated to place him in one of your best fields, by all means you should save it for others . . . ."

Your servants,
Milton Badger[21]

Here is a warm and compassionate response from Dr. Badger, reaching for an explanation of how to accomplish this task. This letter meets its mark, and after being carried on a steamship ahead of Brier, it was delivered in two months time to Rev. Willey in Monterey. Willey has already heard further news regarding Brier's problems, and this time it focuses upon problems with his wife, Elizabeth Brier. We know from family correspondence that she had visited with Jesse Fremont, (the wife of Charles Fremont) before she left Washington, and perhaps this is the source of her fears related to the comforts and culture available in the California frontier. We have no correspondence which confirms her concerns, so it may be through hearsay, or a lost letter from the AHMS headquarters, which conveys her sensitivities as she departed for California. But it does seem odd that the AHMS is not more concerned about the arrangements for the first husband and wife team sent to California. William Brier was single when he applied to the board, and as we have seen, was fairly casual about mentioning his wedding the previous December. Nevertheless, it seems that the board should have been more proactive in securing her comforts.

This poison letter would stain Brier's chances for friendship and support among the missionary community for the following years. And the follow-up letter from Rev. Willey gives us insight that the doubts about Brier continued to swirl throughout the tight knit missionary community. This conversation among the brothers creates a tension that Brier would have to recognize and overcome in the years ahead.

Rev. W. W. Brier's questions to the New York office elicits them to send a letter clarifying their expectations of his performance while he is in their service in California. It is the charter agreement for their support of him for the years to come. It also suggests that they want him to be engaged in gathering information and writing narratives for their newsletters. This letter is sent to the Briers, perhaps in Washington, or in upstate New York while they are traveling.

Correspondence came through private courier of government post in those days. Letters were hand written with a fountain pen and ink, then the paper itself was folded in six creases so it was compact and sealed on its own edges, and the address was written on the backside and often bled through to the text. Many times letters were addressed to the General delivery postmaster in the city where the family was traveling.

AHMS Response

To: Rev. W. W. Brier
April 23, 1850

Rev. Wm. W. Brier
Dear Brother,

1. *In providing you this commission, it is proper that I offer a few explanatory notes before you go, and it is proper that the committee should suggest responsibilities for you while they are responsible for your welfare.*

2. *Mr. S. H. Willey will be responsible to direct your activities in California. We will grant you $400.00 a year for you to live on. If it not possible for you to live on this amount, you will kindly report to Mr. Willey. Your support will be dependent upon the people so they can support you when you don't have this help. We trust that the circumstances shall not diminish the amount, which will add to the support, and eventually replace the support of the society.*

3. *It is the expectation of the Committee, that you will confine your efforts to the appropriate duties of the ministerial offices. We are happy to know that this is what you believe, and to feel strong confidence that you will not allow yourself to be drawn from ministry to the attractions of any worldly enterprises.*

   You will greatly aid the society by giving us full and descriptive views of the state of the things as they concern yourselves. On the abundant detail, of facts which we may gather from the letters of yourself and others, must not only add to our ability to do so what we do in the best manner, but also to have some information so that we may send out future missionaries. The facts you supply are the ones with which we shall be able to more fully inform the committee and the letters will help us to feel like we are fully supportive of you in word and prayer.

   In this historic space and opportunity frames my stressing the importance of the early phase of ministry, which you are now entering.

4. *In the early period, in the history of Protestantism in California, you labors may be arduous, and often times the work may be solely up to you, yet if performed in the true missionary spirit, you can be assured that you will find fruitfulness in you labors. The foundations may be laid strong, but upon them most of the partnership of the glory of the spirit may build a lasting church, which shall prevail—for Jesus Christ who is the chief cornerstone.*

Yours in Christian Bonds.
Brother Badger and Hall.[22]

This letter attempts to sort out some of the conflicts they were having, specifically related to the depth of their financial support for him. It may have been that Brier had done his research, and already knew that the level of support they were offering was woefully inadequate in California. Perhaps he was pushing the limits of what they would do to increase that support, or seeing if they would allow him to work at some other enterprise to increase his income. The society firmly slams the door shut in this regard, and establishes a clear line of communication and authority over him. This may have resolved the issue as far as they were concerned, or perhaps the doubts had just begun.

Setting Sail for California

The American Home Missionary Society sent $1,000.00 for them to sail to Panama and then transfer to California. Finally, on May 2, 1850, they were able to secure their tickets from New York to San Francisco; they sailed for Chagres, Panama, aboard the sailing sloop, *Crescent City*. Their farewell party in New York was quite an occasion and many dignitaries attended, including Ralph Waldo Emerson.

On the way from New York to Chagres, the steamers made a stop at Kingston on the island of Jamaica to fill their coalbunkers. This could be a long operation, but it only took two days for the *Crescent City*. The ship plowed its way through a choppy spring storm, and arrived at Chagres ten days after leaving New York—a trip filled with misery and seasickness for the Brier's. A strange illness struck Elizabeth on the Atlantic trip, which was first assumed to be some sort of seasickness due to the rough water, but it did not abate in the first days of calm anchorage in the harbor of Chagres. She was two months pregnant when they left New York, but would spend the next ten weeks in Panama in the height of sweltering heat and disease. Morning sickness and tropical disease did not mix well.

CHAPTER 9

Heroic Crossing, Heroic Patience

As boats enter the harbor of Chagres, the Briers could see the castle of San Lorenzo on the rock bluff at the left of the entrance, crowning the point of the harbor. In the tropics, there is a different sense of time and urgency—and no timetable for departure or arrival. Shortly following the arrival of any ship, strong Panamanian men in longboats paddled out to offer passage up the river for any passenger willing to pay. Little did the Americans know that there were no ships at the other end of the Isthmus, and that once they traversed the river, they would have to wait for weeks for passage. Most of the passengers had economic interests. They were fortune hunters, merchants, missionaries, and were frustrated that others might beat them to the Promised Land!

The first stop in Panama for the Briers was an overnight on shore. There was only one hotel, and it was reserved for dignitaries and women, in that order. It was $4.00 each for the overnight room. They stopped at the "Irving House", a frame building where the only sleeping accommodation for men was in one room of 125 bunks. William secured for Elizabeth a private room with Jane Beard, ten foot by ten-foot square. This was not their final destination. The passage through the swamp and over the mountain was also a lengthy, expensive venture. It would take them six days to go up the river. The locals created a bidding war for who would be transported first. Most fortune seekers thought that the first one over the mountain, and onto the shore of the Pacific would be first on the slopes of the California goldfields. Prices ranged from five to fifteen dollars. William Brier bargained for a paddleboat passage for twenty dollars.

It is possible to trace their movements upriver and overland through the invoice Brier submitted to the AHMS for reimbursement, with date, and costs for each portion of the trip. Their misery had just begun, concealed by a calm paddle into the mouth of the Chagres River,[23] which seemed like a tropical dreamland. Lush palm trees graced the shoreline at the calm mouth of the water. Calmness was a familiar theme for what was to come. Much of the interior rivers turned into the brackish swampland of the interior, with disease above and dark water below.

On the 13th of May, they put out on the Chargers River for Panama in a long boat carrying fourteen people with Panamanian oarsman, clad only in straw hats and loin clothes, to pole through the swamp. Mrs. Brier wrote that the scenery was beautiful, but the trip very tiresome. On the river, the boats experienced frequent rainsqualls and intense heat. The forest were lush, the river flowed remarkably clear, clean, and swift. The riverbanks were alive with flurry of native parakeets, and the splash of colored flower blossoms in every bright tropical hue.

The bamboo hut village of Gatun was the first stop for rest along the journey. Elisabeth noted, "The boatmen arranged for their employers to spend the afternoon and the first hours of the night in some of the native houses. A notched pole serve as a ladder from the common room downstairs to the sleeping loft under the thatch."[24] Many people indulged in a siesta. Passengers would rise at midnight to paddle while beating the heat, and travel in the longboats till sunrise. Frequent rainstorms would drench the passengers by night, and further douse the spirits of the travelers along an unfamiliar river. The Briers had an untimely arrival in the rainy season.

On the second night, the river began to rush more forcefully. Immigrants could not wait for the nights stop. Briers' invoice to the AHMS states they paid $5.00 for food and sundries on the river. Most passengers would have to adapt to the local meals of chicken, eggs, and rice boiled in cocoa milk.

In the town of Cruces, the mountains stood like a barrier wall between the river and the intended goal of Panama City. In both bookend cities of the mountains, Cruces and Panama City, the cursed disease of Cholera raged. They did not know if they were fleeing from it, or into it.

On the rugged road over the mountains to Gorgona, they paid $4.00 to stay for the night. The winding roadway over the pass to Panama City was long and dusty in good weather: a muddy mule train in the spring weather—which is exactly when the Brier family crossed the river.

The bidding wars were not over yet. Travelers were tested into an auction of prevailing transport. Horses and mules were difficult to find, and the prices were escalated higher the Briers paid $2.00 each for the short journey. The cost of carrying their luggage was eventually bid up to $21.84.

Travelers from Panama to Chagres could go by way of Gongora or Cruces. The Cruces road was considered the best—particularly during the rainy season. The mule trip (which took one day in the dry season) varied depending on the damns, with water cascading down the hillsides and across the trail and switchbacks. It usually cost twelve to fifteen dollars: baggage was transported separately at forty four dollars for 180 pounds. Considering that the bill for the Brier's luggage was $21.00, they had a mere 90 lbs. of luggage. The Beard family must have spent more, as E. L. Beard records that his wife brought considerable supplies of rose bushes and fruit tree grafts, which were crated and aboard the ships when Mrs. Jane Beard arrived.[25]

One traveler wrote of the three days, "The path at the outset was bad enough, but as the wood grow deeper and darker and the tough clay soil held the rains which had fallen, it became finally a narrow gully, filled with nearly to our horses' bellies. Descending the steep sides of the hills, they would step or listed down almost precipitous passes . . . ."[26] Elizabeth Brier could not ride a donkey because she was so ill, she was forced to travel over the mountains of Panama on foot, and in the process ruined all four pairs of shoes she packed for California.[27]

One passenger over the mountains noted the heartbreak of the mountain pass. "The only sounds in that leafy wilderness were the chattering of monkeys as they cracked the palm-nuts, and the scream of parrots . . . . In the deep ravines, and you could see spent mule's lay dead, and high above them on the large boughs the bald vultures waited silently for us to pass.

"The solid men led on to believe that their comfortable route to El Dorado would progress with all the smoothness and what they discovered was a crumbling Panama city, which was packed with angry Americans, weary with delay, disease, and decay of this provincial city. They were challenge by the ruined churches, palaces, grass grown plazas, and dry fountains. The future of their hunting gold lay tarnished and waste if they would not move from this side of the Pacific on a boat."[28]

A lack of ships to California created a bottleneck of pioneers at the ports in Panama. This delay and overcrowding stirred anger and violence in both locals and miners. As the Brier party neared the city they encountered a menacing mob of local Panamanians who had set upon a group of angry miners. The Panamanians had locked their city gates to new migrants. As the Brier's waited, a Spanish priest invited William and Elizabeth into his house until the authorities opened the gates.

Mrs. Brier wrote, "They were a lawless set—for the most part. It was the rainy season. Many died of the fever prevalent. My husband had services in the Plaza (also at the Battery) and attended thirty funerals—all of them young men. It was a long two months before we were able to secure a steamer for California. In the meantime, I had Panama fever badly. Mr. Brier had it (the fever) on the steamer."

But the delay was not to be wasted time for Brier. A passionate missionary spirit had already bitten him. He used these weeks delay as a God given golden opportunity to preach, visit the sick, bury the dead, and conduct prayer meetings in various parts of the city. He later confessed to his AHMS supervisors that he studied the Spanish language during that time as well, and was fairly conversational.

Another advantage that emerged from Briers wait in Panama was the intense bonding between the pioneers from Indiana. Elizabeth Brier and Jane Beard spent the weeks together, and as both of them were from higher social circles, Mrs. Beard took an intense liking to Elizabeth. Jane Beard invited the Briers to come and stay with Mr. Beard at Mission San Jose (fifteen-miles north and east of the city of San Jose). In addition, the Briers deepened a friendship with others from Indiana. These include Emerson Timothy Crane, and Joseph Weller, both whom would connect with the Brier family in the decades to come.

Brier Letter # 12

The original of this letter is not in the file, although excerpts of it were published in the *Home Missionary Magazine*.

In a report to the American Home Missionary Society prior to leaving Panama, Mr. Brier wrote:

"I have preached every Sabbath since the first. I have had as large congregations as could be accommodated, sitting and standing in the houses where I preached. For two Sabbaths, I have preached at 5 o'clock in the evening on the Fort Battery, which is pleasant place.
Yesterday, there were about one thousand persons present. I stood on the carriage of one of other cannons while my congregation crowded around me on every side. Thirty feet beneath, the waves dashed against the strong walls, above where the calm heavens; and a cool breeze blew off the bay. I felt it was not a vain thing to preach the Gospel in Panama." Having visited the sick and attended many funerals he expressed the hope that he had been instrumental in leading one wanderer, at least, into the fold of the Gracious Shepherd. He went on to state that the people who had been so attentive and impressed with the message of life longed for something more and better than they were getting according to what his Romanist friend had told him of their clergy. He thought the contrast of a good American minister would open the eyes of the people. There were a number of vacant churches belonging to the government, so a petition was sent to the Governor of the Republic, just as Rev. Brier left, asking for permission be granted the Americans for a place of worship. Thus it was that God surely used Rev. Brier who was for a time Panama's first Presbyterian missionary. So it was from that opportune place of precious seed sowing that Rev. Brier came to enter upon the great work that awaited him in California."

Historic records from the Brier family recount that Elizabeth nearly died in Panama of illness. This may also explain why Jane Beard traveled ahead without the Briers. Perhaps Elizabeth was too weak to travel. The long wait in Panama for passage to

California called for extreme measures. Although the Brier, Beard, Weller, and Crane parties have sheltered together for these many weeks, there was only so much room on the first steamer. The Beards went with the first boat, the *Panama*, arriving in San Francisco on June 10th. The *Panama* was built to accommodate 60 people, but was now pressed into service for 200. The ships manifest documents that the Crane brothers were on board with Mrs. Beard and her two children, which set sail from Panama on June 17th, 1850, and took 18 days to reach San Francisco.

The Briers and Joseph Weller remained behind for *The Columbus*, which would arrive in July. It was another month that the Briers would languish in Panama before departure. They settled for passage on a steamer *Columbus*, a ship built for 50 passengers, but which also had booked over 200 passengers on board. It was a wooden screw propelled steam ship with two decks. It was relatively new, having been built in 1848, and had only one previous journey between Panama and San Francisco. The Brier's had to pay an additional $107.51 for room rent on the boat. They left Panama around July 18th, 1850.

The Briers were listed as "*Rev and Mrs. Bryan*" in the ship's manifest.[29] Throughout his life, his name was misspelled as Brien, Bryan, and Brayer in newspapers. Their trip was more rugged, than the journey for Mrs. Beard, taking 21 days from Panama to San Francisco.

On the lengthy boat trip, Brier's friendship with Joseph R. Weller deepened. Weller was a teacher of agriculture and theology from New York. In Weller's brief biography, summarized in the 1881 *History of Santa Clara County, California* it is noted that once Weller had crossed the mountains, and descended into Panama City, they waited "with several thousand others, six weeks were passed awaiting a steamer to convey them to San Francisco. At length the almost unendurable suspense was ended by the arrival of the ship Columbus from her first trip to San Francisco. As soon as repairs could be made, he secured passage, and arrived in San Francisco August 7th, 1850. He soon went to the mines at Coloma, El Dorado County. At the end of the month he returned to San Francisco, ill with Panama Fever. In the following spring, still suffering from the effects of the fever, he came to Santa Clara County, and located on the Charles Weber Ranch, twenty miles from San Jose, where he remained until his health was fully restored."

This friendship forged on the final leg of the trip to California would remain a significant one, which would bless Brier some twenty years later. The party of the Briers and Weller, once aboard the *Columbus*, headed off towards the Gulf of Tehuantepec with the sea tranquil, and the sunsets phenomenal. They had an additional three weeks to bounce along the coast of Mexico, waiting in ports along the way for a supply of coal to fire the steam engine. The humidity made the days unbearable. After a week at sea, the Mexican mountains were sighted in the distance. The next day, the ship made the harbor of Acapulco, where a small boat came out and proclaimed the news that no one would be allowed to come to shore because of the fear of disease. Yet the captain curiously took an additional hundred passengers onboard who may have brought disease on board with them.

After clearing Mazatlan, the ship ran around Cabo San Lucas, the rugged point of lower California, and then tacked north toward the California. During this trip Mr. Brier had one of the fevers raging through Panama. It was a treacherous journey with the outbreak of disease, which swept through the ships passengers, particularly the 90 passengers who were in steerage. Many were on the verge of death. Even though he was seriously ill himself, the Rev. Brier gathered on deck with the crew to perform burials at sea during the voyage.

A few days after their arrival, the August 7, 1850 *Daily Alta California* recorded a Cholera outbreak on board.

ARRIVAL OF THE STEAMER COLUMBUS!
Late from the U. States
CALIFORNIA NOT ADMITTED!
Cholera at Acapulco!

The fine, fleet steam propeller Columbus, Capt. James B. Peck, was telegraphed yesterday afternoon, about 5 o'clock, and soon came up the harbor and stood but some distance opposite Clarke's Point, where she came to. Notwithstanding it was blowing very fresh, a number of boats from the shore reached her, but they were not permitted to board her.

After some delay our news collector boarded her and brought on shore one of the passengers, Mr. Mortimer J. Smith, who had kindly prepared us a synopsis of news items, with a list of passengers, of which we have gladly availed ourselves, and return him many thanks for his courtesy!

In consequence of there having been a number of cases of Panama fever on board, and having touched at a cholera port, Dr. Rogers, the Health Officer, ordered her into quarantine and prohibited intercourse with the shore. She came up, however, near the foot of Cunningham's wharf. Up to the time of our writing we believe Mr. Smith is the only gentleman who has succeeded in getting ashore.

The Columbus left Panama on the afternoon of the 17th of July, having been detained two days awaiting the arrival of the semi-monthly mail. She brings the mails from the United States of the 1st of July, which were brought to Chagres in the Falcon. Eight days out she put into Acapulco for fresh water, and was detained there two days. Thus it will be seen she had made the trip up in less than 20 days. Her qualities for comfort and speed are highly praised. On her trip she experienced a succession of head winds nearly all the time, and for the last three days has been compelled to contend with a heavy gale of wind. Her captain and officers are highly commended also for the attention they have paid to their passengers. The captain brings up 300 passengers, including quite a number of ladies.

Up to this time we have received no late State papers, but are informed that there is but little news. The admission of California was still unsettled, but the same belief that it could not remain unsettled much longer appeared to exist. This will be bad news to all of us, as we had expected by this arrival to have heard of some decisive action.

We regret to learn that there was considerable sickness on the Isthmus, and that several deaths occurred on the Columbus among the steerage passengers, many of whom came on board in a debilitated condition. The following paragraph relative to the health of the ship, with the names of the deceased, was furnished us by Mr. Smith:

Many of the steerage passengers came on board the Columbus more or less sick with the "Isthmus fever," as it is called, and on our seventh day out from Panama, one of them, Mr. Joseph Webb, of Athens, Ohio, died, and the following morning another, Mr. Samuel D. Caldwell, of New Boston, N.H., also died, and both were buried at the same time in the "deep blue sea," the Rev. W.W. Brier officiating over their remains. On Sunday, the 28th, four more died, viz: Irving Garrett, Serbia, N.Y.; W.W. and James M. Dodge (brothers), New Boston, N.H.,; and F.H. Hall, Tressander, N.Y.; and the next morning another, Mr. Charles D. Jenks, Pox Sutawney, Pa., also died, and were all buried at sea, the Rev. O. Harriman, a clergyman of the Episcopal Church performing the funeral services. The ship's surgeon, Dr. E. R. Smilie, gave all of the deceased the utmost attention that eminent skill and science could give, and Capt. Pratt and others rendered them all the services in their power, but all in vain—some of them were beyond the reach of medical help when they came aboard, and the others imprudently partook of tropical fruit, on shore at Acapulco, and for which they have paid the dear forfeit of their lives. Others of the sick are now entirely well or convalescent, thanks to an overruling Providence and the efforts of Dr. Smilie."

CHAPTER 10

Anticipated Arrival

The AHMS stipulated that Rev. Willey was the Missionary Coordinator for the AHMS, and would keep them posted on the assignments and movements of the pastors. By the time Brier met him, Sam Willey had been in California a year and a half. His letter has news of the AHMS pastors in various locations, and highlights their eagerness for Brier to arrive. It also responds to the intrigue surrounding Elizabeth's meeting with Jesse Fremont before departure, and responds to the bad news spread by Mrs. Fremont to discourage Mrs. Brier. Willey highlights the political motives and intrigue in Charles Fremont and his run for President of the United States.

Letter from Willey to the AHMS

May 27, 1850

Monterey

Our mail arrived today as it was forwarded to me while at San Jose in Presbytery. I know you sympathize with us in our feeling of disappointment when we read your intelligence about brother Brier. (Brother Douglas and myself read it strictly confidentially and the only part of its contents communicated to others were the facts concerning the arrival of our brethren).

We had been together one day before with Rev. Blakeslee of Marysville (on Feather River), Benton of Sacramento, Hunt of San Francisco, Douglas and myself were attending. We had spent the time in making statements of facts about our different fields of labor and all the destitute places within California. I wish I could give you some adequate idea of the field brought before us! Would that I could map it on the wall in our committee room of your New York Office.

Brother Blakeslee began his report on the extreme north, or rather from the most northern field occupied (by our missionaries). His central point in Marysville on our "Fremont Map" follows up the Sacramento to Feather River who further on the Yuba and in that is Marysville, an within one mile of it on either side are Yuba City and Elisa. (?) Marysville is well defined and growing business town of between one and two thousand inhabitants of who many are immigrant families. The other place are but a rapidly growing and doubtless will be permanent settlement.

Brother Blakeslee preached each Saturday at the above named town. At Marysville he has formed a religious society. It has the potential to become a congregation of 6 members—5 of which are Old School Presbyterians.

There is surely to be one site of the great importance. Mr. Douglas hopes to get a chapel completed this summer in San Jose. He is currently preaching at a tent. He preaches at the Mission of San Jose frequently(15 miles from the town). There are quite a number of families settled there. There is adequate business, and agriculture on that beautiful mission. An important settlement has occurred there. He also preaches at afternoons at the Mission of Santa Clara (5 miles in the other direction) where a still larger population is growing and one of the most beautiful, healthy, and fertile place in the California sun.

There is surely, a singular mystery about Mr. Brayton (gone around the horn) it seems if he was beside himself—or would seem so. If he knew how much he was needed here! Round the Horn!

But Mr. Brier. May he be able to do well at Panama for he will likely to be there for a long stay. The "Sarah Sands" ship has not arrived at San Francisco yet, and the report in this town is circulated on very good authority that she is on the coast 60 miles south of here waiting for fuel to be sent down to her. (This is why the delay) So we turn our eyes away from man, and say with the Psalmist, "I will lift up my eyes to the hills, from whence does my help come from. My help comes from the Lord."

I feel like having a quarrel with that lady who so represented affairs here as to render—or tend to render—Mrs. Brier discontented. That individual (Mrs. Jesse Fremont) was not the last one who has done this. Where peoples husbands are in need of votes in any country to raise them to high office, people are satisfied, pleased, delighted, yea, enraptured with that country and can see no other. Now that the election is passed, positions given, all home again, alas there have been stories of destitution here in Cala—want of civilization—etc. The individual in question did not receive much attention—even extra attention—in this town—whatever she might have elsewhere.

But be assured that Mrs. Brier fell into bad hands. Of this, it will be easy to convince her when she arrives. The improvements in the facilities for living comfortably are tenfold greater now than when the woman who spoke to her was in Cala. It requires

a little talk and planning to keep supplied with all one needs, but that is all easily
possible these days.

S. H. Willey[30]

This letter was both defensive about the local conditions, and also a clarification regarding the misleading information they had. This reveals the negative gossip about Brier's abilities spread amongst the brothers, as Willey and Douglas read the letter out loud at their gathering. Considering the warning they received regarding Brier, it is odd they moved ahead to appoint him to one of the best assignments in the city of Marysville where Blakeslee has been already preaching. Perhaps it was such a marvelous opportunity that they could not afford to pass it up, and were willing to assign a risky, but hearty and proven Indiana preacher.

It is also odd that Rev. Willey would spend so much time defending the cultured state of living, when he himself is battling illness since his arrival in Monterey. To make matters worse, Willey's own wife has been ill for some time, and was not fond of the California culture.

CHAPTER 11

Arrival and Assignment

When Brier sailed through the Golden Gate on August 6, 1850, there were 509 ships in port. Most ships were abandoned and could not sail back due to the fact that most of their crew had abandoned them to work in the gold mines. The ship manifest lists the Brier's as arriving August 6, 1850, but his letter suggests it was August 7, 1850 which may account for the day of disease quarantine before they were able to go ashore.

Brier thought he would arrive and be greeted by a welcoming party who would assign him a growing location for church planting. However, the delay and sickness Panama had taken the wind out of his sails. There would be no welcoming party in California. Most of the ministers were out exploring new ministry locations. Brier would have to rest for a while, and the ministers would have to regroup and confer before making an assignment for him.

In his first day in California they found their way to the Howard street home of Rev. Timothy Dwight Hunt.

The Window depicting Rev. Hunt
Stewart Chapel, STFS Library

Timothy Dwight Hunt is leading the first Protestant Communion service in California at Portsmouth Square in 1849. Out of his work came the formation of the First Congregational church of San Francisco in the same year. Hunt came to California from Hawaii, represented by the clipper ship in the top triangle. The bottom triangle shows the organization of the Presbytery of San Francisco in 1949—the first presbytery west of the Rocky Mountains. The medallions (shown top right) a bag of gold for the hordes of people who came to California looking for gold: (bottom left) the Portsmouth Square school house: (bottom right) a scallop shell and wafer symbolizing the sacraments of baptism and communion brought to California by Hunt.

In those early days, Hunt was not alone for long. The steamship *California* arrived in San Francisco on February 28, 1849, and brought four missionaries from New-York; the Rev. O. C. Wheeler,(Baptist), Rev. S. Woodbridge, (Old School Presbyterians); Rev. J.W. Douglas, and Rev. S. H. Willey, (both New School Presbyterians).[31]

Three years later, Hunt emerged as a leader in the New School Presbyterian movement, working a shared administrative role with Rev. Willey. Hunt saw his role as supportive. His charge from the AHMS was not a direct advisory role, but his voice was weighty with them. At the time Hunt became the "agent" for the A.H.M.S. and as such was assigned the tasks for assessing and supervising the five church planters supported by the A.H.M.S: Brier, Buel, Brayton, Corwin, Warren. Unlike Rev. Willey who had money to dispense on behalf of the AHMS, Hunt had no resources but his income as a chaplain of San Francisco.

He was the sort of figure that would inspire the admiration of Brier. It is natural to see why W.W. Brier was attracted to Rev. Hunt. Hunt's role as Chaplain of San Francisco, made him a model of the pastor who was involved in the community, and used this platform as a bridge point in building a church. He was the lone missionary on the West Coast with previous pastoral and church planting experience, and became Brier's personal choice for a mentor.

This created an awkward situation for William Brier. He was told to report to Rev. Willey, but he prefered to be mentored by Rev. Hunt. Hunt was more "Congregational" in his theology, but more Presbyterian in church government. Both men were financially supported by he AHMS, and each had their own congregations. They submitted reports to the AHMS every other month on the activities of the California missionaries. Willey was given two thousand dollars a month as discretionary funds to be used in support of the pastors and congregations that were most needy. Willey's cash record show that he never contributed to Brier's ministry.

Over the next decade, Hunt would be a regular preacher in Brier's church, yet we have no record of Rev. Willey ever preaching there.

When the Briers arrived at his home, Hunt was away on an exploratory mission survey in the mining country surrounding Marysville. The Briers stayed at his home and awaited his arrival. William and Elizabeth spend the week resting, seeing doctors for their Panama fever, and visiting with friends. The Rev. Hunt arrived a few days later, and the Brier's and Hunt's got aquatinted. By the second week, they wanted to see the countryside. Rev. Hunt escorted the Brier's to the southeast San Francisco Bay area north east to the Mission San Jose, so Elizabeth could see her friend Jane Beard.

Hunt had already been to the Mission San Jose a number of times. In a letter to his wife (who was still waiting in Hawaii) dated, May 28th, 1850, Timothy Dwight Hunt wrote the story of his horse ride around the bay as he looked for places to assign ministers to begin new churches. *"On Tuesday I mounted Mr. Mather's horse and rode 15 miles to the northern side of the valley. I continued up towards San Francisco on the "Contra Costa" to the Mission of San Jose. The American gentleman in charge of the garden and orchards and vineyards courteously entertained me and conducted me through the premises. There are several immigrant families living in the mission houses, and I promised that some one of the brethren should go out and preach to them on the next Sabbath. I afterwards learned that two went. I rather promised the gentleman proprietor (E.L. Beard), and myself too, that I would go and see him again in pear and grape time. But I shall not go simply for that. If I can do so when in the accomplishment of the great object of my life, I shall feel that I may turn aside a little to eat of the Lord's fruit as well as do His work. To seek pleasure for pleasure's sake merely does not gratify me except in connection with it do some good I can also do there.*

On leaving, the proprietor would take no pay either for my dinner or the oats of my horse, so I had only to thank him and lay up the visit for pleasant remembrances. He is expecting his family out this summer and I may see them as they land here (in San Francisco) and may have a chance of reciprocating the favor."

Hunt's comments were significant. True to his word, he met the boat that carried Jane Beard and escorted her to Mission San Jose.

A few months had passed since he had visited. On this trip, Hunt did not stay long, but left the Briers with the Beard family at the mission for some rest. Meanwhile in the city, the Rev. S. H. Willey and Rev. Hunt met to debrief Hunt's trip to the mining area. It was Hunt's urgency about the opportunity there, and his advocacy of Brier, which confirmed the decision for Brier to go to Marysville. Brier was not thrilled with the prospect of leaving the mission and taking his bride to the rugged hillsides of the Gold country, but he would go Marysville.

Rev. Willey wrote to the AHMS society with this report of the assignments. He was eager to respond to the letters of concern about Brier he had received in the briefings from Secretary Badger and Hall. He also corrected an impression he received from Brier about the different styles of ministry between the Old School and New School Presbyterians. In a letter dated August 15, 1850, S. H. Willey wrote, *"Brother Brier arrived on the 6th, much to our joy and gratitude. Brother Brayton was here before him some weeks. Our advice to Brother Brayton is to gone to Sonora. Brother Brier we advised to go to Marysville, a town at the junction of the Feather and Yuba rivers, growing up to be another Sacramento. If this state of affairs takes place we shall have somebody in each of the strongest points in the state, except Stockton. We have printed but little concerning what is going on in our field of labor because we had not timed. From what Brother Brier says to me I have gathered the impression that Dr. Hall thinks the Old School brothers are reaching out more than we are. This is wrong. Nothing could be further from the truth. San Francisco, Benicia, and Napa and Stockton are all (the cities the Old School) talk about. Rev. Albert Williams is doing a good deal here, but is deeply embarrassing. His church has never prospered. They got into a lawsuit about the (property) lot, a year ago, and it has distracted them.*

Brother Hunt visited Marysville. At present there are about one thousand inhabitants. Brother Blakeslee has done something there, but his talent is beginning enterprises not for staying with them. When he gets his mind impressed with an idea, he must go on to new places. We all wanted him to stay at Marysville. But a week ago Blakeslee was impressed with the idea he must preach in the mines and to the mines he went."

The departure of Blakeslee left Marysville empty. This did not distract the leaders of the Presbyterian Church from having designs upon the area for the purpose of church planting, and Brier was part of that design.

The four Presbyterian AHMS ministers in California voted to concur with Willey to assign Brier to the city of Marysville. Perhaps meeting and talking with Brier allayed their fears. Nonetheless, the time was now. They could not wait, as the New York office said that there were no other candidates for service waiting in Panama City to come to California. The current pastors on the field were all they had.

In a way, Brier was the most likely to go to Marysville. He was fresh, seemed to have passion, bright eyes, and boundless energy. Brier was also the most experienced Church planter in California, with three churches already established in Indiana. Other AHMS and Old School missionaries were fresh out of school, including Willey, and they had not helped him to establish any churches. Brier was a long-term man, and they believed he was also the last of the men commission by the AHMS. Volunteers were not forthcoming, and their resources were stretched thin. Hunt and Willey already had contacts with people in the city who said there were enough Presbyterian residents to form a church. The pastors on the field had compassion on Brier, and his concern for his newly wed bride and her need for stability and comfort in her late pregnancy. In fact, they were enamored with the manner in which she had come through the trials of Panama. Since the Beard family had so graciously agreed to host her for some time in the Mission San Jose, this would free up William Brier to go forth to the mission fields of Marysville and establish a preaching mission.

CHAPTER 12

A Conflict of Conscience

He was ready to go, but became briefly sidetracked by a misunderstanding. In the first weeks in California, Brier was drawn into a jealous conflict with the two east coast AHMS pastors who had preceded him in California. Brier was mistakenly already been lobbied by Rev. Douglas' San Jose congregation as pastor of the Presbyterian Church. To unravel this tangled mess, we must first meet the Rev. John Douglas and the Rev. Issac Brayton.

The window featuring John Douglas.
Stewart Chapel, SFTS Library

John W. Douglas is discussing the newspaper, the Pacific, with the printer.
In the top triangle, a copy of the paper is pictured.
The bottom triangle represents Douglas coming to California on the S. S. California.
The medallions show: (top left) Acts 1:8 for Douglas' service under the American Home
Missionary Society supported jointly by Presbyterians and Congregationalists: (top right) the
State Capitol building in San Jose for the services Douglas conducted there until his own
church was built and for his service as chaplain Douglas conducted there until his own
church was built and for his service as chaplain of the Assembly: (bottom left) the poppy for
his work with the State of California bottom right) quill pens for his writing ability.

Rev. Douglas wrote a report of those early days to Dr. Hall of the AHMS, and he included a telling portrait of Rev. Willey, and the committee of five ministers who decided where to assign the new missionaries.

Douglas Letter to AHMS.

> *Before our arrival, the Home Missionary Society had appointed by mail a committee of*
> *five pastors, Congregational and New School Presbyterian, Brothers Benton of*
> *Sacramento, Hunt and Willey of San Francisco, Warren of Nevada City, and I think,*
> *Eli Corwin of San Jose, to advise us as to our locations. Of all these and of all that group*
> *of missionaries, I am now the sole survivor. I was the youngest among them.*
>
> *Among pastors already here, Mr. Willey was evidently the leader, partly by*
> *formal appointment, for I think that he was the representative of the A.H.M.S. in*
> *California, "serving for nothing and finding himself." I never can forget how he*
> *impressed me on my first sight of him, an impression that deepened as I came closer*
> *to him through somewhat familiar intercourse. He had a fine form, tall and straight,*
> *surmounted by a fine head, the face gleaming with intelligence and kindliness. I*
> *loved him at first sight, yet stood somewhat in awe of him. To begin with, he was*
> *the pioneer, the old-timer, I the newcomer.*
>
> *Rev. John Douglas*

Another area pastor who clashed with Brier initially was Rev. Brayton. Brayton is remembered as being a slender man, but had a compelling face with beaming eyes, dark and curly hair. Friends remarked that although he was a slender man, he walked with the swagger of adventurous man, who was also known as a steady and gifted writer. Brayton would first be a critic of Brier, and later become a mentor and advocate for Brier's ministry.

The conflict which would develop is clearly explained by Brier as an innocent misunderstanding of his intentions in preaching at Brayton's church, which was manipulated by the search committee of the congregation. Although Brier was the innocent victim, this conflict confirms in the minds of the Brayton and Douglas, that Brier is a "fumbler", and may have alternative motives for being in California. In the flurry of activity settling into his assignment, he procrastinates writing a letter to the AHMS office for six full months after his arrival in California.

His side of the story is rolled out in Brier's thirteenth letter. It is the longest one—packed full of details, sermonic observations about the missionary calling. He responds to the AHMS rumors that they had heard little from him since he has arrived.

The beginning portion of letter #13 is dated February 26 and is focused upon the conflict in San Jose.

> The circumstances, which I am about to relate, I would gladly omit if you knew nothing of them but it is right that you should know my motives and acts in this case. When (we were) in Panama, Judge Dimmic of San Jose called on me, and said that he was returning to the States for his wife, who is as a Presbyterian. As Mr. Douglas was about to leave San Jose, the judge wished for me to settle there, making fair promises, as he was pleased with my manner of speech, et cetera.
>
> I innocently spoke of this to the brethren at San Francisco, thinking that Mr. Douglas was about to leave his post. It seems however the Mr. Douglas conceived the idea that my intended visit to San Jose was to try to supplant him. So he posted (a letter) home with determination, as Mr. Brayton says, to prevent it.
>
> Such a thing was foreign to my designs, contrary to my nature to perform, and unkind in him to imagine. But, as soon as Mr. Douglas got to San Jose, he learned from Mr. Brayton that he was unpopular, and so determined to leave.
>
> But he also determined to establish Mr. Brayton in his place, so in the middle of the week, before any of the church knew that I was there, he collected privately in his house, a few of his friends to invite Mr. Brayton to fill his place (as pastor) for a few months. Mr. Douglas left before the Sabbath, and left word with Mr. Brayton not to invite me to preach by any means (Mr. Brayton is my authority). But some of my friends from Indiana went to Mr. Brier and did succeed in getting the afternoon hour, in which to hear me preach. On Monday I was about to leave the town, when one of the members of the church came to me, and said that he had seen the record of the meeting which gave Mr. Brayton a call, and that there were five persons present—two of them from the family where Mr. Douglas and Brayton boarded in the country. They also named five or six of the principal members of the church and congregation who had expressed a desire that I should remain and preach with reference to settlement. When Mr. Brayton opposed this they wished me to permit them to circulate a subscription paper for my (salary) support. There are many families there; hence they wish to minister with a family.

> *But feeling that it was by far too much beneath my calling to engage in such a contest, where intrigue was used destructively by the ministers. I retired to the mission, with a strong conviction that Western ministry never treated a brother as I had been treated. I cared but little about that place (San Jose), but my wife wished to live where she could see her friends and has female society.*
> *(We pause in the letter here.) [32]*

Since Brier's letter is long, it is fitting to comment on this first "painful incident" before we read the rest of the letter in its proper place six months later. It seems that William Brier is aware that his reputation is not stellar with the AHMS, and he wanted to sort out this recent awkwardness of being manipulated into be a candidate for the ministry at San Jose. Although his explanation seems straightforward, there may have been more than meets the eye. It was no secret that Brier loved the Mission San Jose area, and he would delight in taking a church fifteen miles away in San Jose, as he wanted his wife to have "female society."

The five ministers of the AHMS in California had already been "warned" by Dr. Badger and Dr. Hall about weaknesses in Brier's social skill, and his character. They were looking for problems, and quickly found one here. From Brier's explanation, it is easily an honest mistake he made in opening himself up to a post, especially because he had not been instructed where he was going before his departure.

But the delay of four months in arrival had changed the landscape of priority. Rev. Blakeslee and Isaac Brayton had been already preaching in Marysville, having beaten Brier to California by several months. But after the first harsh summer in Marysville, Brayton was exhausted and wanted to try his hand in the mountains towards Tahoe. Marysville was certainly a more strategic city, but it was a difficult community, with intense summer heat, Brayton decided to attempt another ministry and leave Brier to the mud and the trees!

Many times the stress of frontier ministry was not conflict with the pastors, but rather the conflict with the congregations that would reject pastoral leadership. It was in the first two weeks of his stay in California, that Brier steps into an awkward conflict that is widely misinterpreted. It began when Brier traveled to Monterey to meet with Rev. S. H. Willey, and along the way is invited to come back through San Jose and preach at the church that had been founded by Douglas. The pastorate was vacant, but Rev. Brayton had been assigned there by Rev. Willey, and was on his way there to take the post.

Following preaching on Sunday Brier was offered the job as pastor of the congregation in place of Brayton. When Rev. Brayton arrived and heard of this offer, he was understandably angry. Brier felt the tension, and offers this humble explanation in his letter to the AHMS. In essence, he was not only attempting to ward off any further erosion of his confidence in ministry, but was also asking the New York office to become an agent of reconciliation.

CHAPTER 13

In His Element in the Mud and the Trees

Brier went alone for his first exploratory trip to Marysville, as Elizabeth was eight months pregnant and still sick with chronic dysentery. The journey to Marysville was a rugged one. First, there was a twelve hour trip on carriage and horseback that would usually be spread across two days to reach the Sacramento Delta. Sacramento at the time was a major staging ground and market stop for mining expeditions in the gold country.

He took the steamer, *Governor Dana*, from Sacramento thirty miles to the northeast, to the landing at Vernon. It was the end of the summer season and the water in the Yuba river was too low for the boats to go any further, although after the spring rains they did go as far as Marysville. Brier took a stagecoach for the 28 miles between Vernon and Marysville, arriving on September 7, 1850.

He had an introductory letter from "Deacon" Leonard of Hunt's church in San Francisco to a business partner, a young fellow by the name of Mr. Tay who ran a wholesale store in a tent on the lower side of the plaza. Mr. Tay received Rev. Brier and helped him to post notices of preaching and worship services the next day. It was a historic day for many reasons. It was Brier's first sermon in Marysville. He represented the first resident pastor, and it was the week California was admitted to the Union as the 31st State.

Brier arrived in Marysville ready to plant a church like a flower in the California hills, yet his earliest work was in the hillside mining camps in and around Marysville. The following is an excerpt from a *Home Mission Magazine*, which quotes it as an excerpt from Rev. William Wallace Briers' journal of those early days: On September 7, 1850 Mr. Brier arrived at Marysville, where he found *"fifteen hundred or two thousand people . . . about twenty families and five hundred houses and tents, more then half of them cloth . . . . There were some large fame buildings, much dust and many fleas."*

"Sunday, September 8. Preached under the shade of a large white oak tree in the morning. All stores open, all the gambling houses in full blast, teams of ocean and a train of mules loading goods. Went the place advertised, and found about twenty men sitting on old wagons, ox-yokes and logs. One said, as I looked about, 'Sit down, and here's the place to hear preaching'.

"Preached according to appointment at half-past nine in the morning under a large oak tree on the Plaza, near the bank of the Yuba. Seventy men were sitting upon the logs, ox-yokes and parts of wagons. I took my position on a little eminence and commenced to sing a hymn. From every direction gathered crowds of care-worn men, in whose countenances could be seen thoughts of loved ones far away and remembrances of Sabbaths of rest, all listening respectfully to the preaching. At night in the Court House, a rough unlined wooden building on the corner of "E." and "Third Streets". It stood quite beyond the limits of the town. On November 24, 1850, I organized the first Presbyterian Church of Marysville, consisting of nine members. It was a day of much prayer and great solemnity, confession and penitence."[33]

The plaza in Marysville was an open area on the banks of the Yuba River near the upper steamboat landing where freight was unloaded from the boats and re-loaded on carts and mules for transport to the hills. That afternoon, Rev. Brier preached again in the courthouse, which he said was "away out of town, on the plains, on the corner of "E "and Third Streets." The courthouse was a room 20 x 30 feet, on the first floor of the Masonic building. It was described as a frame building covered with rough boards a foot wide, no interior wall lining, a rough floor, and a roomful of backless benches. There were about ten people present. The next Sunday the congregation was larger and the people circulated a subscription paper for pastoral salary to raise monthly funds so they could invite Rev. Brier to remain in Marysville.

Sometime in September Rev. Willey became ill. He could not directly visit Brier to interview him, but instead relied on report from other pastors. Whether he had a visit from the "Panama Fever" we do not know. But by the time Rev. Willey became ill, Brier had been on the field for four months. The following letter from Rev. Willey makes a note of Brier's movements.

From Willey
January 9, 1851

"Brother Brier went to Marysville before I recovered from being sick. I have not heard directly from him—though from others I learn that he is an acceptable minister of the gospel there and is pretty much alone on that ground. Brother Benton in Sacramento has a house of good worship established and a good congregation." [34]

Marysville was known as the mining capital, and was largely an all male community. On occasion, a bride would arrive in the frontier, summoned from a romantic letter sent back home. It was big news in town, and Brier was called forth to officiate the marriage. One of these "gold brides" had arrived, and it was time to seal the deal. On December 29th, Sunday evening, the Reverend W. Brier married Mr. O.H. Pierson, formerly of Peoria, Illinois, to Miss Nancy Hight, lately of St. Louis Missouri. [35]

The second half of Brier's letter #14 is important at this point. Returning to this letter, he narrates his journey to Marysville.

Brier Letter # 14

"Ministers here should be men of strength, both of body and mind."

Marysville, California
January 11, 1851

Dear Rev. Badger,

You have long expected a report from me and have commenced to fear (and doubt not) that I have "vanished" to the "mines". But if you knew the work I have had to perform, you would readily forgive the apparent neglect. If the path of cross is the path of duty, I surely have been in the true way since I left Indiana—(Detention and disappointment have met and have lifted their snaky heads at almost every steps of my progress.)

When I arrived at San Francisco on the 7th of August I found Brother Hunt absent. I remained until his return on the 13th. At that time (Brothers Willey and Douglas were present) their advice to me was to locate at Marysville. But as my health was much reduced by my stay in Panama, and as my wife was not in condition to be taken among strangers, (to a place, as this was then, extremely hot and sickly, also destitute of comfortable houses) I determined to go down to San Jose, where my brother resided with his family, (and whom I had not see for five years).

(When) I went down to remain a few days with my brother, I met Mr. Beard at the Mission. I was expecting to visit Marysville very soon.

Now(I am residing) in Marysville. On the 8th of September, I preached my first sermon in this place—All the stores were open and business as on week days—I stood under an oak tree in the plaza, and while I sung an old Sacred song (of camp meeting origin), many came running from every quarter, to hear "what was up" They listened, as audiences always do here, with the attention focused on the word. In the afternoon I preached in the courthouse to about ten persons, some said that this was an unusually large turnout to preaching. (On) the next Sabbath the congregation was larger: and the people gave me an *invitation to preach in this place by circulating a subscription paper for so much more during the winter. After going down to San Jose, on the 22 of September the Lord gave me (a gift) in the shape of a little girl. I returned to this place on the 12th of October. As I could not rent even an inferior room for less than $100 per month, I built a little house, working six days with my hands and preaching three times on the Sabbath.*

As I could save $10 per day (by doing the work myself) I thought it better to preach old sermons, and do as Paul did. We have a house now neatly lined (in calico). One room 10 by 12 and my study 8x10. You would be astonished to step into it and see all the signs of a minister, in a town, which did not exist this time last year. I have made a bedstead, a wardrobe, a book cabinet, shelves, and a lounge chair. I also made a cloth house (a wood frame and cloth walls due to the cost materials) for a lumber-room and wood house.

I removed my family here on the 6th of November. My wife has not been well since she arrived. She has the chronic dysentery. I have preached regularly. My congregations have gradually increased. The courthouse has been filled for several Sabbaths. There is hope that we will soon build a church, but all things are uncertain here. I circulated an agreement among the merchants to close the stores on the Sabbath, which they all signed—I am glad to see a better state of morals in every respect than when I first came to this place. All have seen the change and speak of it. And the glory is given to the Gospel of Christ.

The gambling saloons are not so crowded. Profanity, the incense of the wicked souls, does not rise in such a united constant column as it did. The strange women do not walk and ride the streets in men's attire as much as they did. The prayer meeting is better attended; and Christians upon whose lips the long neglected words of devotion were almost bound, now utter strong and earnest cries for the descent of the Holy Ghost. And I continue to hope that even in these ends of the earth we will have a revival of religion. But even the golden mountain has great power to draw the divine electricity from the souls of men.

Marysville is in the fork of the Yuba and Feather Rivers, 45 miles above Sacramento City. It contains about 2000 people, has improved much since I came to it, but is now declining. There have been only 6 or 7 rainy days, hence the miners in the upper country have been enabled to go to Sacramento City for their goods. The people are disappointed and many have met with losses in having made preparations for a great influx of people to spend the winter on high land. The river also has been low. All these things are against me. Many who had subscribed to my support have left for the mines or back east.

But I trust the Lord, that He will provide for me, and that the seed which I have sown here may spring up in the hearts of those who have heard, in whatever place they may be— I have organized a church of ten members, the first church organized in the place and I believe about the only one. But it is very doubtful where or not I will remain longer than the spring. Then most of my people will go to other places during the summer. I did not think this the best place, from the first to settle; but my commission made it necessary to follow the advice of them, and I was not willing to assume the responsibility of acting differently.

In new countries, missions should be established, not when a number of people may be together at any particular time, but at places where the tide will rise. The Methodists are doing just what we are not doing. They establish their best men at the centers of agricultural districts on those points of trade which will not change with the winds of mining operations; and leave almost entirely neglected these upper country cities of a day. This may possibly be a permanent place of trade, but it depends altogether on the mines. Most of the places mentioned by Mr. Blakeslee will be deserted in a year or two. It would be just as well to send missionaries among the sailors in the port of New York, with the expectation of building up the Zion of California, as to send men to these mining towns because these miners may be sailors in two years, and the sailors will become miners. We know not what a year will bring forth—no not even a month in this land.

But one thing I believe, this will become a great country. This is a delightful climate. This day was as bright and pleasant as any day in May, and so it has been most of the winter. I am delighted with California, but cannot tell how the summer will go off. This is a very difficult country for a minister to succeed.

There are so many here who have apostatized, that the people suspect everyone to be bad. We have five or six persons in this town whose letters are addressed to Reverend, but they sell whiskey, and some do worse. We have men here from all countries and states, and the preacher must please them all. They must read to please the Eastern people, and speak extemporaneously to please the Westerners; Southerners must have fire, Northerners argument and facts. The whole community is composed of men who have seen and heard much. California contains a host of strong-minded intelligent people from all lands of earth.

Ministers here should be men of strength, both of body and mind. It is better not to send any than to send weak men. They will not be supported because people will not go to hear them preach or if they do it is to blaspheme. It is not an uncommon thing for men to tell the preacher that what he says is a damned lie; that is, preachers whom they do not respect. You know that it is better to have no preachers than such as these.

Brother Benton of Sacramento is doing very well. He is a new man, who has a mind to the work. The churches in San Francisco are will attended this winter. Brother S.H. Willey was well when I heard from him last.

I sold one of my drafts ($150.00) because the expense of getting up here and getting settled was very great. I am yet in debt, but will soon be able to pay up all. I have spent $1167 since I left New York including Panama expenses.

Write to me. I will write again before long. I send my love to all. My wife sends her love. Give Christian love to Mr. Hall and all the friends who may inquire. In haste I have written this long letter.

Yours truly
W.W. Brier[36]

Indeed, in haste he wrote them a long letter! He noted that he was alone in Marysville for the first two months while his wife remained at the Mission San Jose. In late September, Brier returned from Marysville to Mission San Jose where his wife was about to give birth to their first child. There was no doctor in the Mission area, so they drove 15 miles southwest to the village of San Jose. That very night, September 22, 1850, at 9 o'clock a baby girl was born, which they named Lizzie. Mrs. Brier wrote, "My husband was my nurse and washed the baby's diapers, because the cost of having someone wash diapers was six dollars a dozen. As a favor, a woman washed some plain pieces for them at $3.50 a dozen." Days later, they returned to the Beard residence at the mission. Elizabeth stayed at the Beard residence until November 6th when the young family moved to Marysville. In those early days Elizabeth and the baby were the celebrities of the town, as there were few wives, and even fewer children present in that community.

Brier also wrote about the transitory nature of the population and the difficulty in reaching the people. The economic and political landscape seemed to change by the day; "We know not what a year will bring forth—no not even a month in this land."

Northern California Churches

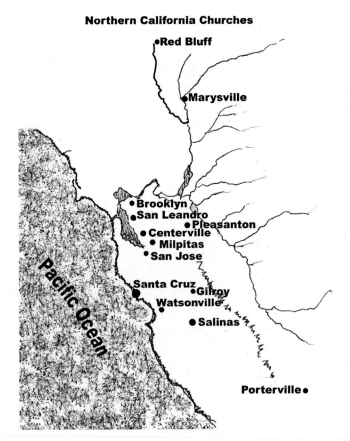

It is remarkable that the church is up and running after just a few months. He commented about the demanding role of the preacher in meeting the needs of so many different people. "Here we have men from all countries and states, and the preacher must please them all. They must read to please the Eastern people, and speak extemporaneously to please the Westerners; Southerners must have fire, Northerners argument and facts."

It is curious that there was so much infighting and overt backstabbing among the ministers as they related to the New York Office. In this letter Brier goes after Rev. Blakeslee. "You know that it is better to have no preachers than such as these. You will wish to know how Mr. Blakeslee succeeds here. If I must speak, it is to say that he is not fit for California." If there is any hallmark of the western spirit, it is the rugged individualism, which resides so deeply in the soul of the people, and finds its place in the life and leadership of the churches. Brier notes, "The whole community is composed of men who have seen and heard much. California contains a host of strong-minded intelligent people from all lands of earth."

Rev. Brier notes Rev. Willey was healthy again—at least for the moment. Here is Rev. Willey's strategy for Brier's move.

Rev. Willey's Letter to the AHMS
March 1, 1851

There is a wonderful place at San Jose Mission where a very respectable agricultural community is gathering. Brother Brayton preaches regularly and every week, as you could appoint a man to get on the ground there they will be able to raise a place of worship. They may be able to teach a while and then the people would support them.

Brother Brier and wife are at Marysville. I have no direct information from him personally, but two gentlemen members of his church say that his congregation is about to build a place of worship, that his influence in the community is extensive and salutary. He enjoys the confidence of good people, and the respect of all. That a visible change has taken place in the community after he went there. Now Brother Brier may give much better information from the north, than I can, but I will tell what I know.

Grace and Peace,
S.H. Willey

This brief note from Willey to the board was a confirmation that perhaps they had misjudged Brier and his ability to establish a church. He was now indeed in his element— out in the mud and the trees!

But to establish a strong church, he had to get there first. In the early days of church planting in the west, there was an informal agreement over territorial rights among the Protestant Christian denominations to prevent competing over communities or in any part of the state. They called this *a Comity agreement*, which basically assigned towns to one denomination or another, and then agreed not to compete with each other. This was honored for generations. And the way to secure this agreement was to be the first church ministering in the community. Thus, like a church mining claim, it regulated who would be probing for the gold of human souls in that community.

Willey wanted to keep his eye on Brier's progress. He was not going to let a failure occur on his watch. Other pastors he would allow to work without regular reports, yet he wanted Brier to report to him on a regular basis.

Brier responded to this intense scrutiny by trying to succeed in the construction of the church building as soon as possible. This did not sit well with Willey, who thought Brier ought to work on getting pledges (subscriptions) for the pastoral support. In a way, Willey was correct. Had Brier worked at getting personal support, this might have worked, except Brier was threatened by the intellectual strength of Rev. Willey. Brier had previously been mentored by some high-powered intellectuals, and was not frightened by scholarly work. Perhaps it was the cool personality and the ivy league accent that put Brier off. Rev. Willey tried to please Brier, but when he needed on the ground support, and not lofty ideas, he turned to Brier.

Even though he was different from Rev. Willey, Brier learned about mentoring and supervision from him. He watched Willey as he supervised a variety of ministers, and he noticed what was required of them. In many ways, Brier bonded more deeply with Timothy Dwight Hunt, but he also knew that Willey would outlast Hunts influence in the agency. Hunt was the leader of only one congregation. Willey was quickly recognized as the Presbyterian leader who was the elder statesman of the Presbyterian community, and the California educational community as well. Sam Willey was a conservative, "by the book" East Coast intellectual. There were proper ways of doing things. His view of establishing a church or a college was to use the same, tried and true pattern of leadership that would lead to success. Brier was in a tough situation; as three of the ministers, Willey, Brayton, and Blakeslee, were trained in the East Coast intellectual rigid environment. Brier was planner and a doer.

Brier wanted to get the job done as quickly as possible. He proceeded with this plan to build the physical structure of the church while he worked on the building of the membership of the congregation. He thought that if they were to raise the building the members would come soon thereafter. Some issues Brier faced were not unique to Marysville.

CHAPTER 14

The Brier Family in Marysville

Sam Hopkins Willey wrote the AHMS office regarding the return of the Briers to Marysville in his March 1st, 1851 letter to the AHMS.

"Brother Brier and wife are at Marysville. No direct information from him personally, but two gentlemen members of his church say that his congregation is about to build a place of worship, that his influence in the community is extensive and salutary. He enjoys the confidence of good people, and the respect of all. It is evident that a visible change has taken place in the community after he went there. Now Brother Brier may give much better information from the north, than I can, but I will tell what I know."

In Elizabeth's Reminiscences, she remembered the drama of that first trip to Marysville. "In four weeks (after the baby was born) we went in four horse stage coach to San Francisco (58 miles in five hours). There was a station every ten miles where fresh, unbroken Mustangs were hitched up. A man stood at the head of each horse, until the word was given to let go. The horses loped all of the way until the next station we reached. We were on our way to Marysville, which was at the head of navigation on the Yuba River. We were obliged to stay in San Francisco a few days. The cholera was in Sacramento City and you should have had to stay over night. The steamer on which we traveled to Sacramento had no private rooms. Berths only on each side of the dining saloon. A common wash-pan for all. Nothing luxurious in that kind of traveling. A lot had been given us in Marysville. Mr. Brier with the help of a cheap carpenter ($10.00 to $16.00 a day was the usual price) had built a house, the dimensions of which were 10x 20 feet. It was not finished when I went into it. We could see the stars through the cracks. But when it was lined with calico, it was very cozy. We had a partition of calico to make two rooms. Two rooms were added the following years, there were more cloth tents in the town than wooden houses. So we were quite swell."

Meanwhile, the return to Marysville was difficult for William. It may have been that he had a second bout of Panama fever, or perhaps he was hit with a new one. It appears that he was ill and depressed.

The following letter is a curious one in that it is not in Brier's handwriting. It is clearly written by someone else in tight, neat handwriting that was perhaps his wife's. The last paragraph is added to, and signed by him. He may have been too ill.

Brier letter # 15

"It has been a dark time with us in this place."

Feb 26, 1851
Marysville, California
To the Secretaries of A.H.M.S.

Dear Brethren,

I have delayed my quarterly report for a short time, as I have completed my 2nd quarter of missionary service this year under your society, laboring in California. I now write in order to send you a statistical report, but am almost, ashamed, as it will show but little accomplished.

It has been a dark time with us in this place. All business in this place seemed to stop for a while, and with it my (financial) support. One half the sum promised to me has not been paid: hence I must send a draft to refund money received for books sold for M. H. Newman and Co. The money was spent in building my house and settling here: now I have completed the sale and hence must pay. But I hope, and trust, this is the last call I will have to make on you for funds.

The people have supported me since I fairly settled here. It cost me much to get to this place. Freight from San Francisco to Marysville when I came was much more than from N.Y. to San Francisco (over $500.00). I would do anything consistent rather than call upon you for money: I know what good a little accomplishes in the great Western valley. But here we may not turn our thoughts to secular objects. If I should do it, I suppose, I could make more money than some of your agents collect, in the states, but you did not send me for that purpose, and I have given myself unreservedly to the work of the Ministry. I feel that any labor has not been in vain in the Lord.

Since my last (letter) congregations have been as large as I could accommodate in the Court House—they have given deep and serious attention to the truth. The change in morals is marked. There is a strong public opinion rising to Heaven against the sins, which have been rife in this place. I have organized a Sabbath School, which promises *much good. It has only met twice. We are raising funds to build a church, and I trust in three months it will be dedicated to holy purposes. We do things in haste when we commence—as you have seen in the papers. I suppose that we have obtained a City Charter. The business of a City is now done here. I heard one of the many merchants of this place say in recent days he had sold $50,000 worth of goods in the past month. But we know not what will be next month. Business and church matters are alike uncertain— I have no idea how I will spend the summer. It may not be best to stay here, that I may go to the mountains to preach. One of the members of our church, who now lives fifty miles distant, last Sabbath, with tears streaming down his cheeks, asked if I knew anything about the Home Mission Societies operation in California. "Will they send any one to preach in the mountains this summer?" There are many good people in the mines but an awful state of morals.*

Mrs. Brier's health is better than it was: at present she has chills and fever: she has not been well since I came to this place. It may be necessary for me to leave this locality on her account. Our "Chicuela" is growing very fast.

Our second communion will be next Sabbath. I preach three times on Sunday and have much other work to perform, as the minister here must do most that is done in a religious line. We have few people, however who have not defiled their garments in sin. The people have paid me $420 for Ministerial Services in this place. My expenses in California (including building and freight) have been $1,000.00. We are now perfectly delighted with our beautiful country. Had we society this would be a land unequalled by any other on earth. This we hope soon to have—Many are bringing their families to settle in this region of eternal summer. Next week, March 5th, I attend a convention to ordain and install Brother Benton, of Sacramento City. He is doing a good work. All the Ministers in San Francisco have full churches. We could dispose of some more good men here. The name Presbyterian is a great recommendation to a Minister.

The Western Presbyterians take hold of the work in new places and help the ministers. They do not distinguish between Old and New School Presbyterians here. Several of my church members were Old School at home. I do think the Presbyterian name and system will succeed better than the Congregational, but I sincerely hope that we may all unite and have our three churches in one.

Yours Truly,
W.W. Brier.[37]

If it were ghost written, it is certainly his tone and style of letter. He must have dictated it to someone. Brier boasts of the influence of the church upon the Marysville community. "I feel that any labor has not been in vain in the Lord. Since my last (letter, the) congregations have been as large as I could accommodate in the Court House—they have given deep and serious attention to the truth. The change in morale is marked."

Of interest in this letter is his comment about the lack of division between Old School and New School Presbyterians on the frontier. This became a hallmark of his ministry for years to come, as his heart pushed him to become a bridge-builder at every level throughout the Old School and New School Presbyterian Church families. He also sold his personal library to fund the building of his house. He foreshadows the disaster and departure from Marysville, and he claimed he is poor and under-supported.

Attached to the report was a short note in Brier's handwriting to Mr. Ripley, the Treasurer of the AHMS, whom he stayed with while in New York. Ripley must have expressed an interest in the geology of California, for Brier notes in great detail a large granite outcrop which rises from the midst of the valley floor some fifteen miles north of Marysville. It was called Sutter's Rock, visible for 100 miles in every direction. Perhaps it is a result of Brier's college training at Wabash, which included a class on Geology. It appears that since he was submitting his voucher to the secretaries of the AHMS, there was a member of the staff who has had specific fascinations with geology that Brier refers to. These geologic interests could have raised further concerns and added to the board's intrigue and fear that Brier's motive for going to California was in the "gold getting" mode.

Brier Letter #16

To Mr. Ripley,

My Dear Friend,

I took a ride yesterday to the Buttes, a clump of mountains 12 miles west of this city. As I examined their geological structure I thought how you would be delighted to ascend their rocky steps. The peaks are numerous and show evident volcanic action. They have been thrown up in the middle of the Sacramento Valley and are unconnected to any other mountains. I had no means of measuring the heights of the peak, which we ascend: it was the highest and lifts its heads among the clouds. For a great distance up on the outside the formation is the same as the plane, but when you got within 3 or 4 hundred feet of the summit we came to rocks heaped up in awful majesty. They are synitic (sic) granite, having been subjected to great heat and there is an unusual proportion of quartz in them. These peaks have been the escape pipes for fire and gases—But I have not room to give any more.

Our love to yourself and daughter.
W. W. Brier

While things may seem curious in Brier's letters and actions, there is never any evidence that for a moment he showed interest in commercial activities other than farming. The following letter from the AHMS office is a response to Brier's letter, four months after they received it. It clarifies that they were concerned about not hearing from him, and were celebrating the arrival of the first child.

AMERICAN HOME MISSION SOCIETY Response

New York,
May 27, 1851[38]

Dear Rev. Brier,

Your January 11th letter was received by our office three weeks ago. I now embraced the opportunity of Rev. Hunt's departure to San Francisco to send you a response.

Your long letter was truly a relief. I can't even imagine why so long a time had elapsed without our hearing from you. I was sometime filled with apprehension, lest unwittingly we had done something or left something undone, which had hurt your feelings. That the narrative of your labor and that various changes through which you and yours have traveled, assured us that you have had an abundant reward for all your time and strength. We can most cordially unite in sympathy with you and Mrs. Brier's thankfulness that you were carried safely through the various emergencies and trials of your voyage. I have continued to enfold in our prayers a praise of God's goodness and your mutual affections. May (your daughters) arrival as a gift of an ounce of domestic joy. May she become an instrument of blessing to the country of her birth!

Considering the rudeness of all new settlements and especially the elements, which compose the first population of a mining town, I am supportive of the history of your first quarter of labor in Marysville. Truly no parallel ever will be found on this side of the continent of an equal advance on the heart of the Gospel: the desecration of Sabbath. If Mr. Hunt could not face its population, which you express some apprehension, I cannot but regard your prospects of useful influence (and that also of ultimately conquest) quite as much as if you had settled at San Jose.

In your account of the occasion which you allude to in reference to that place, it surprised all parties about your being proposed as the second pastor of San Jose. But it is past, and while it was very difficult, it may seem disastrous, so far as you're own comfort and Mrs. Brier is concerned. Still if you have the conscientiousness of having acted in a true and honorable manner, you will have nothing in the end to regret. It is difficult (to judge) when every one is so new, and to form many definite conclusions. As the part of greatest influence a few years hence, I see that the capital is to be removed to Vallejo of Camden, San Jose will not retain its relative prominence.

Other changes must continually be taking place for some years, so that it will change if most of the ministry in the new state spirit will be compelled to shift their position repeatedly. What is due, in your case more than any other, must be left for the light when radiance shall be seen from time to time.

Unless the illness of Mrs. Brier, to which you allude, will compel your removal, I hope you will make full proof of your experiment, which this far seems to grow auspiciously.

Our Treasurer desires me to ask you to send us your account of expenses. You will remember that there was an advance made to you for the purpose of expenses on the Isthmus. He is unable to balance, it on his books, until you shall file us your bills and particulars. Also state how much of your time since your arrival in California you consider the Society responsible to you.

I beg you to present affectionate regards to Mrs. Brier whom we remember with fraternal interest. Many other acquaintances made in New York have inquired after her, as well as yourself. Your Mission to that interesting land is upon our hearts and brought to the Mercy Seat. If there be any thing which we can provide for your welfare or comfort let us know. You will aid the purpose of the mission if you will freely communicate any facts that may come to your knowledge, or facts of what's needful and expedient by which we may be guided in conducting to you.

May the Lord help and keep you,
Rev. Dr. Badger[39]

This is an interesting note of fatherly support from Dr. Badger. For one it reflects the level of pastoral support an accountability that has taken place between the AHMS and the supported missionary. He wrote a compassionate letter which responds to Brier's explanation of the conflict in San Jose with Brayton's church, and the early days of establishing his ministry in Marysville.

Rev. Badger hails his support for Rev. Brier's condemnation of the lawlessness of the age. His words of admonition to: *"Considering the rudeness of all new settlements and especially the elements which compose the first population of a mining town, I am supportive of the history of your first quarters labors in Marysville. Truly no parallel ever will be found on this side of the continent of an equal advance on the heart of the Gospel, and the desecration of Sabbath."*

This paints a bold contrast between the good of the gospel, and the evil that is resident in the mining camps. If nothing else, it focused Brier upon the good ministry he was doing.

CHAPTER 16

"I will build a church in Marysville"

Early in his California ministry Brier began to express his frustration with the financial troubles of serving as a pioneer minister. He submitted his Panama expense voucher (for one thousand dollars) which helped us to understand his every move across the Isthmus. Here in this voucher he writes to the AHMS a letter scribbled on the back of his expense voucher from Panama:

"I have been very economical, more than any other in the country"

Brier Letter # 16

Dear Dr. Badger and Hall,

I have been very economical, more than any other in the country. We live in a house too small for comfort and have not been able to buy furniture. This I have done because I knew that every $100.00 saved to your Society would assist some minister to live one year in Western field of labor. I receive but little at present. The people have been contributing to build, and my subscription run out in March. Since that time it has not been renewed. The church spoke of making another effort to raise funds, but has not done it yet. This place is improving and will probably be a large town. Our church lot is the best site in the city. When we get into a new church there will be more certainty of support.

In the meantime, on April 6, 1851 a Sunday school was organized with 27 members and a library of 100 volumes was collected which, undoubtedly, was the first public library in Marysville. At the end of the first year all the money received from your Society will constitute about one fourth of my expenses: that is from August 7, 1850 to August 7, 1851.

William Wallace Brier

It is true that Brier was economical. He was known as frugal and ran very frugal congregations. It was part of the Scottish legacy and part of the legacy of the Presbyterian Church. It is true that other denominations were better equipped to bring financial resources to California. Although they had fewer churches, they were more strategically located, and more substantial in their buildings and structures.

Brier was already active in the community, making connections and ministering through weddings and funerals. The San Francisco newspaper, *Alta California*, notes that on March 28 the Rev. Brier performed a wedding for Mr. George Livingston of New York City, to Miss Eliza Jane Fairrow, of Illinois.[40] This informs us that in March he went to San Francisco to collect money for the church building among his friends and colleagues in the city.

Signposts on the Frontier: Raise the Church Building!

The difficult issue facing the pioneer church planters of that age was the contrast between the miners that bristled with wealth and the church members who were on a fixed income. Farmers were dependent upon the erratic weather conditions in a land they did not fully understand. Merchants and traders were tied to the breezy news of first gold strikes caused a stampede of miners and fortune seekers who would march in and out of the area seeking the latest bonanza. Cities were founded overnight, and rolled up the streets just months later as the claims proved empty. Still, good God-fearing people were determined to found a church that would last. The Presbyterians of Marysville were determined to find a way to get the church built, and Brier was in the lead helping them.

Most pioneer ministers would contact leaders in the community, both Christians and non-Christians, to gain pledges, referred to as subscriptions, for their personal support and for the construction of a church structure. Frequently, non-Christian business leaders thought that a church edifice would insure the stature and permanence of the community. Their contributions were often rooted in the hopes of future profits, and the permanent success of the community.

The task of securing financial support was not an easy one. Pastors asked new residents to sign subscription papers as pledges of support against future income. Rev. Brayton notes his difficulty in gaining support through subscription in the burgeoning capital of San Jose.

"Leaving around a subscription papers was anything but congenial; yet I found in the end that it gave me the but feasible introductions to the action classes of the community. It was hard work, which property and businessmen declining to obtain promises of money. It was harder still to collect the money promised."

Sometimes, the tithes were not simply in cash but in the donation of timber or laborers to finish the task. Brayton continues, *"A generous farmer in San Francisco sold us*

the building frame and materials not only for credit but without any other security than the
word of promise of a compassionate stranger. The bright side to this place was the paying the
workmen lifting their hammers moderately at from eight to twelve dollars a day." [41]

Here we begin to see the various styles of fundraising that Brier employed in the
construction of a church. He utilized the church erection fund, which was a national
denominational fund that would offer modest grants to both the Old School Presbyterians
and among the loose connection of the New School Presbyterians. He met with influential
citizens to sign subscriptions to pledge support over time—both for building materials
and for support of the pastors. He also worked in getting non-believing individuals to
give money to his church both in Romney and in Marysville. Now he branched out and
networks the social circles of Marysville to be involved in throwing an auction and
dramatic comedy show. A fire destroyed the theater in San Francisco earlier in the year,
and so the theater troop traveled to regional cities for performances. Brier recruited the
group to be featured at the Marysville fund-raisers.

The Marysville Herald reported the following fundraising events: *"The subscription*
list was started in February 1851, and in May, the ladies of Marysville associated for the
first time and held a "Ladies Faire" as a means of raising money to help pay the cost of the
new church building. This "Fair" was held on the evenings of May 13, 14, in rooms over
Perry's Brick Store on Second Street. It was largely a sale of homemade commodities at
auction to the gentlemen, who became so bewildered at "the array of bright eyes and straightway
deposited into the hands of the fair ladies who were conducting the affair." Mr. Fairchild, a
comedian with Dr. Robinson's theatrical company, in town at the time served as auctioneer.
His function is described in their words:

"The funny Fairchild was holding forth . . . selling at auction. When we went in he was
selling a piece of gingerbread and had got a good bid of two shillings on it. 'Gentlemen will
you allow me to throw property away like this? Who wouldn't give more than two shillings for
a piece of gingerbread in aid or building a church . . . ? Look at the style of ginger, going, any
advance—gone!' And up walked a man from Pike County and the gingerbread disappeared
immediately. A very "handsome sum" was realized from this Fair." [42]

Aside from this high society fundraiser, the building fund languished. Marysville
was a tough city to labor in, and a tough place to raise money in. Brier collected most of the
money to pay for the building of the church himself. He went to the mining camps on foot,
preaching, and soliciting funds for the church building. He raised several hundred dollars in
gold dust on these trips. He traveled to San Francisco again in May to obtain building
supplies for the church structure, and provisions for his home as well.

By many accounts, he thought he was doing well. The church was organized, and
the building was on the way to completion. Yet his colleges suspicions about his
abilities continued. In a note critical of his financial approach, his supervisor on the
field, Rev. Willey wrote to the New York office on May 1, 1851, saying, *"Brother Brier*

is in town today getting materials for a fair in Marysville to raise funds to build a church. Business in Marysville is growing very much. The town is becoming more and more permanent and prosperous. Brier will get a house of worship soon, but he began at the wrong end. He must not work up a salary for himself first—and then the building. Had he done this— looked first to the getting of a plain church—he might have one done by this time—and arrived at his support from the pew rent. But he may have a building up soon."

After much difficulty in obtaining materials, by the spring of 1851 they constructed a small church on the northwest corner of 3rd and D streets on a lot 60 feet on D Street and 40 feet on Third Street. At the same time the church bought its property, he purchased a lot for his own home, and began construction with wood and fabric to create a home.

By May of that year, the population of Marysville was booming to over 3,200 residents, who positioned themselves at the supply headquarters and stage departure center to the sprouting mining communities 30 miles northeast and beyond. The city had become a provisional banking center, with clusters of gold assay offices, hundreds of lawyers to defend claims, hotels, mining outfitters, and stables.

Yet all was not well with Brier's soul. This letter from the AHMS board validates the receipt of a letter by Brier to the AHMS board, and validates his feelings of distress about the ongoing problems in ministry there.

Letter From the AHMS board to Brier

March 17, 1851

Rev W. W. Brier,

Yours of February 2nd has been received. We regret that you experienced much embarrassment, disillusionment, but this must be the order of the day in California. I am fully sympathetic with our heart now and from equal to learn the lessons that of the day. I apprehend that are all to have a new breath of faith in references to the missionary call in your heart, but that a bright new day is coming, though distant. I have no doubt. We have conferred with Dr. Bushnell and Mrs. Hunt in regard to your interest in Education in California.

The committee has granted this request for your scholarship application. Herewith is a draft for $220 is the balance due you on the 1st of February. We should know about this except the last Steamer delayed for Mr. Pierpont of the meeting Mrs. Hunt on the subject which was very practical till yesterday. We forward your report for the current quarter, as even as you receive this we will send a draft in the first mail. If the increasing *liberality of your people were to lead to commission we would be delighted—at least after these recent years.*

Commending you to the care of the Chief Shepherd.
Yours truly,
Dr. Hall.[43]

He was commended for his hard work. Meanwhile, in the flash and flair of 15 months of ministry Brier began to crack. His health broke first, then his pastoral performance, and finally his emotional life.

The response from the board was encouraging. Dr. Hall sent a compassionate letter with a number of interesting facts. There was the foreshadowing of the Brier's reaching out to Rev. Horace Bushnell, his former pastor and professor. Dr. Hall mentioned that he has passed on the letter with Brier's interest in establishing a college in California to Bushnell. This will be a note for future interaction, as Brier's connection with Bushnell will have a significant impact in the future history of California.

Marysville had quickly moved from a mining camp to become one of the most promising and vital communities. It is ironic that Brier was sent into the mud and the trees of the backward California, and in a years time Brier is ready to start a university there. In both his October and November reports to the AHMS, Willey includes a statement about Brier's illness and progress.

October 1, 1851

"Brother Brier has been suffering from bad health for months, we now hope he getting up. He is at one of the most important points in the State."

Brier suffered through the return of the dreaded Panama Fever, which could have been many things; amoebic dysentery, malaria, yellow fever, or hepatitis. In the days before effective antibiotics a disease like this never really went away, and would stay with the person for years, only to resurface when they were weakened by fatigue. Willey notes Brier's poor health again in his November 14th letter to Badger and Hall. The delay is timely news in updating his next letter to the AHMS Board. He may have gained dysentery or Cholera from his visits to the logging camps of golden hills above Sacramento.

November 14th, 1851

"Brother Brier is recovering from impaired health from which he as suffered during the summer and he is seeming to have more energy and success than before."

CHAPTER 16

Floundering In The Tide

Brier's letter of May 29th, 1851 stressed his growing acceptance by the pastors in California who were supported by the AHMS. They trust his ability to discern new opportunities, and his ability to make connections with New York office of the AHMS, so they urge him to write with his observations and concerns. Brier's writing emerges with a pattern that would paint picturesque visions of the landscape, stirring brush strokes of the spiritual needs, and a hungry cry for more financial support. This letter also shows that Brier is angling for a new assignment in San Diego, where he thinks there was a better assignment for he and his wife. Though he has never been there, there are reports that it must be a more temperate climate. He also reveals to his supervisor that he studied the Spanish language during his months in Panama.

We are like babes lifting up our hands against the inbound tide,
which comes thundering amid huge rocks.

Brier Letter # 17

May 29th, 1851

Drs. Hall and Badger
Home Missions Society

Dear Reverend Brethren,

I was appointed by our Presbytery, which met last week in San Francisco to request your Board on the subject of sending more missionaries to this state and Oregon. Since I last wrote, there have been great changes in this country. The tide of immigration, into this wonderful land, has changed in character. The people have also, almost unanimously changed their views in respect to the promise of our prosperity. Great multitudes are determining to send for their families and friends.

Brother's Hunt feels we should be increasing our activity in each community to overtake the raw march of migrants, which every three months changes its course and character of the community. These changes are great and frequent, yet they are all for the better.

The cities with promise spoken of at our meetings are to follow, each requiring at least one minister.

First. Napa and Sonoma valleys reveal a beautiful agricultural district surrounding the beautiful cities.

2nd. Trinity Bay, which will soon be very important.

3rd. Humboldt Bay north of Trinity—a pleasant countryside.

4th. Sonora and other places in the Southern mines. This region has been neglected.

5th. San Diego and the coast country. We should have a man who will be useful among the Spanish who can speak their language. I would like that field myself. I became interested in the Spanish at Panama.

6th. The mining country in this northern region. These are places where 5,000 people live within two or three miles of towns in the mountains. A man of the right kind would be supported in many of these places. We have tens of thousands in these mountains who need to hear the words of life. Not much can be done of which will be permanently benefit our churches here, but immortality might be sustained.

I fear that these people are unrestrained and will form habits and characters, and learn vices, which they will carry back with them to curse many a fair portion of older states.

Infidelity grows very rapidly among a people in the condition of our miners. I have found some whose minds are deeply tainted with loose notions and whose opinions are unsettled in respect to the great principles of our holy religion. Men, who, at home had been members in good standing in orthodox churches—and many others who have forsaken entirely the covenant of their God and pride of their youth.

But I write to say something about the men who should be sent there. No country in the world requires such men as this. There are no crooks or corners where a man of narrow capacity can be placed. Unless you can obtain the right men, do not put others of less importance forward. We do not wish men who will require others to take care of them. A man sent here should be a learner who can hold his own in a hostile territory.

There are several points that we felt important (in qualifying men):

1st. Have a wife as necessary assistant unless he is sent to travel into the mines.

2nd. He should have experience and knowledge of human nature. Young men who have seen nothing but the walls of college are dangerous persons to labor here: they may sincere, but they end up failures. They should be strong as steel. There is no room to grow up, everything must be ready or else or cast aside.

3rd. Western or Southern men are best, from the fact such are permanently settling this country and they have their own unchangeable nature and customs. But a man would be able to show a north, east, southerner and western side. They should not be like the young Easterners. They ought to have some measure of established character and reputation. The world has no fields where "seed wheat" is to be raised to the same extent as here. One of the members of my church has written to her brother to come out and train as a preacher, but I wished to see a few who will have strong arms to beat back the dark waves and give character to our efforts.

We are like babes lifting up our hands against the inbound tide, which comes thundering amid huge rocks

We are getting short about money, as usual, our church has not made advances as fast as was expected. Have raised about $3,000.00: it will repay the costs, but later.

Mr. Brier wishes to remember her kindly to you. Lizzie is growing. We are all well at present. We were glad to get Dr. Hall's kind letter and hope to hear often. Ask any questions and you shall have the best answer that I can give.

Yours Truly
W.W. Brier.[44]

In the previous letter, Brier points out what sort of leader it takes to survive on the western frontier. His goal, of course, is to induce the society to send more missionaries. It is interesting is that he creates a description of a leader that exactly matches him. He is married, strong, and comfortable with a farming community. These new leaders need to hit the ground running, like a rugged Western man hewn from the swamps of Indiana. Eastern men or New Englanders are not able handle the frontier situation, as they were seen as bookish, and prissy.

In this letter, Brier also shows himself to have the classic temperament of an evangelist. He is brash, self confident, and always restless. He is a planter, not a harvester. He is eager to get things moving, and then is ready to move on to the next assignment.

William Brier was focused on the task. And this task was the organization of the New School congregation in California, at the mother community of all the mining town churches. This was such a single-minded concern to him, that he paid no attention to his own body and soul. The cold weather became unbearable in January when Elizabeth returned to the Mission San Jose. For the next three months, William worked flat out. In April of 1851 Elizabeth and the family joined him once again, and stayed through the long sweltering summer.

The heat was unbearable during the day. There were a number of fires, but none as great as the great August fire, which swept through the burgeoning tent city of Marysville and destroyed three quarters of the town. On the night of August 31, 1851, a Chinese washer man fell asleep leaving a candle burning near some clothes. The candle burned down, igniting the clothes, and before the Chinese awakened, his shop was in flames. Eighty buildings are completely destroyed. Three-fourths of the business section of Marysville was destroyed in a few days.[45]

CHAPTER 17

Continued Mistrust

In the early years Rev. Benton emerged as a stalwart leader for the American Home Mission Society and was seen as the "bishop" of the Congregational churches in the Sacramento valley. Benton had arrived in 1849, and had already established a solid congregation. He was an intellectual. Some called him a poet of the pulpit, as his sermons would be packed with visual images of the divine calling of the pioneers to conquer the land. Although he was settled in his Sacramento ministry, there was some evidence of restlessness in his soul.

W.W. Brier considered himself a friend to Benton, and was invited to Sacramento to participate in Benton's ordination and installation at the church. The First Congregational Church of Sacramento, in their Sesquicentennial history recalls, "The ordination of Mr. Benton was the first such Protestant ceremony in California. The council included pastors from San Francisco, Marysville, and Monterey. After an extended examination of the young pastor, which was satisfactory, the service included the reading of the Scripture and prayer by Rev. J. W. Hinds, a sermon by Rev. J. H. Warren, the ordaining prayer and charge to the pastor by Rev. Albert Williams, the charge to the church and ecclesiastical society by Rev. W. W. Brier, the right hand of fellowship by Rev. S. H. Willey and benediction by Mr. Benton."

But all was not well with the Benton and Brier friendship. In a letter to the AHMS, Rev. Benton issued his own request for new missionaries to work in the Sacramento valley, and in the process he shares a negative comment on Rev. Brier. This letter was more than just a poison pen. The letter revealed that Brier was considered very serious, with a stern demeanor, and could not share in joy of others. Benton says he was "the least successful" of all the men who have been sent.

Rev. Benton's letter to Milton Badger, AHMS
Sacramento,
October 13, 1851

Dear Brother,

As a lover of Christ's cause I am grieved that no good men are coming of themselves to our aid, and that the New York Society has been able to furnish so few. Our Methodist brethren quite overwhelm us in numbers, and they seem determined to keep the land. We do not wish their supply stopped—but ours much increased . . . .

The men you have sent are able, diligent, faithful, and acceptable. You have no reason to keep any back because of past mistakes. Brother Brier is the least successful of all sent, considering the fine field he has and his opportunities. He may have done as well as anyone could but it does not appear so to me. He has abilities enough but he is not popular. He lacks the "Gravity in mood", I suspect.

Yours in Labor and Love
J.A. Benton[46]

This is a curious conclusion, because Brier was centrally involved in the network of ministers, and seemed to be growing in his influence.

Although we are uncomfortable with the spirit and conclusion of his comments, we must trust Benton's observations. There is something Benton saw: a personality style, a brusque argumentation where Brier wanted to be seen as serious, forceful, and right. There was a great deal of maturity to come. There is more to come as the true plan for his life is developed and revealed to him.

It is curious to compare this reflection of his ability and style, with the reference provided by seminary professor Dr. Charles White two years earlier," *He (Brier) is a good scholar, of strong intellectual powers, of sincere piety, of great religious influence and energy, and quite forceful and prophetic in the pulpit."*

Brier must go through the darkness of rejection for some time before things turn brighter. There may have been another dimension to Benton's evaluation. It seems that there was a bit of jealousy in the churches, and ministers who were frustrated with their assignments were always looking at other pastors and congregations. In effect telling the AHMS society, "I could do better than he has!"

Several months later this proves true when it was mentioned that Rev. Benton had his eye on Marysville. Brier could sense all along the palpable tension between him and the brothers and did not know what had created such suspicion. This awkwardness led to paranoia, as if he felt he could never "do the right thing".

Marysville was the rough landing for Brier. Captured by the intrigue of pastors who wanted this boomtown, this treasure in the rough placed him in the center of intrigue. There were many who would have brought him along and could have cheered his progress. Instead he found, to his dismay, a number of people who were vindictive. They wanted his removal.

1852

William Wallace, Elizabeth, and Lizzie, 1852
Photo courtesy of Elizabeth Thompson

Again in September of 1851, Elizabeth joined William in Marysville, when the baby, Lizzie was 1 ½. Since the August business district fire, much of the city continued in ruins. The church had not yet been fully built, however the materials for the church building purchased in advance of the fire were safe. Their home was not in the path of the fire, so they were able to return to their "calico cottage" shortly before the fall rains began. Little did they know that it would be a rainy and devastating cold winter.

Weather records for that winter note that the temperature was in the low 40's, yet the homes were not well insulated in those days, and there was little heating. Brier himself complained that they were living in a drafty cottage. It must have required tremendous courage for Elizabeth to return to join him in the city with such a tiny baby. Cold, wet, and muddy streets still reeked of ashes from the fires. The stress of having his wife and young child live in these conditions, his ongoing affliction with tropical diseases, exhaustion, and the church conflicts diminished his health. William began to crack. In late January, Elizabeth became pregnant with their second child, and if history was to repeat itself, she struggled with sickness in the early months of pregnancy. At least this time she would not have to walk over the mountains of Panama and ruin her shoes. By February the cold was too much for her to bear. Brier sent Elizabeth and Lizzie back to the Beard residence at Mission San Jose. William stayed through the winter and sent this letter to the board as a sign of sunny success in ministry.

Marysville, California
January 12, 1852
Brier Letter # 18

To the Secretaries of the American Home Mission Society.

Dear Brethren,

You will readily pardon me for not writing more frequently, when I tell you that my health has been to bad for six months that I have hardly been able to discharge the duties of my office.

I have had nervous dyspepsia induced by warm weather. Yet I have been able to preach every Sabbath: and I now thank my God that he is giving me health to study and labor—I feel that it is good to have been afflicted. At a time, when my energies were taxed to the utmost, by taking them away, God taught me that I should only trust in him. Although, I am not well yet, I am much better and hope to recover. Mrs. Brier is in excellent health, and is delighted with this country. She would not live in any other, if she could. Our little Lizzie is a fine specimen of humanity. She runs around and talks a little. We now have many excellent families in this place.

The ladies connected with our congregation, have a sewing society at the first meeting took in $75.00 in "initiation fees." It seemed like home to meet together and hear the sweet voices of ladies and there take notes of the piano a forte. Our little church has been almost doubled within the last three months. Only one had united by profession of faith and baptism, recently a young man from New York City. We have a choir, which is not inferior to most towns in your cities; for we have several that have been choristers there.

The material for churches is furnished. But all our prosperity does not satisfy me. I mourn for the desolation of Zion, that the majority of those who have been members of churches at home here neglect the ordinances of God's house and many are openly profane. It is a solemn truth, that a large supporting of our church members have never been converted. Multitudes of impenitent go on heedless of the call to life. Yet I labor on.

I have representatives from all countries within my field. A few days ago, I visited one small corner of our city, in which I found fifty-six persons present. I distributed tracts in four languages, and yet discovered that their tract society gift of tongues failed me for I had nothing for a family of Sandwich Islanders. If I could speak five or six languages I would like it.

I feel that my labor here has not been in vain. We have raised for church purposes about $6,000.00. This is about three times the entire sum which you expended in sending us out, and we hope we long to commence returning the original, this we consider the interest at California rates. I was very glad to receive a letter from you to hope often to hear by letter and otherwise. Our city is growing in importance. Our mines are rich. I go into the mountains and preach on occasion. Once I made a tour of two days, preaching every night. The people were very attentive to hear the good news.

I wish again to present the subject of supplies—I am now prepared to say that we want twenty good men. This country changes so fast that it requires the heart of the prophet to see what will be required one year hence. Thirteen hundred persons came by the last steamer. Within the past year the future destiny of this country has been settled. If we get help we can maintain our position and hold this land, for the Lord is with us.

The Methodists are sending out very many, and yet this field, is not as accessible to them as to the Presbyterian Church. Those "who first occupy will have the advantage." I have written for Rev A. F. White of Attica, Indiana, to come out to California. Send as many men as you can.

W. W. Brier

Brier found at the outset that the complexity of ministry in the hills of California required that he respond to the multi-cultural diversity of the population. In Marysville he encountered Chilean, Hawaiian, Chinese, and Irish immigrants who were plying the gold fields in search of sudden riches.

CHAPTER 18

His Dark Night of the Soul

Rev. Brier was not ready to give up. He had hoped he would recover, that he would secure a permanent call to Marysville, and that the reconstruction of the central business district would turn the tide of negative events. Yet this could clearly have been the dark night of the soul for him. How could it possibly be worse for him?

He has been working so fervently to get the church built, confident the recognition of the congregation would follow. He did not listen to his body, and pushed beyond his capabilities. Ministry became an ordeal. He invested his life in teaching some members of the church, only to have them leave as the prospects of new mines shifted to other communities. Depression began to settle in upon him, and it seemed as if he was operating in slow motion. The toll upon his body and soul began to mount and he slid deeper and deeper into depression.

It couldn't have come at a worse time. He was on the verge of a breakthrough as the first New School church planted in a mining community. It was easily the first church organized in a mining community, and the first church structure to be built in the mining areas. Yet it seemed the test is too difficult. Perhaps he was flawed. In the best of times Brier was considerate of others—but in the worst of times, he must have been testy to work with. His impatience with his progress, and his intense focus to please the mission society backfired, in his passion and rage.

His breakthrough became a breakdown. He developed a malady called dyspepsia that seems strange to us today. The newspapers of the day had many advertisements for medicines, which touted a sure cure for whatever ails you. A newspaper advertisement describes the symptoms of nervous dyspepsia.

Dyspepsia: Liver Disease

When you have Dyspepsia, you may experience pain in the right side, under the edge of the ribs, an increase in pressure, the loss of appetite, head pain, back ache, there is generally

*a considerable loss of purpose. Accompanied with a painful sensation of having left undone
something, which ought to have been done.*

The symptoms they describe could be diagnosed today as either yellow fever or
hepatitis; both are water-borne diseases that are common in overcrowded facilities with
poor sanitation. In the days before good medical treatment, symptoms could resolve
with significant rest, or could leave the liver damaged. If Brier had yellow fever, it could
reoccur and plague him.

Fragile health was not the only problem he was facing. The bottom seems to fall out
of his life, as the storms of conflict revisit his ministry. There was trouble brewing in the
congregation, and he was blind-sided by the dissent.

In March of 1852 a congregational meeting is hastily called to take a vote on
issuing a permanent call to Rev. Brier as pastor. It was routine to have settled
congregations vote to call the itinerant as permanent pastor, but the timing of it and the
procedures were highly unusual. In some churches, these were used as a way of placing
the financial burden upon the congregation to fully support the pastor. We do not know
if Brier initiated this meeting, or if there were more complex dynamics within the
congregation. At this congregational meeting, the vote was eight for him to be the
installed permanent pastor and nine votes against him. What offended him most is that
most of the "no" votes were not by people present, but by those who had voted as
absentees. This practice was technically illegal in the Presbyterian Church. He resigned
under the pressure, and left in defeat.

In his lament to the Mission society, he explained this debacle away and dismisses
any underlying cause. But the combination of his broken health and his broken
congregational leadership caused him to conclude he should leave the ministry. His
letter of March 29th spells out the conflict.

*"My Physician says that I must desist from preaching, that six months more preaching in
this climate would demand my life."*

Brier Letter # 19
March 29th, 1852

Marysville
To the Secretaries of the American Home Mission Society,

Dear Brethren,

*I write to lay before you my condition and position. Last fall I wrote you that my health
was not good. The warm weather here gave me the nervous Dyspepsia, which made it
desirable to wean and even desist from preaching for a time. Dr. Hall answered that it
was important that I should remain in a place where I had been so successful. I did so.*

Three weeks ago a meeting of the church and congregation was called for the purpose of deciding whether to extend a call to me to settle as Pastor or not. It was a stormy day and only a few attended. The vote stood eight for me and nine against. More than half the church members were absent, and most of the votes against me were out of the church. (A new feature of Presbyterianism to me, to give the option to church petition.) I knew of no dissatisfaction. The kindest feelings are expressed by all (people) towards me, and the only reason given for votes cast in the negative, was my (weak) health. The congregation wished me to remain as stated supply: this, by the advice of the Rev. Mr. T.D. Hunt, I refused to do. The Rev. Brayton and Rev. Benton are candidates for this place. But there is great dissatisfaction in the community on account of the vote, and I fear that much injury has been done to the cause. It was a great error in those who take the lead in the church, not to have told me of the dissatisfaction. I would have been glad, at any time, to resign my charge, which has almost brought me to the grave. I could have received a larger vote to settle, but think the indication of (God's) providence is clear that I have finished my work in this place. My Physician says that I must desist from preaching. Six months more preaching in this climate would demand my life.

I will give you the outlines of what I have done. I believe I have received about $2,000.00 from your society since leaving Indiana (I would be glad to know the exact sum). By the response of people to the gospel, California interest and all the principle has been doubly paid into the common treasury of God.

I have labored in Marysville nineteen months. When I arrived at this "trading post" there was no church, no Sabbath. I had collected $4,000.00 to build a church to hold the largest church bell in California weighing with fixture 1450 lb., and at a cost of $550.00.

My congregation has doubled within three months and when I left was very prosperous condition. I had devised a system of subscription and giving by the congregation by which I expected in short time to return into your treasury all that I have received. I still hope that gifts from this church will soon commence to flood into the treasury of the Society—a river that will irrigate the desert places of our beloved Zion.

What shall I do now? I suggest you can advise me in such a case as this. I have denied myself rather than ask aid from you. And I think that it would be better for me to turn my attention to some secular employment than to ask money to support my family, which could be applied in sending a man to labor in this destitute field. I hear that you are about to send Rev. A. F. White of Indiana to California. I rejoice in this. I think he will do well.

I need men with experience in the wild for churches. A young man from the East who has lived in an ancient church has a new trade to learn. A man ought to know how to stake the best lead at once. Oh how I long for health to go forth so I can really preach. But my God has humbled me and my strength has been taken away. And yet I trust that arm which has been stretched out to afflict. It leads me and mine by a way, which I knew not. My wife and little daughter are well and happy. Mrs. Brier would not exchange this place even for Indiana. She joins in sending love.

Will you give me your counsel?
Yours in the Gospel
W. W. Brier.[47]

This final letter from Marysville holds some foreshadowing for his future. Brier had vision and passion, but seemed exhausted and depleted in ministry. He was humbled by the brokenness of his health, and facing another summer of intense heat, he played a card, "that he is not an Eastern man." He was not easily adapted to the work in this intensity. It was not his skill, nor his stamina, but the pressure of the unique ministry setting in Marysville, the demands of the congregation, and the intrigue within the Marysville church that eventually ruined him.

The church split over his call to be the installed pastor. It is ironic that the very controversy that erupted regarding Rev. John Douglas' call to San Jose, comes back to haunt him in Marysville. And to add insult to injury, one of the pastors rumored to replace Brier is Rev. Douglas himself!

The question of the day is whether his poor health affected his performance and the congregation wearied of it, or whether his style of ministry was too serious and bombastic for them. One thing was true, the movement of populations in the early swirl of the Gold Rush made many communities into a continually revolving door. Fortune seekers lost everything and returned home destitute. Businessmen made great fortunes before seeing the business cycle peaking, and they cashed out and left. Families first flocked to Marysville, then fled when the late summer fires swept through the city and leveled it. It is no wonder that Brier was exhausted from the strains of ministry.

His call for help and advice went unanswered. A letter may have been written and sent, but in the days prior to the Pony Express, mail often was damaged, lost, or undeliverable. Brier wallowed in the throws of depression. Now it seems he was finished in his work of planting churches. He is spiritually, physically, emotionally burned out. And he is no longer a hero to his wife. He had convinced her as he was the major church planter and missionary, and had promised to support her on the California frontier as a minister. This dream had become a nightmare. He did not hear back from the New York office, nor did it appear the local ministers gave him a directive.

In April, 1852, Brier returned to his wife and family near the Mission San Jose. He retuned as a broken man. The Beard's welcomed him and wanted to provide a place for him to be restored. By this time his wife was in good health and spirits. If there was any cheer, it was to be away from the rejection of Marysville, and gladly reunited with his family in a more stable environment. But he was haunted with guilt, and inadequacy. It was a repeated cycle for him.

Brier was paranoid too, that Brayton, Douglas, and Benton orchestrated the plot to stir up others to oppose his leadership in the Marysville church. Evidence led him to believe that Brayton will follow him as Pastor at Marysville.

Vindication came when Brier left Marysville. The brothers were whispering that it must have been his style or his weakness that led to his failure. It was in fact Rev. Brayton who was assigned to replace him in Marysville, and Brayton's health failed after only one year in the heat of that region.

For William Brier, leaving Marysville seemed like the end of his missionary career. Surely it was the end of his days of being a pastor. In bitterness and defeat, Brier left the ministry and returned south to join his wife and his friends. It was the dark night of the soul. He rehearsed the events of that fateful congregational meeting over and over again in his mind, wondering if he had been done in by the intrigue of others. Was it a betrayal by his friends and by other ministers who had sown the seeds of discord? Did they envy the work he had done in building a church structure, and chartering a church?

He may have been broken, but he was not beaten. Contrary to the advice of his doctors, Rev. Brier did not give up on the ministry. He had gone on preaching trips in 1850 and 1851 to the gold mining districts along the trail northwest toward Lake Tahoe, twenty miles west along the supply line into the gold fields. Grass Valley was a burgeoning town nestled in the ponderosa pine covered hills, sprinkled with gold mines and ore refining mills.

He organized the Centreville Presbyterian Church of Grass Valley, on February 8, 1852. James Woods in his *California Pioneer Decade of the Presbyterian Church* remarks that Brier was the temporary pastor of this congregation and renamed it as the First Presbyterian Church of Grass Valley. It appears that Brier continued to preach there for a number of months until it was clear that he needed to remain with his family at the Mission San Jose, in the San Francisco Bay Area. The church in Grass Valley was turned over to Rev. James Pierpont months later.

Even without a steady call to pastoral ministry, Brier could not stay out of controversy. Some time during the months of transition Brier wrote a letter which was printed in the Home Missionary Magazine. It was so extreme in its discouragement that Rev. Willey wrote a forceful letter of response to correct Brier's remarks about eastern values and western hardships. Although we do not have access to that letter, we do have his remark about the "Shady Side of life" and the way in which his letter of complaint was reprinted in the national newsletter of the American Home Mission Society.

Rev. Willey Letter to the AHMS
May 4, 1852

We are sorry to see some remarks in Brother Brier's letter that overstates the truth very much. His remarks read by many people leads to a misunderstanding that there are many drains on the financial allowance we give. It would draw a very strong inference concerning a deviation in Christian integrity here. The truth is hard enough in that direction, but it cannot be "the only way "of Eastern Christians to abandon their consistency here! We know some do. There are many, but nothing reaching a majority in my judgment. Brother Brier's health was miserable last year and he needs his best entreaties to maintain himself in a congregation.

He must have relaxation. He was here the other day and he told me he had communicated with you concerning his leaving Marysville. I suggested to him that Monterey would afford him a change of climate and I wanted to introduce him to the officer of the post as a candidate for chaplain at Monterey, now vacant. He went down there at once. I hope he will get it. If he should, it will afford him an easy and excellent post in which to recover. Brother Brayton is supplying at Marysville at present.

S.H. Willey[48]

This letter highlights the Brier journey more fully. Although Rev. Willey was sometimes harsh on Brier, he was also focused on getting him a useful place of ministry. After Brier's returned to Mission San Jose, Rev. Willey sent him to the Monterey Presidio to interview as a chaplain to military men stationed there. This could have been a stable assignment. But Brier was never interested in a stable assignment because the passion of his heart was church planting! There is no record of what happened at the Monterey interview—if Brier declined the position or if they thought he was unsuitable. Monterey was now considered the backwater of the state, and considering Brier's commanding attitude, he would not have been a good match as pastor to the military. But we do know that he had another invitation that was beckoning.

Willey noted Brier's fatigue and his purity of heart to preach the gospel. With his observation came the caution that Brier may be too serious to be successful. "He needs his best entreaties to maintain himself." This means they think he is a loose cannon! The inference is not that he is out of control, but he must be careful to not crush others in his passion to speak the truth.

This latest stir Brier created does not help him to win friends and influence people. His evangelistic tendency to state the problems he faced in overly dramatic terms created good text for the magazine, but when the other pastors read the magazine, they suspect that he had poisoned the well watering their expenses. Rev. Badger and Hall in the AHMS office did not understand the controversy over Brier's remarks, but they had their suspicions about his motives. In June Dr. Hall sent a compassionate question to Rev. Willey.

AHMS letter to Willey
June 22, 1852

AHMS Secretary Charles Hall writes,

We are sorry to hear of Mr. Brier's health has been feeble. Is he placed unsuccessfully? And how is he engaged? I hope he will not resort to gold hunting.

Charles Hall[49]

Again the doubts surface; doubts about Brier's motives and potential for pastoral success. They wonder if he was placed in the wrong place. What action by Brier would have led them to think that he would join the miners in search of riches? Surely many a pastor left the call to hunt for Gold because of the pressure of rising prices, the lack of emotional support, and the flourishing promise of easy money. But it is odd that the office does not respond by saying, "What can we do to support him? Does he need time off?" Or the AHMS home office does not say, "Do everything you can to support him, as we cannot spare one worker in a field so vast as California." There are only seven more missionaries who have been selected to serve in California.

It was a desperate time. One of the symptoms of a liver disease like dyspepsia was chronic dysentery, total exhaustion, a lack of motivation, and unclear thinking. In the fog of this illness, rejected and dejected, Brier left the ministry and returned south, so his wife could stay with her friend Jane Beard.

With no response from the AHMS regarding his resignation and future calling, Brier returned to the serenity of the mission. It was breathtaking. From the Mission San Jose, you look northeast into the horizon of the Pacific. On a clear day, it looked like the land was kissed by God with brilliant sunshine and gentle breeze. There were few places in the world a pioneer would rather be.

Beard let him stay in the room in the back of the mission in the wing of the mission compound used as a guesthouse for visitors who came through the area. While recuperating there, William spent many long days walking through the lush gardens of the mission compound. He struggled with bitterness over the way he had been abandoned. But he could not remain there.

During his early weeks at the mission, Brier began to reflect upon his giftedness and calling. His social skills left him restless in dealing with people's long-term problems. He came to the realization that he was no longer gifted at the pastoring. He would turn to some other profession and stay in California. In previous correspondence with Dr. Badger, he had anticipated the possibility that his health might be damaged while in California and had pressed the AHMS directors to concede that they would pay to relocate the Brier family to Indiana before their obligation to them was complete. Yet Brier did not pursue this option of relocation, and was strangely silent while he recovered at the mission. Perhaps he had an indication that God was not finished with him yet, and the Lord did not send him on an errand into the wilderness.

He was haunted by the call to ministry he received while in Indiana. Yet his fear of financial ruin drove him out of ministry and into a new job. Farming was something he could understand, and in the pattern of Henry Ward Beecher, he found inner peace and tranquility in the farming community.

CHAPTER 19

The Light of Restoration
The E.L. Beard Family

Mission San Jose
Photo from Fremont Museum of Local History
(R.B. Fisher Collection)

It could be the end of his career as a missionary and church planter. Surely it seemed to be the end of his days of pastoring in that community. In bitterness and defeat, it was his dark night of the soul. Brier wanted to reinvent himself. In his brokenness, Brier sought sanctuary and refuge in the mission. Mission San Jose had a spiritual quality to it, which attracted many pioneers, soldiers, gold seekers, and farmers. It held the images of missionaries, Catholic Church, Spanish rule, conquest over the Ohlone Indians, and now the frenzy of the Gold Rush.

The buildings of the Mission San Jose crown the valley, as a citadel of secular religion, with the St. Joseph sanctuary as protectorate of the Mission compound. The whitewashed adobe was scarred from neglect and earthquake. The Spanish had secularized the mission, and moved the priest into the city of San Francisco. Its position in the valley reflected a towering position of strength, and yet the Mission building itself was in disarray. The Beard family had purchased a questionable title to the land, taken possession of it, and had added considerable improvements to it.

Pioneers typically networked friendships in order build a community and congregation. W.W. Brier found a clustering of friends. Within close proximity to the Beard family, lived the Pattersons, the Wellers, the Crane brothers, and Abijah Baker, all of them from villages surrounding Lafayette, Indiana. The Briers found that there was a bond in the context of the ancestral homeland, a bond that was deepened with support and loyalty in the swamps of the Panama crossing.

A portrait of Elias Lyman Beard and his son
Fremont Museum of Local History (R.B. Fisher Collection)

At the time, Beard was the key figure in the valley and a courageous and bold pioneer in the annals of California. His crops were legendary in the fruitfulness of his early years of farming. He was one of the early agricultural pioneers and raised the most valuable crop ever raised in the state. In the year 1853 his crop of potatoes exceeded eleven million pounds.

The *Pacific Newspaper*
May 19, 1880

According to the Rev. Dr. Willey in the Pacific of May 19, 1880, 'The size of some these potatoes was something marvelous. It was common to find some of the 3 pounds and frequently those from 3 to 5 lbs. Willey writes, 'I remember one day at Mr. Beard's when there were nine of us grown persons at the table, and a single potato weighting four pounds served all us, and there was plenty left for three people who came afterward, and both the quality and flavor were exceptional. "

As a friend and mentor of Brier, Beard was a man who was enamored with religion but was careful not get too close to it. Perhaps a clue to his warmth and distance from religious things is contained in his obituary. It was notes that at the age of 16 years old, "he had visited the society of Shakers at Lycea, Livingston County, New York, where he remained several months. He greatly admired the simplicity of the social life of that peculiar people, but did not join their ranks." [50]

This may have been why E.L. Beard was so respectful of his friendship with Brier, yet Brier was unsuccessful in converting him to join in the congregation. His wife, Jane Beard, was a significant leader in the congregation, and E.L. Beard's daybook repeatedly notes his friendship with the Rev. Brier. There is, however, no record of his being a member in the life of the Alameda or Centerville Presbyterian Churches. His father, wife, and son, were active in the church.

Beard moved to Lafayette, Indiana, in 1835 and remained there until 1849. During that time he assisted his father in large-scale farming, in working the flour mill near Attica, and in the construction and contracting business that would take him 1847. [51]

His obituary also notes that as a young man he was *"engaged in building, milling, keeping a hotel, and buying and selling country produce. He engaged in grain and saw milling, being the shipper of the first load of grain on the Erie Canal. Later he engaged in the pork-packing trade and owned a stone quarry. His real bonanza came as a contractor when he was selected as the sole contractor for the Wabash and Erie Canal. He shipped the first load of corn from the state of Indiana to the New York market. In 1844 he built for the Government the docks of Memphis Tennessee."* [52]

E. L. Beard was a man who took risks in his ventures, and he might also be noted as a man who took risks on his friends and the community. He took a risk on the burned out Rev. Brier inviting him to begin teaching classes in the mission. To sustain a growing community of nearly one hundred farmer families there needed to be an opportunity for them to go to school. Beard asked William to reach back to his college training and begin teaching. Brier consented, and set up a school room in the mission compound.

Beard made some requests of his friends in San Jose and was successful in securing county funding to pay Brier, and in so doing he became the first paid school teacher in Alameda County. Brier felt as if he was raised from the dead, and his season of darkness began to turn toward the light.

His training at Wabash had prepared him for education, as one of his mentors, Caleb Mills, was a premier educator and saw part of Christian ministry to be a public school teacher. Local History notes, "*In the summer of 1853, the school was opened in an adobe building north of the church: the class consisted of seven or eight small boys and girls in their ABC's. The term was three months long, and the teacher's salary was $150 per month, collected by subscription.*" [53]

On July 30, 1852, the Rev. Willey wrote a note to the AHMS Board with the news about Brier. It should be remembered that Willey had been a guest of Mr. Beard in 1849, as evidenced by the article he published in The *Pacific Newspaper* about the lush yields of the Beard estate.

"*Rev. Mr. Brier removed to San Jose Mission (15 miles from San Jose) to recover. Have been there some months. He requests, and requires relief. He has some purpose toward "gold getting" beyond the support of his family. But (confidentially) his manners and spirit (socially) are against his success here, but we hope he will be directed rightly.*"

Rev. Willey carefully kept track of Brier but still had reservations about his ability to fit in, adapt, and relate to the Californian church context. Brier's manner and spirit were the issue. We can guess that he appears to bumble things, and perhaps his serious and forceful demeanor is a concern. It is interesting to notice that the congregations Brier led were always appreciative of his ministry. But four of his colleagues did not agree, and sent notes to the AHMS office regarding their concerns about his social skills.

Benton is critical because of Brier's "gravity of mood". Perhaps he is too serious. Why the contrast? He was so successful with people in the villages, yet he was so much of an irritant with those in authority. One possibility is that Brier had a problem in relating with authority. He reacts in an awkward, even combative manner, when people in the chain of command criticize him. And yet, there other pastors who follow Brier's unusual voice of authority, like the Rev. White, a new missionary who would only follow Briers advice.

In Rev. Willey's November letter there is confirmation of their conflicts with him and their suspicions. Willey sees him as "not adapted to build up a church" in this country. In his role as coordinator for the AHMS, Rev. Willey traveled to the Mission San Jose on November 30, 1852 and wrote a second note to the AHMS board. "*I have recently visited the San Jose Mission, and I suppose I may as well say in confidence that from my knowledge of the impression our Brother Brier makes on the people. It is my opinion, reluctantly entertained that he is not adapted to build up a church in this country. I called on Rev. White, but he was out(of town) and he had gone to see Brother Brier. The facts are, that everyone will encourage him if he will enter (into ministry) heartily for some place in the world. He will not be advised, (unless it be by Brother Brier) to go into any new field in the State, but of course he will not be persuaded. He must follow his own judgment."*

It was uncertain why this lingering question about Brier continued to color Willey's evaluation of him. Perhaps Brier was depressed and had not yet recovered from his illness. Family pressures were on his mind, as Elizabeth Brier gave birth to their second daughter, Mary, on November 27, 1852.

In those early months of waiting at the Beard residence, events took a turn which shaped the remainder of Brier's life. A new humility and reliance upon the Holy Spirit in his life emerged in his ministry, and letters. He realized that if anything were to take place it would be a work of God, not his efforts. The Beard family had improved the abandoned Mission San Jose property significantly, but there were continuing challenges on his claim to the title of the property. Brier had several students at the time.

He was with his family, and opportunities were opening up for him as he was connected again with many of the Indiana farmers who had come to benefit from the Gold rush. Deep within his heart he knew that many of the men and women flowing through the mission compound had no fixed religious expression, and no professed faith in Christ. He so desperately wanted to see the Kingdom of God established in the community.

Jane Beard knew of this too. She had been the one who had invited visiting Presbyterian pastors to preach in the mission. A long history of church leaders had seen the potential of the site. Brayton, Douglas, Hunt, and Willey, all had spent time there and saw the potential of this beautiful place. Now it was the reluctant Brier who would see if it would work. In the compound there was a small chapel set up, with a low entryway, painted adobe walls, exposed beams, and benches that would seat twenty. Jane went to Rev. Brier and asked him to lead a service on Sundays. It was music to his ears. Here was the light at the end of the tunnel.

M. W. Woods highlights Brier's next move in his 1883 *History of Alameda County:* *"Mr. Brier, with his wife and child, lived in the Mission a few months, he taught the first public school for which funds were drawn in the bounds of Santa Clara County. Alameda County, as yet, had no existence. At the same time he preached to small congregations in his schoolroom each Sabbath. In the beginning of 1853 the Pacheco Ranch was sold, and he bought his place near where Centreville now stands, and began to hold services in a building called, "Horner's School House."*[54]

Teaching school at the mission location was short-lived for William Brier as the claim for the Pacheco land in the valley below became available, and an agricultural land grab took place. In February of 1853, Brier was at the front of the pack, gaining 40 acres at the crossroads of two main roadways. Documents reveal that Brier got the land from Beard, although the title was not recorded for a year or more, and we do not know if Brier bought the land or it was given as a gift. Brier suggested in his last will and testament that he bought the land in late 1852, using the bequest from a family estate. The original title for the property it is unclear the larger tract of land was a partnership between Beard and Horner, but the original sketch of the land and deeds identify Brier as the owner of the forty acre tract. He was into farming again.

What is interesting is that he joins Indiana families from surrounding the mission in farming that fertile valley. Discovering that a large land tract was going up for sale, they all purchased land and moved to the farms in close proximity, and regrouped as a small community.

The History of Alameda County notes the relational networking that took place in this pioneer community, as many of the immigrants were living together and purchasing farms side by side: *"Emerson Timothy Crane is a pioneer resident of San Lorenzo, and one of the leading fruit growers in Alameda County. He is a native of New York, but started for California from Lafayette, Indiana on the 12th day of February, 1850, and arrived in San Francisco on the 6th day of July following. In the same party came Rev. W. Brier and wife, Mrs. E L. Beard and two sons. He spent the first two years of California life at the Mission of San Jose, farming and removed to San Lorenzo in the fall of 1852, where he had since resided. He is a brother of Addison Crane, the first Judge of Alameda County."*[55]

CHAPTER 20

Centered in "Hardscrabble"

1853

In order to make the transition to farming in Centreville, Brier sold his house and property in the center of Marysville. He built the house when it was one of the few "calico shacks" that had survived the citywide fire, and was highly valuable. He may have also owned a farm outside the city as Court documents refer to his fruit crops in Marysville. Now with the home sale he is cash rich.

A creek flowed across the roadway two miles from Brier's property. Locals called the area "Hardscrabble", and it was quickly renamed Centreville. The Mormon farmer and community leader, John Horner, had a small house there that became identified as the community schoolhouse and Mormon house of worship.

Early in 1853 the Farmer John Horner invited him to teach at this school in Centerville. It was called "Horner's School House." Brier transferred his Mission San Jose students to the Centerville schoolhouse as quickly as possible, so he could live and work on his property nearby. He clearly planned to set up roots in the community and make it his home, regardless of his vocation.

Other families followed him down into the valley, and he began preaching on Sunday morning at the schoolhouse, as John Horner led the Mormon congregation on Sunday afternoons. Woods notes, *"Mr. Brier and the Methodist minister preached alternately every Sunday morning when weather would permit, as the horse wagons bogged down in the muddy roads if there was rain. A small creek offshoot from the Alameda Creek flowed down through the valley and past the land where they would build the church."*

The Town of Centreville

If you were looking around for a prosperous community, Centreville was not much to look at. The ground was a flat alluvial plain that stretched for thirty miles to the southwest toward San Jose and thirty miles to the northeast, with the only boundary being the mission hills to the east, and the San Francisco Bay on the west. Yet to the discerning eye, it was a fertile crescent. There were clusters of trees that lined the creeks and tributaries of the Alameda Creek which created green borders for this a growing community. The area had water from the Alameda Creek, and became a midway point on the road from San Jose to Oakland. Historians at the time recall the formation of a new community.

Here is a quote from one of their neighbors *"The adobe houses of the Spanish ranches and a few tents or shanties were the only dwellings in the valley, when my husband and brother bought a ranch about 7 miles from the Mission. We built the first house that was there. Soon we had neighbors, Reverend W.W. Brier and others built houses that winter, and within the year we had formed a friendly and pleasant community. There was one small building where Centerville now stands. It was called "Horner's School House." We came together from far and near all the family, babies and all. It was a great privilege to gather for worship on the Lord's Day. Soon after Mr. Brier built the church at Centerville and then we went there."*[56]

The New Gold Rush: Land for Farming!

There was a land rush taking place! There were some regional factors that made farming the area quite attractive. The miners needed lots of food supplies, and the food stocks brought overland were quickly exhausted. The rains had devastated the harvest of produce in the hillside mining towns and created a true gold rush in the farm field. Brier put down roots in the Centreville/Alvarado area, both as a preacher and as a farmer. He had not farmed for twenty years, but it was clearly in his blood and was the ticket to financial security for his future in church planting.

The forty acres were bare when he purchased the land. He began with walnut, maple, and sycamore trees around the edges, then quickly planted a diverse orchard with cherries, apricot, figs, and other fruit trees purchased from Niles orchardist John Rock. In 1867, with proceeds from the early crops, he diversified the crop with apricots purchased from Bernard Fox's Nursery in San Jose. Brier caught on quickly and became an accomplished orchardist. In 1880 he and his son William Jr. patented their own variety of apricot, called "Briers Royal Golden Apricot Variety."

Brier was serious as a farmer, believing that he would provide food for the growing inland mining community and the burgeoning city of San Francisco. Like his church planting strategy, he was planting for the long term. Fruit crops, which he planted aggressively, often took five to eight years to harvest a mature crop. The local newspaper reported, *"Forty acres of the land which Mr. Brier owned is devoted to apples, peaches, apricots, and cherries. A cluster of fine maple and walnut trees lined the driveways that led to the main house and several small cottages."*

He was also a farming innovator. An article in the *California History Quarterly*, titled *California crops that succeeded*, notes that, *"while in Alameda, W.W. Brier of Centerville raised Kona coffee from Hawaiian seeds. The first severe frost dashed all hopes."*[57]

Rev. Brier was already seen as an influential leader in the community and connected with the farmers. He was invited to be a founding sponsor to promote the State Agricultural fair. Brier was seen as someone who could draw others from the agricultural community into the movement of the state fair. His friend James Shinn, chaired the event its first years. He then began attending Brier's church, and the Shinn family became church members.

The Brier farm had been plowed and planted with trees. Now all that was left to do was wait. Most fruit bearing trees needed three years before they would bear fruit, so in the center of the forty acres, there was a large plot where Brier planted wheat, and corn. This crop would carry him through the first few seasons. Farming fed his family, but he was still passionate about the church. This church planting was his true destiny, and he wanted to focus more and more upon the ministry he was called to Rev. Timothy Dwight Hunt had not given up on him, and he encouraged him to begin preaching once again. Rev. Willey had become ill once again, and did not contact Brier for a number of months.

Meanwhile, he taught a growing group of students at Centerville. The schoolhouse was not much to brag about, built as a wood frame structure forty-by-sixty, with wood clapboard siding. It was a beginning, but like many of the early school structures in California it was not built for beauty or permanence. Brier may have moved the students to Centerville to join the families of John Horner, and enlarge the school. There are no records of the continuation of the school at the Mission, but the Centerville school became the center of a network of schools, which covered the communities in the fertile valley. The schoolhouse was subject to the same problems much of Centerville experienced in the early days. The streets were muddy in the winter, many times impassable, and if the Alameda creek and its tributaries overflowed, there would be standing water throughout the district for weeks at a time.

John Horner's extended family and Mormon Church began to gather on Sunday afternoon in the Centerville schoolhouse for worship. Brier's friendship with him began three years earlier, when they clustered around the Mission and enjoyed the hospitality of Elias Beard. There is no record of the financial arrangement between Horner and Brier, whether Brier was paid to be the schoolteacher at Centerville. But his tenure as teacher lasted just over a year. He wanted to do bigger things in the area.

It was while teaching at the schoolhouse that Brier began to dream about ministry again. Horner opened the house to Mormons in the afternoon. Brier approached him about having Presbyterian worship services in the morning hours. Horner agreed.

It was resolved that the church be organized on June 5, in J.M. Horner's schoolhouse. The minutes of that meeting tell, *"At the close of the sermon, Reverend Brier read the petition contained in the foregoing minutes, and after a Solemn Act of Prayer, declared the persons whose names are thereunto subscribed duly and regularly organized into a Church of Jesus Christ. By a unanimous vote Charles Hilton was chosen to the office of Ruling Elder."* Two weeks later, on June 19, 1853, after public services, Charles Hilton was set apart to the office of Ruling Elder by a prayer offered by the minister, Reverend Brier.

Four weeks later, Sunday, June 17, the first administration of the Sacraments in the new church took place; the Lord's Supper to the congregation and a baptism. It is interesting to note that the person baptized was Mary Brier, seven-month-old daughter of Reverend W.W. and Elizabeth A. Brier, born on November 27, 1852. The Reverend A.F. White performed the ceremony.

Forming a church in any community was no easy matter. Sometimes there would be enough historic Presbyterians from the East Coast to form the nucleus of a strong congregation; other times it was a mixed bag of traditions that began the process. Charles Howard Shin recalls,

"When there was talk of a Presbyterian Church, Mrs. Breyfogle, who was a Methodist, Mrs. Coombs, who was a Baptist, Mrs. Henion, who was Episcopalian, Captain Richardson, who lived below Sam Marston's Old farm and was a Baptist, Charles Hilton, Captain Bond, and a few others got together. Captain Richardson said that he was "The very hardest shell Baptist, and yet he was willing to have any kind of Christian Church to take his family to." I go with the Majority," the bluff old pioneer reiterated. At that was nucleus, of the old brick (Presbyterian) church." [58]

This was a tough bunch to pull together into the Alameda Presbyterian Church. The Brier's had an unusual friendship with the Beard family, which was strengthened by Jane Beard's historic ties with the Presbyterian Church. Years later, the Centerville Presbyterian Church records mention, *"On February 26, 1854 Mrs. Jane Beard was received into membership by letter from the Second Presbyterian Church of Lafayette, Indiana. Mrs. Jane Makemie Ellsworth Beard was a great grandniece of Francis Makemie, the Presbyterian minister who came to the Maryland—Virginia region from Donegal, Ireland in 1683. The tireless zeal and energy of Francis Makemie resulted in a large increase in numbers and the consolidation of the Presbyterian elements, so that in 1706 a Presbytery was organized in Philadelphia—the first on the continent."* [59]

CHAPTER 21

Brier's Role as Educator

Brier was looking for a way to support his family in ministry. This is a great portrait of blended ministry that was part tent-making, part preacher. It worked well as the Presbyterian church has always been a democratic institution that draws the educated into leadership roles of the church and society. Shortly after taking the job as schoolteacher and preacher, Brier was elected as Alameda County Superintendent of schools.

There were three to six candidates for each position, and the election was spoken of for years afterwards as the "steeple chase". "So little regard had previously been paid to the proper names of persons, that until the election some were known only by nicknames."[60]

It is remarkable that Brier would be elected, considering that he had only lived in the district a few months before the election. We can assume that his backing from local farming legends of Beard and Horner were the decisive factors in his election. It may have been that he was the only county paid schoolteacher at the time. Or it may have been that as a "Reverend" and with a Scottish name, he was clearly not a Roman Catholic. This was an advantage as many pioneer families were nervous about the efforts to strengthen "Catholic" schools, which were present in the Bay Area, when they arrived. In the 1851-1852 the state Legislature specified that each county and district would be paid on the basis of the number of school children ranging in age from five to eighteen years. Fifty percent of the county funds paid for the teachers were added to the state educational trust fund proceeds. The county tax assessment was not to exceed three cents per one hundred dollars valuation of assets.

After his 1853 election as Superintendent of Public Schools, Rev. W. W. Brier had an unusual challenge. There were few schools for him to visit, but he launched an aggressive program to expand the number of schools in the county. In this role, he would drive his horse and buggy around the farming communities of the East Bay, and do an assessment of the need for new schools. He would then report his findings to the County Board of Supervisors, and request more money to establish schools and pay teachers' salaries.

In his report to the state Superintendent of Public Schools for the year 1853, Brier wrote that there were few publicly owned schools. Early schools were often housed in rented buildings, or buildings donated by local farmers. Education was taking place due to the heroic work of teachers who were underpaid and under appreciated. Many of the public schools were referred to as "charity schools" because the students who were attending were from homes whose parents were too poor to place them in denominational or private schools.

"The number of school age children enrolled in public schools in 1856 was 847, but actual attendance was only 387. Countywide, fourteen school districts were spread out across the plains and valleys, with 19 teachers employed. In 1856, the district budget totaled $4,937.36 for teacher salaries and $2,512 for school building structural repairs. The school year instructional average was five months."[61]

In 1856 the Centerville and Alviso school districts united, and built a schoolhouse on the Alvarado-Newark road, two miles west of Centerville. The teachers initially were not paid from public funds, but Rev. Brier lobbied the County Board of Supervisors to provide twenty cents for each child schooled. Brier then recommended that the board adopt a resolution making schooling compulsory. He was successful in having this resolution pass, although it would take decades to fully implement. He organized the first Alameda countywide public school convention at San Leandro on November 6, 1858. This gathering brought together school trustees and teachers from nine school districts in every township. By sharing common struggles in the growing county, the convention voted to pass a resolution they gave to county officials which declared, "That the value of property depends upon the intelligence of the people, and therefore, the property of the County should pay for the education of the rising generation."[62]

In 1859 a tradition was begun by Superintendent Brier: the first May Day festival for children of Alameda County schools. This linked the cooperation of the agricultural association with the schools to celebrate the arrival of spring planting season. Three school picnics were held on April 30, 1859. Students and school teachers within the twenty mile radius, would gather in the park to play games, recite poetry, sing, and walk around the Maypole, and picnic. *The History of Alameda County* notes, "The first festival was at Fruitvale, the second at Hughes' Gem Valley, and the third on the banks of Alameda Creek above Vallejo Mill. The first May Day picnic was held in 1854, on Ellsworth's Island, then owned by Daniel and Osmond Sanborn and planted in grain: they cut a few acres and after the picnic, regretted that the entire field had not been cut. Invitations were sent out to every body in the township. It is estimated that there were present fifty women, one hundred and fifty men and about fifty boys and girls. The Rev. Mr. Brier and Noble Hamilton were speakers of the day. These picnics sometimes lasted for several days and preparations were commenced months before these great social events." And in the next two years, there was additional growth and continued resistance from farmers and merchants who wanted to either home-school their children or do limited teaching for the elementary grade levels. Brier was a regional crusader for changes in the systems, and lobbied county and state for compulsory education.

The enrollment statistics of the 1859 school year were full. There were 1,174 children of school age, and the total expenditure for school purposes was $10,138.33. "Andrew J. Moulder, State Superintendent, in his report strongly urged immediate measures for founding a State University on the military plan. W. W. Brier, Superintendent for this county at this time, recommended the adoption of the compulsory system of education, but was opposed to military school as a State University. He gave the Trustees of the county credit for having done well this year."[63]

Brier was elected to a second term as Alameda County Superintendent of Education. It was not simply an honorary title. Many farming communities wanted to organize a school as a way to train their own children, as well as to attract and sustain families for their industry. We can see that the job of being Superintendent was not an easy task from the following letter that highlights the many calls for help in founding schoolhouses, and a sidelight on the freewheeling lawlessness that troubled the remote parts of the county.

A letter in possession of the Brier family today is from a friend in Redwood City. Redwood Landing—November 6, 1854

Rev. W. W. Brier

Dear Sir,

I wrote you concerning the schoolhouse I believe about two weeks ago, and I am disappointed in not receiving an answer. I fear matters are "moving slowly." If there is not now an answer to my first on the way, will you please write me our expectation of this that I may know what to expect? If the schoolhouse is not to be built, I must make other arrangements than those I have anticipated.

My horse was stolen about two weeks ago. Probably I shall not find it again, though Jose now in confinement in S. Francisco, and Domingo Phales says there are several hundred stolen horses in the mountains near San Jose. Discoveries have recently been made concerning thieving operations in these parts that are sufficient to sicken one of the countries. Will you please notice whether my mare comes your way. Brand is MC on the left shoulder, and three or four Mexican brands on the left hindquarter. Mrs. White's family is as well as usual.

Sincerely yours,
J.A. Chattered. [64]

Brier was looked up to as a regional leader in many areas. The growing Irvington community was at the junction of five corners on the road from Centerville to the mission and San Jose. Irvington had significant paleontological beds in the near-by Irvington Gravel pits. *The History of Washington Township* recalls that *"the Rev. W. W. Brier called these ancient fossils "the bones of fallen angels." Perhaps they are."* [65]

Setting down roots in California

Few personal letters survive for the William Brier family. The only letter we have was handed down to a relative, Mrs. Jean Fraker Roath, the great niece of William Wallace Brier.

Brier Letter #19
(Post Office) Union City

Nov. 14ᵗʰ, 1853

Dear Sister Mary,

I wrote a letter to you in June last and left it for wife to write in but she laid it up and forgot it until it was too old to send. So now I write again.

1ˢᵗ. We are all well. I am better in health than I have been for two years. Wife is healthier than ever she was. Lizzy is growing and learning her 'a-b-c's. Mary stands alone.

2ⁿᵈ. Our worldly prospects—I am largely in debt about $4,000. But I have a worth $7,000 in money, and $1,000 worth of stock, &c. Also about $7,000 worth of potatoes and grain and my lot in Marysville worth $1,500 this I am offered for it.

After my debts are paid I will be worth ten or twelve thousand dollars. All but two thousand of this I have made this year.

You speak of pigs—I bought four in July. Now they are nearly ready to bear an increase. I paid $100 for the four. Last Feb. I bought $58 worth of chickens 28 hens. We have sold $160 worth of eggs and have $250 worth of chickens.

Our house is comfortable. You enter a yard with a neat railing fence and walk 8 rods to a cottage with a door and a large window on each side of it. Enter the door and you see my table on the right with shelves and pigeonholes and all filled with books and papers and me sitting in large rocking chair writing. In front is my bookcase with glass doors and containing 300 volumes a well-selected library. The floor carpeted neatly with a "turkey carpet." Other parlor furniture I have not yet procured but shall as soon as my debts are paid—but off this you enter a small room which has a French bedstead and a carpet same as the parlor. This is to be my study if I ever study anymore.

Through another door you enter the dining room and turning to the left you enter our bedroom which fronts on the front of the house. It has a bed, a crib, stand, etc.— carpeted with a plain carpet but off the dining room you go through a door back into the kitchen which contains a stove, table, wash table, pump, and other kitchen things. Back of the kitchen on the same floor you enter the pantry 5x7 feet and through another door you enter the bathing room 6 ½ by 7 feet. In front of the kitchen there is a porch 16 feet long. Back of the house is the barn—haystacks, chicken house, and tent for men, and hog pens. I have sent to the States for $100.00 worth of trees. In time I shall have a fine place.

You have seen my house. You may listen a little.

You hear my wife ask Liz, "Who made you?"

Answer "God"

Question, "Where is God?"

Answer, "Gone to San City" (meaning San Francisco City). So you see we teach our children religion. Of course the child was informed that God is in Heaven. Lizzie is a very bright child. She is as quick as a squirrel—all life—her muscles are as hard as those of a cat. The baby is growing brighter and healthier.

I hear that you have another boy. I would like to have a boy, and then I would be satisfied with children. If you do not look out you will get ahead of us entirely. Juliet has a baby girl. They are well as usual. James has squatted on 160 acres of land but is preaching; is poor.

Potatoes are very low, only worth 1 ¾ cents a pound. They will be worth 3 cents this winter. I have about 300,000 lbs., which I intend to keep (until winter). We have tomatoes yet on the vines. Here we raise garden vegetables all year round. We have had one frost, which froze about 100 bushels of potatoes, which were in the ground in the field exposed. I have 6 men at work—Chinese and two Americans. I have had all kinds of people working for me. Wife does all her own work so you must excuse her from not writing this time. She sends love and says she will write the next time. We will not always be so busy.

I preach every Sabbath. We only missed about 5 or 6 Sabbaths since I came to Cal. Yet I am not able to be a professional minister. I receive nothing for preaching. Church matters in this country are flourishing, but alas there is but little vital piety and but few turn to the Lord. You have had Mother and Ide with you. I wish we could have them here for a time but this I cannot expect. I do not know what I shall do this year. If I farm I may make a visit to you next year. Frank White and wife are within 20 miles of us at Oakland. Write us soon all about your affairs. I have told you all I can think of. Ask all the questions you please. I can answer everything you wish to know about California. Last week I attended Presbytery. We had a large meeting. Goodbye—God bless you and your little ones.

Yours truly
W.W. Brier. [66]

There are a number of fascinating observations we can make from this letter. William is boasting to his sister, obviously assuring her that everything is fine with the Brier family in California, and he is taking a breather from the intense work of claiming the land and building the house. The dust has finally settled after a year and a half of tumult.

The Brier family home in Centerville (photo after 1900)
Photo courtesy the Fremont Museum of Local History
(The Robert Fisher collection)

He celebrates in the symbols of success and culture, a home with adequate furnishings, carpeting in the rooms, and "a well-selected library". This was a two-story farmhouse, with bedrooms upstairs. There are a few things that are noticeably missing. There is no mention of the church or his calling there, but he does say he has continued preaching. He apologizes for not being paid for ministry, and the curious note, "this is to be my study if I ever study anymore." He describes his livestock, hogs and chickens, and his crops in rotation, potatoes, tomatoes, and wheat. He is back in business in farming what he did as a child in Indiana. He is doing well to have six workers, two Americans and four Chinese.

He was already a successful farmer, a leader in the county educational system, and an emerging community leader. But there is something still gnawing at his soul. He wants to respond to the call to return to full time ministry of developing churches. His primary love is to do this full time. Brier had already exhausted his AHMS support while serving in Marysville, and having left under those difficult circumstances of ill health, now needed an advocate in order to get back on the payroll so he might devote full time to the ministry at Alvarado/Centerville.

1854

The Brier family began to settle in. Rev. Brier was fulfilled in farming, economically stable, esteemed by society, established in teaching school, and called once again to preaching. This was his first report after leaving the staff, and like his Romney farewell letter, he tries to show that he really is doing the job of missionary and church planter.

Brier letter #20

"My way seemed dark, but God led me."

File # 01085
Dated 1854

To the Secretary of the AHMS
Bible House
Astor Place
New York City

Dear Brothers,

It is with sincere gratitude to God that I make this quarterly report to the society under the patronage of which I set foot upon these shores four years ago. I am constrained to bow in silence before the Almighty when I remember His hand, which has been upon me.

Deep indeed have been the shadows through which we have passed. While health continued, we joyfully submitted to privations, want and toil, for the hopes, which were before us. But we commenced to be comfortably situated. My health, which had never entirely returned after my residence in Panama, declined, and brought about the resolution, which has fixed my location in this beautiful valley. By the advice of the brethren, I determined to break a vow, which I had made "never to turn aside to worldly business". I knew that it would require a year or two for me to recruit supporters, and that I should be compelled to make heavy drafts upon your treasury for my support and that there was even a great uncertainty whether I should ever recover so as to do the full work of the Minister.

I therefore thought it better to save the society one or two thousand dollars, with which you might send a man to take my place: indeed I felt troubled that so much money had been spent on me for so brief a period of labor. My way seemed dark, but God led me. My health improved constantly, and I soon commenced to preach a "free gospel"(as some westerners call it) that is, without salary. The example of Paul's tent making consoled me wonderfully. (Although as the pile of old sermons decreased this example was less appreciated).

Society has improved. Families have settled about us. Nearly a year ago, a request was made and I organized a church. Then the Mormons held meetings every Sabbath, and I must confess I envied them of the large congregations, which assembled to hear their senseless harangues. They were principally the tenants of a wealthy Mormon preacher who owns this house we nest in. Now the congregations fill the house at my hour, while but few attend the Mormon meeting. The above I have written as a report of the past four years as I always have and still consider myself your missionary on this coast. I wrote when I left Marysville, and was anxious for your advice, for Dr. Badger and then lamented Dr. Hall seemed like fathers to me, but I received no answer.

Report.

My parish contains about 180 square miles, and a population of some 1500 souls. I preach at three places presently. At two of them there have been Sabbath schools organized within three months, and $87 worth of books procured. One common school of high character has been in operation four months. Congregations have increased gradually; at Union City I have been visiting and inviting all those who did not attend in my attempt to doubled the attendance.

It is often remarked that there has been a marked improvement in the morals and religious aspects of community within a year. Three years ago this entire territory was an open plain covered within Spanish cattle, now every acre is under fence and most of it is under cultivation. Young orchards and comfortable houses are making their appearance.

The Old Catholic Mission church stands on an eminence seen from every point in the valley, yet its power even over the Spanish population avails but little. The old Padre lives in his ancient adobe houses, almost as solitarily as the owl, which builds its nest under the tiled roof. "His people" are carried away by the Spirit of the "American Dream" and even manifest a desire for their religion and the Bible as well as the language; I acquired a partial knowledge of the Spanish language and am known far and wide as "Padre". Most of the people have been supplied with the Bible and tracts. I trust that the Lord has a work here to be done and I shall commit myself to it with all my strength.

There are many difficulties to surmount—Sabbath desecration, intemperance, large land holders, with transient laborers, and tenants, a mixed population, Mexicans, Indians, Chinese, Chileans, Irish and German Catholics, Swedes, and all of them bent on making money and leaving. The people are improving also and in debt. Produce is low.

Yours Truly
W. W. Brier[67]

This is a landmark letter for Brier, testing the waters of the AHMS Society for financial support after being cut off for some years. It is also holds a clear and compelling portrait of the conditions of the valley he is called to serve in.

There was a certain shame in the eyes of the missionary who had to turn aside to work in the farm field outside the field of the Lord's ministry. "Because the American Home Missionary Society contributed substantially to the salary of frontier ministers, those ministers were expected to spend full time in the ministerial duties. Farming, merchandising, or even teaching was frowned upon. These were not unworthy occupations, but for a missionary they were diverting." [68]

Yet Brier would establish a new model for a dual career ministry by returning into ministry, first as a volunteer, then as a professional.

His work as the Superintendent of Schools has taken him far and wide. He has been a faithful minister. He has passionately worked the farm for two years and preached for free. Now as the call of God is upon him once again, he does not sell the farm, but continues a combination of what would be considered "tent-making ministry". At this time Brier had already established a congregation as a volunteer minister, and he went further north in seeking a second opportunity to preach in San Lorenzo.

The following letter is written as a letter of advocacy on behalf of Rev. Brier. The AHMS society would support a missionary for only two years. Then the missionary would be dropped unless some church body appealed to the society for support.

Affirmation of Support
Letter to the AHMS

Union City, Alameda County California
May 1ˢᵗ, 1854

To the Secretaries of the American Home Mission Society.

Reverend Brethren,

The Alameda Presbyterian Church in order to secure the services of Rev. W. W. Brier for one half his time would make the following representations:

1ˢᵗ. It contains eleven members and was organized nearly a year since, by Mr. Brier. The attendance is about seventy. The nearest congregations are from twenty to eighty miles, except a Methodist circuit preacher who lives twenty miles distant and passes this way.

2ⁿᵈ. It is known to you probably that Mr. Brier by the advice of Physician and his Brethren in the ministry, has been engaged in farming in order to restore his health which had declined, much while in his farmer field of labor.

Although he had not devoted his time to pastoral labors, yet he has preached in this city, really preached, really labored for two years, and his labor has not been in vain.

3ʳᵈ. Interest in the religion of Christ has sprung up and recently is much increased. Previous to this time Mr. Brier has refused to receive anything for his services as he was engaged in farming.

Now he has resolved to devote his entire time to preaching the gospel and we with to retain him in this field. But in order to do so it is necessary to secure him. Will you grant a salary of eighteen hundred dollars for one year, commencing on this first day of May 1854? We have raised a subscription in this congregation amid that of Union City 1,000 population.

Mr. Brier proposes to preach at this church one Sabbath and in the San Lorenzo settlement and at Union City (a county town) the other alternate Sabbath.

At San Lorenzo, the people have never had any preaching until within last month. Mr. Brier has preached for them three times. There is no church organization in that settlement which is distant eight miles. In two weeks the people will have completed a temporary house of worship and expect to build a church in the fall. As we also hope to do here on the entire field we think that $1,200.00 can be realized and are willing to pledge this amount.

Can your advance us six hundred dollars, not for this church, but for the field where
Mr. Brier is to spend the other half of his time. That is a field of much importance in a rich
valley across the bay from San Francisco. It contains some five or six hundred people.

Yours respectfully,
Charles Hilton, (Elder), and James Selfridges M.D. (Elder)

There is a note attached to the application by the Rev. T. D. Hunt. The continuing field director for the AHMS weighs in with Brier to reinstate the financial support. It is interesting that he is not overly praiseful upon Brier's transition back into ministry, nor does he comment at great length about his readiness for ministry. Instead he focuses upon the potential of the ministry to become "self-supporting" as a church within a short period of time. The AHMS listen to Rev. Willey, and respond to his recommendation to support Brier once again. After all—why not go with someone who is on the field, instead of sending out a new one from the East Coast!

This letter revealed that Brier was now preaching in three places: at Union City/ Alvarado, at Centerville/Alameda, and at San Lorenzo/Eden. This new preaching point in Union City came about through his relational networking from his early days in the Mission San Jose. Brier followed up on farming families that attended Presbyterian services at the Mission. The Hawley family and the Cornell family had purchased tracts of farming land in the valley at the same time Brier did. The Cornell family was located further northwest, on the shores of the San Francisco Bay. At the same time, John Horner had purchased a large tract of land in the neighborhood and was farming wheat. It is apparent that John Horner trusted Rev. Brier, as he welcomed him as both teacher and preacher, and accommodated the Presbyterian congregation in Centerville on a Sunday morning. Once again, Brier and Horner teamed up in schoolhouse teaching and preaching to the community of Alvarado. Horner started the schoolhouse on the property, and opened the doors to Brier to form a Presbyterian congregation during the afternoons, while he would gather the Mormon families in the morning.

It is not surprising that Brier would team up with Horner, and that Horner would accommodate the needs of Presbyterians. Like Brier, John Horner seemed to have a heart for innovation and cooperation. Horner was credited with inventing one of the first horse-team-driven thrashing machines to harvest wheat and bale the hay.

As the Centerville Church began selling cemetery plots, they remembered the kindness of the Mormon community and made these family plots available to the Mormon families who farmed the surrounding valley. Horner and others bought plots and were buried side by side with the Presbyterians.

His reputation with his colleagues was improving, as they saw the fruit of his ministry. As a sign of his blessing, Rev. S. H. Willey adds a cool and reserved note to the AHMS society requesting their support of Rev. Brier.

San Francisco May 15, 1854

I am personally acquainted with the field from which this letter comes, and believe this ministry is one where a self—supporting church will grow up in a few years. The support of the inhabitants is a human indicator, and in my opinion, points to the extension of these years, and in my consideration, is precisely worthy of the funds, which he asks for.

S. H. Willey

CHAPTER 22

Signposts on the Frontier:
Teach Your Children the Faith!

Both William and Elizabeth Brier were known for their involvement in the Sabbath School Movement. The New School pastors used a strategy of Christian education which would initially launch a Sabbath School in the community which would enroll future "Sabbath Scholars". The history of Sabbath schools actually precedes the modern-day children's Sunday school programs, and finds its history more in the educational model of teaching. Within the broad American evangelical church movement, Miss Lydia Adams established the first Sabbath school in Boston in 1812. This school brought new children into the church and trained them. The lessons taught were almost exclusively taken from the Westminster Shorter Catechism and two hymnbooks: *Divine Songs for Children*, and *Hymns for Infant Minds*. The movement spread throughout New England, and then into the growing Frontier of the Middle West. The Brier/Naylor family had a pioneering history with this movement. Elizabeth Brier's Mother, Mary Naylor, established the first Sabbath school in the Frontier State of Indiana.

Sabbath Schools attempted to engage the children to study the Scriptures. Two or three families would be placed into study groups and would meet on Saturdays in order to drill the kids in Christian topics. The goal was to help the kids to become a scholar of the Bible. The scholars learned as many as they chose and would often memorize whole chapters. In a class of six or eight, so many chapters had been committed to memory that many members would have time during the session to recite.

The excellence of the school seemed to be in the memory work. In a spirit of friendly competition, rewards were given to stimulate the scholars in their work. A ticket, on which was written or printed "Merit" was given in some schools for every ten verses; when ten tickets were obtained or one hundred verses had been recited, a tract was given. When five tracts were obtained, a book was the reward.

The movement began to grow and mature. After a few years, the workers began to think that instead of crowding the minds of the young with whole Chapters of the Bible, a better way would be to give out from six to ten chapters as a lesson to be committed to memory, and studied, so that the scholars would be able to answer the questions their teacher might ask them on the subject. Question books and catechisms were introduced in some schools quite early based on the Westminster Assembly's Shorter Catechism.

Very early in the history of Sabbath schools there were comparatively few books published for the young, a library was considered as indispensable to the existence of a school. Rev. Brier notes that the Centerville Sabbath School library held 200 books. This would become the first library in Centerville.

The Sabbath School movement became an important social function in rural communities. One feature of the Sabbath school was the monthly concert for recitation of verses, children's choral work, and general music recital. They also had worship with singing and prayer that was spontaneous, and simultaneous, like an orchestra to God.

Church members went door-to-door with invitations to the Sabbath School. Workers created a benevolent society for the young to help out one other, taught musical instruments to their children, visited families who dropped out of the school, and helped provide childcare for families who wanted to attend. This school was a foundational part of the church outreach strategy wherever Brier went.

1854

In 1854, Rev. Willey wrote to the AHMS to confirm that Brier was settled again. Some would say that once Brier was farming, he was focused and began to enter his most mature phase of ministry. He toned down his doubts, and was glowing in praise for Brier. This was a letter of blessing, about as good as it comes from the AHMS supervisor. He confirmed that Brier may now be in the right place in Centreville.

Rev. Willey to the AHMS
San Francisco
May 15, 1854

Dear Sir,

The accompanying from Mr. Brier's people speaks for itself. I think on examination that the request is reasonable. I have been out to his parish more than once. It is one of the most beautiful and fertile valleys in California, and is fast settling all over. His crops last fall broke even, instead of being a loss, this request would not have been sent to you.

Nor is it likely that another request will go to you from this ground. Mr. Brier is
liked in this region. He was out of his climate, erin out of his sphere in Marysville (and
he came to California with wrong notions of himself) but he is now in good health, and
he has a good promise of a congregation where he is, and what they have done is, I think,
for this year all that could be expected.

I sincerely hope the Executive Committee will answer this request in the affirmative.

Yours Again.
S. H. Willey[69]

Rev. Willey confirmed that there has been a clear change in Brier's self-understanding, and his giftedness in ministry. Brier was climbing out of the valley of depression. Either he was maturing and reaching his stride in ministry or people's perception of him were changing. He was highly effective in organizing the launch of a church, identifying leaders, getting them together, finding a place for them to worship, and setting them free to run a church. Examine the record books of the churches he founded and we find a clear pattern of how Brier instructed others how to start the church, how to examine members and elect elders for, and how to keep the church organization going.

Many times Brier would be at the church when the founding pastor was assigned to the congregation. Other times he would found the church himself and would preach regularly for the first year or two until a suitable pastor would become available. Some of his peers would think that Brier had grown as a preacher; others would say that he always had solid content but dry delivery. He was certainly not a flashy leader. But his unusual passion for church planting, his solid approach to organization, and his ability to connect with the immigrant community, made him a legend in the church planting community.

CHAPTER 23

The Boom and Bust of Agricultural Crops

1855

The local economy had a dramatic effect upon the health and growth of the church. In the first decades the members of the Centrerville congregation formed a literal "Who's Who" of major farmers (and street names) in the Centreville community: Beard, Blacow, Decoto, Eggers, Hawley, Logan, Mac Intosh, Overacker, and Patterson. Farming was difficult in those early years. Crops came in unreliable yields, depending upon the rain. It was feast or famine. Crop market prices fluctuated up and down. But the church endured.

Nine months after the first letter seeking support, Brier wrote of the pressures that would constrain the growth of the church and the results he had seen. Brier lists the classic categories of growth in the church.

"Metallic Insanity"

Brier Letter # 21
February 1st, 1855

Alvarado, Alameda County
To Secretaries of the Home and Mission Society

Dear Brothers

By the blessing of a kind Heavenly Father I have been able to preach without interruption during my third quarter of missionary labor in this country.

There has been only one rainy Sabbath this winter, Sunday is almost universally a pleasant day in California: this has observed for five winters and others have noted the same.

My people are mostly farmers: and the price of grain has been scarcely to pay the expenses of harvesting, leaving the people ruinously and hopelessly in debt. Yet I trust that the lack of earthly comforts and wealth will lead them to seek a more enduring treasure. The third of my salary, which you supply, is my principal reliance for a living. I had hoped to replenish my library this year, which is the same one I shipped from New York five years ago. But this hope is deferred.

It may seem strange that in a land of gold there should be want and poverty, even among ministers; but it is a fact, howsoever much we may wish to conceal it.

There are here a number of worthy ministers, who are hard pressed by debts and with difficulty sustain the reputation of honesty. They handle what in a different state would be considered large sums in order to secure comforts far inferior to those enjoyed by missionaries in Indiana and Illinois.

There are many places in our State where ministers are much needed, but not one where a man will not be called upon to endure hardness as "a good soldier of the cross." This has been a dark year for California in a financial point of view; but there has been more light of heaven than ever before. The delusions of hope of sudden wealth have been broken. There are not so many cases of metallic insanity. We can now find men clothed in their right minds, and willing to sit at the feet of Jesus. That expression of our Savior, "You cannot serve God, and Mammon." has been fearfully illustrated in this state. Oh we need the power of the Holy Ghost. Pray for us, who are surrounded by so many chilling influences. A short time since I rode fifty miles to a place where I had heard that the Holy Ghost had been, and preached three days in conjunction with Brother White. We had large and attentive congregations and some determined to seek the great Salvation. They have only preaching by a Methodist preacher south once every four weeks. I was disappointed. I had hoped to find some whose souls were warm with the love of God. But the times of refreshing will come. Although "the heavens have been brass for seven years", yet the Lord's able to break them asunder.

Yours truly,
W.W. Brier[70]

Brier wrote a compelling picture of the difficult economy, and glowed at the response of those who have been touched by the gospel. He notes, "There are not so many cases of metallic insanity." The boom and bust cycles of California have always contributed to the rapid transition of the economy and population. Early emigrants chased the dream of finding buried treasure in the hillsides and riverbeds, and as this dream faded, so did the prospect of settling in California. When the bubble of the gold economy burst, they were forced to come face-to-face with poverty and the need to evaluate their lives.

Brier Letter # 22

February 27th 1855

Alvarado, Alameda, California.

March Report

1st Name of Churches, Alameda Presbyterian Church
And Eden Presbyterian Church, both of Alameda Co.
2nd Number of hopeful conversions 2
3rd Number added by profession of faith 2
4th Number added by letter of transfer 7
5th Number of Sabbath Schools 50
6th Number of Sabbath books 300
7th Temperance lectures none
8th Number of Churches organized 1
9th Contributions to benevolent society $25.00
The Eden Presbyterian Church will have a building complete in three weeks, which will
be dedicated before this reaches you. All is well.

Yours Truly
W.W. Brier[71]

Brier experienced a measure of brokenness through his failure in Marysville, and began to preach about the power of the Holy Spirit. It was with the infilling of the Spirit that the church stood strong. His remark about being "fully clothed" was also a comment about his life and ministry. At the end of the month of February he submits the above statistical report without comment. The church was growing in both neighboring communities: Eden (Union City) and Alameda. He has been successful and the building of the church is in progress. It is interesting to note that the church building in Alvarado was completed before the church in Centreville, yet the Centreville congregation had already been meeting for five years and was the stronger of the two churches. Two months later, he sent a brief letter to the New York office.

Brier Letter # 23
April 29, 1855

This month completed my fourth quarter of labor in this field. I have had unusual good
health, and by the blessing of God I am permitted to rejoice in seeing some fruit of my

labor. Since I wrote last we have dedicated a neat little church, erected by my Eden congregation, at the cost of $800.00. It will seat 120 persons, is paid for, and finished and painted in the best manner.

I should give you a more extended report if I had time. We are holding a protracted meeting in our new house, and have indications of good. I am propelled to labor to the extent of my capacity.

The churches will be under the necessity of applying to you for aid during the coming year in order to support me in this field.

Yours truly,
W. W. Brier[72]

In response, Dr. Badger sent a letter of blessing, reward, healing, and honor. Brier noted that elders of the church show surprising warmth for his leadership, but it showed no fruit. The reason for the churches struggle was that it was wrongly located, and the population demographics were shifting away from favoring the growth of an English immigrant congregation. Both W. W. and Elizabeth are finally established to help others. There was a surprisingly warm letter in response was sent from the AHMS administrative team.

AHMS Response
September 1, 1855
Rev W.W. Brier

I am happy to find you here with a restored man after a year. The committee felt compelled to increase the sum to the support of your support amount. This may be your best year. They are also compelled to assign additional burdens in consequences of the indirect expense of being supported.

Support for your family in California from the society has naturally diminished, within a year. They hope within a year, therefore, that you will find the amount sufficient and adequate to support you or your people will be fully willing to supply the deficit of the amount of your support. So please accept the enclosed one hundred and fifty-dollars. Rev. Willey will aid you in obtaining amount needed from the society.

We rejoice with you that God has restored your health and your work. May you be sustained and changed in your work in California and may your rich labors be the constant presence of the Lord's presence and of the Lords prosperity in your hands.

I send you kind greetings with this $150.00 for your work.

Yours,
Dr. Badger

As Dr. Badger wrote this note with surprising warmth, it reflects that Brier was back in the good graces of the AHMS. The support would not continue forever, as the society hoped that the Centerville church would make up the difference.

CHAPTER 24

Signposts on the Frontier:
Support Your Local Church!

It was a miracle to build a church and support a pastor in the early days. *The Treasurer's Book* from the Centerville (Alameda) Presbyterian Church for the years 1855 through 1870 records an interesting history of some of the inner workings of starting a church during the years following the Gold Rush.

The 1855 ledger begins in the fountain pen handwriting of the Rev. William Wallace Brier, founding pastor. It was customary at the time for the pastor to begin by raising subscriptions pledges for his salary. In the first five pages of the ledger, there were 56 pledges amounting to $1597.70. There are a few interesting notes about this list of patrons. The most generous patron listed, was the treasurer and pastor himself. W.W. Brier registered a pledge of $165.00 for the year. The second largest pledge of $100.00 came from his Indiana friend and farmer E. L. Beard. The remaining 54 family pledges range from $50.00 to $10.00. Eleven of the final names are marked with the words, "Collected by Mrs. Brier in San Francisco". It seems that Elizabeth Brier maintained her contacts among the Presbyterians in the city of San Francisco, and was quite successful in visiting them from time to time and sharing the vision for what God could do in the East Bay, if only they would help. And so they did.

The Briers ministered in Centerville from 1852 through 1855, without having a clear mandate to be there. Brier was partially supported by the American Home Mission Society at the rate of $400 a year to explore the possibilities of ministry throughout the region. During the first six years of his ministry, until the year 1858, the church paid nothing to Brier for his role as pastor. Cash was difficult to come by, due to the crashing produce prices and shifting population at the close of the Gold Rush. As immigration continued, and as towns grew, so did the need for churches.

Many prominent community members are listed as church subscribers and supporters; most are not mentioned later as members of the church. In frontier communities many businessmen wanted the status of having a parson in town. They believed that any proper long-term community needed a good church and a pastor. These businessmen would support the launch of a church building or ministry just for the sake of community "good will".

The church was struggling deeply with the economics of supporting a pastor. In the Presbyterian tradition, the trustees handled the management of the financial and physical details. On February 24, 1855 a meeting of the Alameda Presbyterian Church was held at Horner's School House in Centerville for the purpose of electing Trustees of the Church. Jessie Beard, Henry Clark, Chancy Cornell, Charles Kelsey, and J.A. Mayhew were elected. It was stipulated that *the Board of Trustees and their successors were to be styled forever "Trustees of Alameda Presbyterian Church" to hold in trust all property, real and personal, of the Church."*

Besides having a pastor living in town, the community needed a church building. "The Old White Church" was originally the old red church. It was constructed in 1856 as a red brick structure with no steeple.

There are some interesting features in financing this structure. The congregation still did not have enough money to build the church but was gaining some momentum and wanted to step out in faith to complete the building. They borrowed $500.00 from the wealthy farmer, G.W. Patterson, whose wife attended the church, at 2% interest. Although he attended the church on occasion, he was not known as a deeply committed Presbyterian. The loan was repaid to Patterson in the following two years.

In 1856, there was a special offering to raise money for the purchase of the church bell from Rev. Pond's abandoned church in San Francisco. A total of 28 donors raised the $139.00 needed to purchase the bell, the pulpit furniture, and two oil-burning lamps to illuminate the interior of the church. Once they had a bell, they needed to add a steeple to house it. The cost of lumber and a carpenter to build the steeple was $250 dollars.

There is no reference to "pew rent" collected at Centerville. Many New England churches made the money to pay the pastor by allowing families to purchase pews. Their reserved seats were located in the church based upon the price of their support.

In 1856, Brier again contributes the largest amount of money: $400.00. He was still drawing no salary. By 1857, with the church fully paid for, the new treasurer, Mr. Hilton, notes a personal responsibility of each member to pay the pastor's salary. The total contributed for that year was $470.00.

The shortfall of giving to the pastor's salary is one factor which leads them to look for outside sources. Elders Charles Hilton and James Fair wrote a letter requesting the AHMS to support part of Brier's salary, and the society agreed to do so for a few years. The Presbytery of San Jose got involved, after realizing this was a poor example for any church to neglect paying the pastor fully, and ordered the church to make amends with Rev. Brier and fully repay the years he drew no salary.

Here is the I.O.U. that was issued to Brier by the elders of the Centerville/ Alameda church.

January 8, 1856

The Trustees of the Alameda Presbyterian Church do hereby obligate themselves in this corporate capacity, and their successors in office, for services rendered as Pastor to pay to the Rev. W. W. Brier, one year from this date, the sum of three hundred dollars and interest at ten percent per annum until paid.
Signed on behalf of the Trustees

James Shin
President

Dr. Selfridge, secretary

This helpful note was to secure the financial amount the church owed Brier, and to make them feel more responsible. At the same time, the Centreville church was making a strong effort to support a new pastor. They issued the following note to Brier of their intent to repay him for his ministry, $300 each year until the debt was paid. Yet the good intentions were not matched with income. Brier held the notes for the year, then began to ask the church to pay his doctor bills. Dr. Selfridge brought the matter to Rev. Brier with a concern that the church had not honored its commitment. Somewhere over the conversation they struck a deal. Brier had outstanding bills to Dr. Selfridge for medical assistance surrounding the delivery of Brier's child. Brier also knew that the church was still struggling to pay its current pastor. He was well supported through the proceeds from his farm crops and from the support of the AHMS, so he worked out a trade of debt. He would ask the church to pay Dr. Selfridge, and the doctor would pay the church the money to free up money to pay the pastor who replaced him. The books would be cleaner.

Brier Letter #24
Centerville

November 21st, 1862

The Trustees of the Alameda Presbyterian Church will please pay to Dr. J. M. Selfridge the sum of seventy dollars and 50/100 ($70.50) the amount of his bill against me rendered this day, for medical services prior to this date, to be credited by me on a note bearing date January 8th, 1861 against said church.

W.W. Brier

Building the Church at Alameda/Centerville

The Alameda church was first named for the tributary to the Alameda Creek that ran alongside of the cemetery property. A bit of friendly church competition emerged as the Eden (Union City) church building was completed, so the AlamedaChurch renamed itself to match the growing village of Centreville, and became known as Centreville Presbyterian. Just two years later, the growing village changed the spelling of the name from Centreville to Centerville.

The congregation was not an easy one to begin. One of the problems associated with crafting a church from a group of European immigrants from so many different traditions is that they had no identity as Presbyterians. There is little to hold them together except the charisma of the pastor in leadership. Often a congregation would be formed, and members would see it as a temporary place to worship until they had formed a church like the one they belonged to back home. So they joined and became a part of this faith community.

Brier's local role also held a regional vision. He was designated as "Exploring missionary". He advised congregations throughout the state of their need to be organized according to Presbyterian law and the laws of the state. There was often great energy placed into the building of a church structure. A church then needed a board of trustees separate from the board of elders whose members were called to build and maintain the property of the church, while the elders continued to focus upon the spiritual health of the church.

"According to the usual notice, the Alameda Presbyterian Church and Congregation held a meeting in the Church at Centerville Alameda County, California to elect a board of five trustees. W.W. Brier was called to the chair and the following persons were elected trustees according to the custom of said church. Brigadier Michael Overacker, Richard B. Hall, M.D. William W. Brier, James Shin, and John Proctor. These persons to hold office for

one year and until their successors are elected; and are to be with said successors a body
corporate to be known forever by the name and title of "The Trustees of the Alameda
Presbyterian Church." [73]

On May 12, 1855, the trustees met and elected Jessie Beard as president, Reverend
Brier the treasurer, and Chancy Cornell the secretary. Reverend Brier was authorized to
take subscriptions for the purpose of building a house of worship for Alameda
Presbyterian Church, and to purchase a lot. The trustee's minutes tell us that on July 2,
1855, the trustees met and Rev. Brier reported financial subscriptions of $1500.00. He
also reported the donation of a lot of ground by G.A. Lloyd on which to build the house
of worship. At this meeting the trustees voted to contract with Charles B. Tool to build
the church building. The construction contract called for the building of a small brick
chapel, forty-four feet long and twenty-four feet wide. The walls above the ground were
to be seventeen feet, six-inches with high gothic gables. The work was to be done within
nine weeks. It was a simple construction, with a complex challenge to locate materials
and craftsmen to complete it. Most men were engaged in the building of businesses and
farms and could not help. Because no one could be found to take on the supervision,
Reverend Brier was appointed to superintend the building of the church.

The original old brick church, 1856
Photo courtesy of Centerville Presbyterian Church archives.

All was well for the first few years, until the earthquake of 1868 shattered the brick
walls of the structure. The cost of remodeling the church was $945 to remove and sell
the red bricks and replace them with white tongue and groove boards. It was fitting that
the church appeared like a white New England church. This delayed the plans to fully
repay Brier for his labors.

Paychecks to partially pay Brier as pastor begin to appear in the ledger in these years. But there are notes throughout the ledger that suggest they provided much of their support in donated goods and services. Mr. Hawthorn donated fruit trees, coal and candles were provided by C. Hilton, and Mr. Durant provided the trees around the church. Two cords (of firewood) delivered to William Wallace Brier. Mr. Beard provided 2 tons of hay and 1 mattress delivered to Brier to fulfill the subscription for the year. Mr. Eggers delivered sundries to the Briers and the church to fulfill his pledge.

CHAPTER 25

Signposts on the Frontier: Obey the Law!

All was not rosy in the early days of the church. Presbyterians teach that the church should be governed decently and orderly. But the emerging society had a long way to go in becoming orderly. There was a continuing struggle between the lawless society, and the desire to establish a new community in California. Many residents saw ministers as the prophets of a new social order, and looked to them for leadership in promoting and enforcing better a better moral fabric for the community. On a community level, William Wallace Brier was involved in attempting to build the community through a variety of roles. His name is listed in a variety of activities in the early days of Washington Township, speaking at the Arbor Day at a local college, and acting as Secretary of the township water board.

On a more curious note, he was a member of the famous Washington Township Vigilance Committee of 1855, which was part of the movement by communities across the Pacific Coast to once again put down disorder and reestablish the authority of the courts.

In Washington Township, vigilante reaction was provoked by a new wave of cattle rustling. Late in the summer of 1855 some livestock were run off and several farmers went in pursuit. The thieves were overtaken and after a short skirmish, in which one of the thieves was wounded, they were captured. Two were white men by the names of Hill and Harris; two were Mexicans. They were brought to Alvarado and delivered to the sheriff who was told that they must be guarded, tried, and if found guilty, punished, or the settlers would begin to take the law into their own hands. There was no jail at the time in the county, so the prisoners were placed in two rooms in the old hotel in Alvarado.

Horse and cattle theft were only a part of the lawlessness that was resurgent throughout California. Some would say it was because of the economic trauma shattered economy when the bubble burst on the gold rush, and the migration of miners to the farmland. James Shinn notes that in the face of this lawlessness there emerged the Vigilance committee in southern Alameda county area of Washington Township. This was the perfect area for cattle rustling, as the valley rolls out beneath the golden oaks of the hillside range of hills. Frequently bandits would steal cattle, and then escape into the canyons and over the hills.

Shinn wrote, *"It was about the year 1854 that Alameda County became thoroughly aroused by the depredations of a band of cattle thieves, whose operations spread through out the county. Seemingly no man's cattle were safe while this state of affairs existed. A mass meeting of the citizens was called to meet at Centreville in the Methodist church. The meeting was largely attended, officers were elected, and an executive committee of twelve appointed. In November 1855, thorough the energy of this committee, four of the thieves were captured and taken to Alvarado, where they were placed under guard in the old Brooklyn hotel. During their first night of confinement, two of the Mexicans, escaped. The irate citizens determined that the other two should not follow in the footsteps of the fleeing ones, so formed a posse, took the prisoners from their place of confinement, carried them to "the Willows"(on what is now part of the Patterson estate), and hanged them. During the afternoon following the lynching, and inquest was held, at which Justice Marshall or Mission San Jose presided, and from the evidence presented the following verdict was brought in: Found hung, by some person, or persons unknown to this journey". The two Mexicans who escaped were pursued, captured, and on the same night met their fate on the banks of the Alameda Creek at the hands of the infuriated and despoiled citizens."*[74]

In his newspaper article for the *Oakland Newspaper,* printed in 1887, James Shinn remembers that that among the local dignitaries involved in the organization of the Vigilante movement, although not necessarily present at the hanging is . . . . Rev. W. W. Brier!

This was not inconsistent with the position of his colleagues. Early in 1951, Brier's friend Timothy Dwight Hunt was asked to comment of the first wave of vigilante justice, in connection with the hanging of Mr. Jenkins by the San Francisco Vigilance Committee. "T. Dwight Hunt preached a sermon on Sunday morning, June 30, 1851, based upon Romans 13:1, "let every soul be subject to higher power for the powers that be are ordained of God." In this sermon, which was reviewed in the newspapers, he condones the activities of the Vigilance committee and laments the civil unrest in San Francisco." [75]

The AHMS offered that there were ways to change this lawless spirit. "Something more is needed than a good constitution and equal laws, Laws are but cobwebs, without public virtue. There are but two great methods of governing men—by moral motives or by physical force. If our patriots will not sustain and spread the Gospel that provide the former, they must put the musket and the sword into the hands of the latter." [76]

Brier voiced a number of concerns in August of 1855. Elizabeth was ill once again, and William feared for her life. In his next letter to the board, he celebrated the ordering of a church society. A reference to this new organization in *The History of Washington Township*, notes that this was the first fraternal order in the township, the "Sons of Temperance," called the Alameda Division, which was organized June, 1855, in Mr. Brier's study. [77]

Brier's letter is both newsy and powerful.

Brier Letter to AHMS #25

> *Yet we have a Father whom in the darkest hour*
> *has given us a place in his bosom*

August 1, 1855

Alvarado, Alameda County
To the Secretaries of the American Home Mission Society

Dear Brothers,

The churches under my care made application to your Society for aid during the year commencing May 1ˢᵗ 1855. The application was delayed and yet I have such confidence in respect to receiving a commission that I make my regular quarterly report. Indeed I hope that a few statements in respect to my humble work in this part of God's vineyard would not be entirely destitute of interest, even if I were not your Missionary, sent to this land in an early day.

I have preached regularly at two places every Sabbath, except two, and on those Sabbaths at one place during the past three months. My health has been good, but that of my wife has very much declined. She has labored during the long night, which hung so darkly over our prospects; while I was afflicted, and exhibited that fortitude for which woman is so distinguished. I shudder at the thought that now, when I feel the life-tide returning, and she might be permitted to rest from anxiety, she should be called to bodily afflictions. Yet we have a Father who in the darkest hour has give us a place in his bosom a peculiar character.

The churches are small and poor so that I am not so much the minister of the churches, as the people. From outsiders comes most of my support, with the money to build a house of worship, according to the custom in California. I am now collecting funds to erect a church. My labor does not consist in going to men with families and houses alone: no, it is a pleasure to "beg" from such. Much of the money must be squeezed out of the hard fist of men who have but one idea and purpose, and that idea—to get money enough to make them comfortable or rich, when they return to their families. Often, very often, I am repulsed by the news of New England and the roughest thrusts are made at the Bible and the Church. "Free Thinking" as it is termed, prevails to an alarming extent in this country. Yet I try humbly to bear testimony to the truth and blessedness of our holy religion, and to show the benefits conferred upon this land by the gospel.

We have a division of the Sons of Temperance which has recently been organized at my house. I can see a great improvement n this community, and yet the discouragements, there and elsewhere in California are numerous, our ministry is called to struggle with many cares, in building up the outer walls of the temple. This is a necessary policy. We are heartened to establish self-supporting churches. How is this to be done? The answer is, "Set up houses of worship!" How is this to be accomplished? "Go out and collect money from every man you meet, and superintend the erection of the church. Preach in the meantime in a schoolhouse or under a tree, and keep up your courage and spirituality." This is ministerial life in California. Woe to the man who cannot count dollars and drive sharp bargains with men of the world, all the week and on the Sabbath preach learned and eloquent sermons, and gain the reputation of being a good pastor.

For while all this labor is performed he must live in the hope of a future settlement. It would not do to raise money for a minister while he is raising the funds to build a house (of worship). Your society comes in to help us during this important and interesting probation. May it long continue to sustain the linking of Spirits of God's servants on this land.

Yours Truly
W. W. Brier[78]

Look at the force of this letter! There are three things worthy of comment. First, Brier is on the verge of rage, and questions the integrity of the Church Mission Society under which he labors. How can he do this? Does he think that it is simply putting good copy in the newsletter, *The Home Missionary*? This letter is focused the multi-tasking nature of the ministerial calling. California ministry was challenging because of the complexity of life, the pace of the activity, and the difficulties in ministering to an ever-moving population of people.

Second, this letter sheds light on a number of economic issues. It includes a reference to the first "bust" in the Gold Rush boom, as he talks of commercial business seeming to stop and the church financial pledges slowing up. He sells his theological books in a pawnshop and asks the Mission Association to reimburse him for the loss! This may be his way of obligating them to pay him.

Third, there was the passion for the Presbyterian Church to be a moral influence in the community. Brier writes, "We have a division of the Sons of Temperance that has recently been organized at my house. I can see a great improvement in this community."

CHAPTER 26

Signposts on the Frontier: Liquor is Evil!

Organized efforts to promote temperance appeared in the 1820's as part of the extraordinary outburst of reform that transformed the United States in the first half of the nineteenth century. Inspired by religious enthusiasm, democratic hopes, and moral concerns, temperance reformers joined sabbatharians, abolitionist, women's rights advocates, pacifists, and crusaders.

The focus was to seek significant reform for the sake of health, education, and treatment of disease, crime, and poverty. A growing sense that the country was being held back from true moral and economic growth emerged in the 1830's and 1840's, which led temperance organizations to begin pressing for political power

Many temperance societies prohibited only distilled liquor (whiskey, rum, gin, and other spirits that contained between 40 and 50 per cent alcohol), but they continued to allow fermented alcohol such as wine and beer which had only 12 percent alcohol.

The temperance movement found its roots in the Massachusetts Society for the Suppression of Intemperance (MSSI), which took shape in 1813. This society was heavily supported by the Congregational clergy of the day. Its moral principles was wedded with the New Haven theology that heavily influenced the Beecher family. It was later merged into the New School passion to be a leadership force on the western shore. Lyman Beecher, stated in his sermon series in 1825, "Intemperance is a national sin," carrying destruction from the center to every extremity of the empire, and calling upon the nation to array itself, en masse, against it. "Beecher passionately taught that as the nation struggled to remove the roots of slavery from our soil, so we would have to labor in our destiny to battle alcohol. This is significant for the Centerville Church and for the entire New School Presbyterian movement, as Rev. W.W. Brier was mentored by Lyman Beecher, and Brier was a friend of the entire Beecher clan.

Members came together for many reasons: to protect themselves from the evils of intemperance, to elevate their character, and to enroll family and society in healthy living for the sake of the Kingdom of God. Members kept watch over each other to keep the temperance pledges.

The temperance movement was effective in battling many social evils. Male leadership was the first driving force until it included the role of women. Women became the passionate proponents of total abstinence as they witnessed the damage of alcohol to family budgets, morals, and stability. In a very real sense, the issues surrounding temperance became both a leadership training ground and a political appetite builder for the suffrage movement of the next decades.

Brier's next letter was a financial report to the society. While there was no new information in this letter, it is interesting that he continued to report to them the growing statistics of his outreach. Church attendance was slightly up, with 31 church members, and an attendance of 50.

Brier AHMS Letter #26

To the Secretary of the A.H.M.S.
Statistical Report

1*st*   *Alameda Presbyterian Church, Washington Township*
      Eden Presbyterian Church, Eden Township
2.   *Number of Stations 2*
3.   *Number of church members 33: 17 females, 16 males*
4.   *Average attendance 100 for both*
5.   *Hopeful conversions 3*
6.   *Profession of faith 4*
7.   *Transfer by letter 6*
8.   *Sunday school scholars 200*
9.   *No new church buildings*
10. *Thirty three hundred dollars ($3300) contributed to build two churches. Both*
      buildings finished and your missionary installed pastor of the two churches.

William Wallace Brier.

P.S. Will you please hold the mortgage herewith transmitted until the church erection committee delivers the funds to be transmitted to us and oblige yours in Christ?

W.W. Brier

It is interesting that he sent the mortgage papers of the church to the Society in New York for "safekeeping". This appears to be a clever way of preparing an invoice for the Society to provide funding for the mortgage. Yet what is beneath the surface is that he is playing the two societies off each other, as the AHMS has no funds for the erection of a church. The Presbyterian Church General Assembly Mission Society had a "Church Erection Fund". Rev. Brier pledged the church mortgage to the interdenominational AHMS society in case the Presbyterians did not come forward with the funding. Such were the hopes and concerns regarding the national Presbyterian denomination.

The next letter he wrote is noteworthy for a number of reasons. The AHMS society agreed to support him for another year. He was still farming, and life was good. There were abundant harvests in the summer of 1855 and 1856. He noted in the letter that his farm had a staggering profit of $2,500.00 but he does not want to devote so much time to the farm. It was clear he would rather continue as a leader in the life of the church. The congregation decided to build the church, but not go into debt. He had purchased a horse and buggy for travel. He requested that the church pay him $800.00 for the year.

He also noted that there were many growing communities in the area, as the number of immigrants began to grow and spread. This was the first letter from Brier following he construction of the Alameda Church at Centerville.

I am willing to labor in any part of the Lord's vineyard,
willing to do the most humble work . . .

Brier Letter # 27

November 1, 1855

Dear Brethren,

I received your commission dated May 1st, 1855 a few days since. I have preached regularly and un-interrupted to the two congregations under my charge. In addition to this I have, during the last quarter raised $1800 towards the erection of a church. I have been the contract superintendent for the church, and have provided all the materials. We had no church member to attend to the business. It has been a long tedious task, and yet I have enjoyed it. Our house of worship is 24 feet wide, and 44 feet long. It is enclosed and will be completed as soon as we get the money to pay for the work. The trustees have committed the entire management into my hands, and I feel that the safest plan is not to go in debt. I have addressed men on the subject of giving as a duty, they owe to God, and find that in this way I obtain money more *successfully, and leave a good impression on their minds. Nearly all this money has been received from those who are not professors of religion. Five days in each week has been spent in this business and yet my congregation here has not diminished. You may easily see that little is raised for the support of a minister in a community when all the people were giving liberally to build a house of worship. In this congregation no effort has been made.*

In the Eden many of my supporters have sold out to Germans and left. Where, last spring, I had the best congregation, where they had built a church without my aid and agreed to raise $500 towards my support, there is now a very small congregation. Germans have settled all round the church, Catholics who rely on formalities and speak the English language very imperfectly. I fear that it will be necessary to move the house three miles to get away from them. In addition to your draft of $150 I have only received $50.00 within the last six months making in all an amount not equal to my traveling expenses and the expense of keeping a house and buggy.

It was only the great prospective importance of that, the richest of all valleys in California that induced me to remain here. This is regarded as one of the most important fields occupied by your missionaries on this coast. Your agent Rev. T.D. Hunt had been here and endeavored to persuade me to live by giving part of my time to farming, but this I would not listen to for a moment.

While laid aside I was willing to work and preach old sermons and receive nothing for it. But now that God has granted me health. I feel that it would be breaking my vows to him. Last year I rented the 40 acres of land, which I bought 3 years ago with money, received from my father's estate, and gave myself to the work of the ministry. The land without my attention has only kept itself in repairs and yielded $100. I am willing to labor in any part of the Lord's vineyard, willing to do the most humble work, and as I told Mr. Hunt to go any place, but I am not willing any longer both to preach and attend to business. I have tried this and found it a vexation of Spirit (as Solomon did). The last year I conducted my farm I cleared $2500 and could do it again if I should give my attention to it. Dr. Badger remembers that when I stipulated to him in order to come to this country, I was to be treated as the foreign board treats their missionaries. I was not to be supported here in case of a failure in health, and was to be returned to my former home.

Six months have made a great change in California. I think that it is a universal opinion of the members of our Presbytery that it is inexpedient to send more men to this state unless you can greatly increase your expenditures. Your last missionaries have traveled more than the former ones before settling. No man will go to a place without knowing something of its comparative importance. You may forward the $150 at your convenience. I have been living from funds, which are now exhausted and know not where the rest *will come from. When our new brick church is finished, I hope an effort will be made to rent the pews and thus secure to me a living.*

Yours Truly
W.W. Brier [79]

Brier was still seeking the Holy Grail of missionaries who are church planters: the establishment of Zion! But he realized this was a strange way to build it. He modeled a new way of addressing the economic realities of tent making, farming the land, working the community.

Here Brier noted the common struggle to be fully supported. "Your agent Rev. T.D. Hunt had been here and endeavored to persuade me to live by giving part of my time to farming, but this I would not listen to for a moment!" This also shed some light on the conflicted conversations Brier had with Dr. Badger before he left for California years earlier. This highlights why Brier was so demanding for their support before he departed for Panama, and so embittered by presently having to farm to make a living. There was some implied promise they made to him, or something he heard that assured him that the Brier family would be cared for in California if they succeeded or failed. Yet the directors of the society feared that he would depart from the pure preaching of the gospel to some commercial concerns. This folly, this *gold getting* was viewed as a shift from the mission of the Kingdom. What began as survival strategy became a God blessed vehicle for security and blessing. The farm provided for his family and the Presbyterian church. His dual roles as preacher and educator became a valuable asset for the future.

Centerville Growth is Slow but Sure 1856

The congregation at Alvarado faltered significantly, but the Alameda/Centerville congregation was growing. The *Oakland Tribune* made note of this historical fact at the time of the congregation's hundred-year birthday. "Not until June 27, 1856, was the Pastor, Reverend W.W. Brier, duly engaged and installed at the Centerville Presbyterian Church. His salary was to be $1000.00 for the ensuing year, having donated his services up to this time. His generosity made it possible for the trustees to pay him only $700.00 as he had agreed to reserve one month as a vacation. With the aid of the women giving a festival at Thanksgiving time, the trustees were able to liquidate all debts on the church building, including the interest on the notes."

On September 19, 1856, Briers third daughter Caroline was born in Centerville. His family was growing too. After four years of living in Centerville, Brier has a six-year-old girl, a one-year-old girl, and a newborn baby boy.

"We dedicated our new brick church last Sabbath in connection with my installation. "

Brier's Letter # 28

Alvarado, Alameda County, California.
February 2, 1856
Secretaries of the A.H.M.S.

Dear Brothers,

Yesterday ended my third quarter of Missionary labor. I reported (to you) at length three months ago, but have not yet received the money draft. I have been very busy during the last quarter and have enjoyed excellent health. We dedicated our new brick church last Sabbath in connection with my installation. It is a model for a small church 24x44 feet, with a sacristy above the entrance, and ten windows (that are) each ten-feet long. Front windows and doors are Gothic—also gabled.

We raised a collection with which we bought the bell and furniture of Rev. Mr. Pond's church. We have raised on this field in less than a year $3300 for a church building, beside(beyond) what has been paid towards my support. Not a cent would have been given if you had not sent your missionary here. This is more than five hundred percent return on the money expended by your society on this field. Our prospects are very good. This is Saturday I have four preaching appointments requiring 23 miles travel over muddy roads. Will you please send money as soon as possible, especially the $300 now due on my commission?

Yours truly,
W. W. Brier [80]

CHAPTER 27

Signposts on the Frontier: A Church Has Failed!

Brier noted in this letter that they had bought a used bell from Rev. Pond's church. Rev. William Pond was a college friend of Brier, and their paths crossed in more ways than one. The story began with a failed strategy to plant a California church. The Rev. William Pond's missionary labors in California proved more challenging than most. As a young graduate from Bangor Theological Seminary, Pond greeted his commission to the Pacific Coast with enthusiasm. Assigned by the American Home Mission Society to a district in the northern part of San Francisco, he arrived expecting to be greeted by a community of Euro American immigrants, earnestly seeking the influences of a Gospel ministry, and a modest but workable building in which to conduct services. He found the Greenwich Presbyterian Church of San Francisco, a church newly constructed and paid for, but without members. "I had, in my simplicity, and in accordance with all that I had known respecting the organization of new churches in New England cities, supposed that when the edifice was ready for occupancy, if not before that I should learn of a colony, large or small, going with me as nucleus."

Confused, Pond appealed to the local who had assigned him to the post, to ask which church members would be joining him in his work, "I don't know of nay one," replied the agent, "You will have to do as the rest of us have done."

Pond nonetheless proceeded to build a congregation. He soon had thirteen members and an average attendance of sixty people, and after two years of labor, the church was independent of financial support from the AHMS. Then the San Francisco banks failed. Rev. T.D. Hunt reported to his eastern superiors about the effects of the financial catastrophe on Pond's church. Apparently "Deacon Higgins," a prominent member of the congregation, "the very member whose liberality last year enabled the church so soon to become independent," had suffered severe losses. The church relied almost exclusively on his support, and with his downfall and the departure of several other committed members, the church was left in financial ruin. Pond dissolved the church.

Rev. Brier heard of the situation at Presbytery meeting, and offered to purchase the bell from the church, as well as the pulpit furniture. The weight stamped in the neck of the 1852 Boston cast bronze bell was 300 lbs. It had already been abused and chipped by its shipment around the horn of South America, but it was sound and rang true. The trustees of the Centerville Presbyterian Church sent a four-horse wagon team to the city and walked the pulpit and bell around the bay to its new home in the little white Presbyterian Church.

CHAPTER 28

Signposts on the Frontier:
The Immigrants Are Coming!

During the entire gold rush period, powerful waves of people migrated in and out of the region. Some were those who found their way to the gold fields as whole crews were organized in the Midwest, traveled together, and were operating mining operations together. Sometimes these groups came from the same city, state, church, or school. And when they had arrived, they staked a claim to one mine and wanted to recreate a church as a symbol of their homeland community.

In a clipping from the *Pacific Newspaper* June 15, 1856, this news item highlighted the movement of Rev. Brier and Rev. Lacy to organize the immigrant church:

"An interesting incident occurred in connection with the late meeting of the Presbytery of Petaluma. During the session, a company of immigrants from Missouri sent a delegation to Presbytery and requested to be organized into a church. Thirty immigrants, all members of one New School Presbyterian Church, had taken letters at the same time, all signed at the same time.

They had journeyed together to this State, and they had fixed their homes near each other in the Petaluma valley, and now, in accordance with a previous intention, they desired to connect themselves together as a church, with the name of the church which they left, the Mount Zion Presbyterian Church, that they might retain the name and the polity to which they were attached, and that whether they remain where they are or remove, as somewhat contemplated, to a point farther up the valley they may continue to bond together as a church colony. Besides their children, many of the old neighbors, also, are included in their community. The request of the delegation was complied with, and Rev. Messrs. Brier and Rev. Lacy, were appointed to visit the settlement on the following day and organize the church. Twenty-one members were received: the remainder of the thirty not being immediately accessible. A sermon was preached at the house selected, and a large company of men, women, and children were in attendance; the company was literally a band of pilgrims, covenanting together, and offering their children in consecration. Some of them are aged, and have large families around them. Although coming from a slave State, they were all opposed to the system of slavery. Besides attending the church of Rev. Mr. Baker, at Petaluma, they have occasional preaching from him in their own neighborhood. The ministers who visited them partook of their hospitality and returned pleased with the interview as a deeply impressive and interesting occasion." [81]

This article stressed that whole extended families migrated to California, and often came into the life of the Presbyterian Church at once. But more interesting, there was a morality test applied to believers before they were admitted to the church. The observation made about the members of the congregation was. "although coming from a slave State, they were all opposed to the system of slavery", as if it were a test issue that was used to screen members before they became church members. In northern church states, slavery was considered a moral issue, a faith issue, and a political issue as well.

CHAPTER 29

A Friendship With Horace Bushnell

Brier reached out to one of his college professors to help with a local problem, and in the end Brier rescued him from broken health. In a note to the AHMS, Brier mentions that he had written to the Rev. Horace Bushnell about a concern in founding a school. Badger and Hall were surprised that Brier knew Bushnell, and they were even more stunned when word came to them that Bushnell had traveled to California to stay with Brier.

Horace Bushnell was a frequent visitor to the campus of Wabash College when Brier was a student there and later lectured at the campus of Lane Theological Seminary in Cincinnati, Ohio. His nephew was a student for ministry and was a classmate with Brier at Lane Seminary—in a school where there were only eight students in a class.

In 1856 Bushnell wrote an endearing letter to Brier in California, saying he was on his way to visit him in Centerville. Bushnell came to California and to meet with a few of his students, but stayed near Brier for the majority of his visit. Brier was always fearless to engage his professors and related to them as close friends. It makes sense that Bushnell met up with William Brier when they attended a ministers convention in Marysville on April 3, 1856. Bushnell wrote to his daughter about the experience,

"I have been here now two days, attending the two Conventions of the Presbyterian and Congregational ministers; also their joint meetings and exercises. I have partly agreed to stay here over Sunday, and assist in the installation of Rev. Mr. Walsworth, with whom I am staying, and whom I like mightily. They have an excellent body of ministers here, and I like them very much,—fine spirited, talented, and generally accomplished men. It has been a real satisfaction to me to find how much of real promise there is in them. The two bodies that meet here now contain about thirty, and their number is all the while increasing. They come together from points three hundred miles apart, and some of them have not seen the face of a co-laborer for nearly a year."

Bushnell stayed on for a few days with Rev. Warren in Grass Valley. He was thrilled with the views of the ponderosa pine and the clamor of people in the gold rush. In mid-April Brier received a letter of confirmation that Bushnell was indeed on his way and would be joining him in a week or so. From the letter we learn that Bushnell has a friendship with both Rev. Brier and with E. L. Beard.

Nevada City, California.
April 14, 1856

Reverend Mr. Brier,

Dear Sir,

I am staying here much longer than I expected. But I design at present to reach your place some time next week. I thought perhaps you might begin to wonder what had become of me as indeed I do myself. But I have found myself pleasantly conditioned here since the day I arrived. It was like a breath of health. I suppose I might try to come soon—yet it is neither gain nor loss. If you have spoken to Mr. Beard will you be kind enough to repeat the impact of this (regarding my arrival) when you meet him.

Yours with Christian respect,
Horace Bushnell[32]

Bushnell's visit would honor Brier and would create a delightful stir in Centerville, as a national figure, and the prince of the pulpit would dwell in their congregation for a number of months. Bushnell was a fascinating character, an enigma as a preacher and leader in American society. In *Horace Bushnell and the American Republic*, Howard Barnes notes that Bushnell was a man of many interests and many legends. While he had preached for years about the need for advanced educational institutions in the west, he was forced to travel west to convalescence for his failing health. During the journey he lived with the Brier and Beard families for many months, staying and preaching at Centerville and traveling throughout the Bay Area to explore a site for the University of California.

Six days after sending a letter regarding his delay to Brier, Bushnell wrote to his daughter, confirming his plan. "I am going over, day after tomorrow, to visit Mr.

Durant: and then, after a day or two, I am going down to Mr. Beard's, at the San Jose Mission. I have just heard that he will take me, and invites me to come. This will be my new home: that is, home without home."

On April 28, Bushnell wrote a letter from the Mission San Jose. *"I have just come in from my first morning ride in this place, and sit down to give you my impressions while they are fresh. This is Monday, I came down, or rather up, as they say from Oakland on Saturday, riding through the richest garden of the creation almost all the way. I never saw the like. Fields of wheat and barley two or three miles across, and such a growth! I was very cordially received by Mr. and Mrs. Beard, as I expected to be. Mrs. Beard is one of the finest and most interesting of women: sensible, easy, simple as a child, and practical as one of the out-door characters who has seen all sides of the world, the rough and the elegant, and meets them all with a welcome. Their house is one of the old adobe structures, walls four feet thick, built by the monks on three sides of a square of about two hundred feet on the sides. It is only one story high, and one room wide, with a piazza all round, covered much of the way with vines. The connections between the rooms are mostly on the outside, from the piazza, which is the hall universal.*

San Jose Mission, May 2, 1856

"I continue to be pleased with my new Western home. I could not be more comfortably fixed away from my true home. I spoke of Mrs. Beard. I am also greatly pleased with Mr. Beard. He is one of the noblest native characters I have ever seen. He had bought a property here at the Mission, seven or eight miles square, the very richest land of the world: he had fenced it at an expense of over one hundred thousand dollars. But the squatters came on, went directly into his fields, took possession and built houses; threw him out of the income from the land, by which he was to pay his debt, and left him to be eaten up by the taxes and his interest-money: so that, while he was getting his title established, he was absolutely ruined. And just now his principal creditor is with him, selling out his land to the squatters, now that the title is gained, in a hope of merely squaring the debt. Still he never speaks resentfully, meets the fellows with kindness: does them, one and all, any favor he can: and shows a big human heart, full of trust, and public spirit, and personal beneficence, as if they had done him nothing but good."[83]

Brier put Dr. Bushnell to good use while he was in the area. Brier notes that it was the Rev. Dr. Horace Bushnell who preached at the Centerville Church while he lived in California. In his next quarterly report, Brier confirms this.

Brier Letter # 29

"I have had the advantage of having in my congregation the Rev. Horace Bushnell"

May 1, 1856
To the Secretaries of the AHMS

Dear Brothers

The Alameda (Centerville) Church has been engaged in building a house of worship and feels the exciting effects of it. The Eden Church has been reduced by emigration—but there is a fair promise of prosperity when we shall have sold this present building, and moved out from among the Germans. Since I last reported to you, I have become fully convinced that I could not stay here without aid for at least one more year from your treasury. But I do hope and trust that we shall present a better report by next May.

I have labored in the usual round of preaching and visiting, lecturing, and attending to all kinds of public priorities and wants of the community.

I have had the advantage of having in my congregation the Rev. Horace Bushnell D.D., who has encouraged and strengthened me in my cheerless work in this godless land. He also relieved me occasionally by preaching of his excellent discourses. Also last Sabbath the Rev. T. D. Hunt has preached for me and knows the wants of my family and the community.

During the last year, the people have only paid me $220.00. No effort was made in the Alameda church. Yet I think that they are determined to do better. I have been drawing to the bottom of my (sermon) "Pile" made while engaged in farming. Now I have set down my foot either to be supported or desert the field. I am on the whole encouraged. We had a convention of trustees today, and they manifested zeal to work. I hope you will not give us up.

Yours Truly
W.W. Brier[84]

In this letter, he noted that the Eden church was up for sale, and the congregation was passionate about moving away from the German immigrants. It must have been thrilling for the Centerville congregation to have Horace Bushnell as a national leader as a guest preacher. But even the efforts of such a wonderful preacher could not cause dramatic growth in the life of the congregation.

The story of Bushnell in California is commemorated by his biographer, Albert Barnes. "Another lasting contribution (of Bushnell) involved California. In 1856 Bushnell spent about ten months in the San Francisco area, and although it was one of his "health" vacations, he took it as his special occupation to find a site for a new California college. In several letters he described his adventures in scouting the countryside, looking for the best combinations of climate, convenience, beauty, and the all-important water supply.

Finally one of Bushnell's sites was secured for the college and was named Berkeley. Bushnell later declined an offer of the presidency of the College of California because of his dislike of administrative affairs, his (frail) health, and the distance from his ancestral home. An interesting postscript to the whole episode was the adoption of a California route for the transcontinental railroad that Bushnell suggested."[85]

Rev. Bushnell was to remain in Centerville for another three months. In those last months he was often seen heading up Niles Canyon on horseback with a backpack full of surveying tools and a tube full of maps. He was spying out the most level ground for the route of a railroad. It is unknown how his plans were eventually incorporated, but his route was the one eventually selected to link the transcontinental railroad with the western ports of San Francisco Bay. In 1864 the construction of the western leg of the transcontinental railroad was given to Cox and Arnold, to be punched from Union City through the Niles Canyon, up through the Livermore Valley, across the Altamont Pass, and into the Sacramento Valley

Meanwhile, Brier continued to report his progress in Centerville, as a means of lobbying for financial support of the AHMS for his efforts in growing the church here.

Brier Letter to AHMS #30

May 1, 1856

This day ends the 4th quarter of missionary labor under your commission. During the last three months I have preached 26 sermons, attended three funerals, visited three sick persons, and performed two marriages. I visited sixty families, conversed with 109 persons on the subject of religion. I traveled 1400 miles, received into the churches seven members, preached a sermon on Home Missions, and took a collection in the Alameda and the Eden Churches amounting to $25.

I fear the Eden church will be compelled to apply for aid again and desert the idea of securing regular preaching. I had hoped to be entirely free from the necessity of calling on your society for funds, have done all I could to bring the people up to the duty of self-support. Here in Centerville where I live the church has rented the pews and will

probably succeed in raising their portion of my salary, but the Eden Church cannot. If an
application is made you shall be informed as to the condition of the church in full.

W.W. Brier[86]

Brier was struggling to gain support and was eager to put pressure upon the AHMS for both direct and indirect support. While it was possible to regain the regular support of the AHMS, he further appealed to the local AHMS representative who had been handed discretionary funds. Rev. Hunt traveled east, and left Rev. Brayton in charge of the funds. The letter from Rev. Brayton proves that every member of the AHMS team does still not love Brier. It has already been noticed that Brier loves to paint a picture of the hardships of California in a desire to get support from the East Coast. He was controversial with many of his friends, and some felt they needed to correct some of his problems. Isaac Brayton writes while he is filling in for Rev. Hunt, who has gone to the East Coast for some rest.

Brayton Letter to AHMS
San Francisco

February 20, 1857

In the second paragraph, Brayton notes. "Brother Brier wrote me an urgent letter, saying that Mr. Hunt had engaged to give him $200.00 above your appropriation, of which he had received $40.00 and being in distress, he desired a further amount. I could only reply that Mr. Hunt transferred to me no instructions upon that point, neither discretionary power, but that I would refer the subject to the secretaries and wait for instructions. Mr. Hunt will undoubtedly have given you a full report of the case and I can only add that Mr. Brier writes, "We are in a state of starvation." The crops of San Jose valley were injured by the droughts of last summer, though not very seriously in Mr. Brier's neighborhood. The abundant rise of this winter's crops promised prosperity not only to that community, but also to every part of the state. Brother Brier, I believe, is doing a good work and increasing in influence everywhere.

Rev. Brayton[87]

Again the pattern is evident. Brier demanded support from the AHMS and he had a distrust of authorities like Brayton regarding the timeliness of his financial support.

Brayton's conflicts with Brier in the past are part of the baggage of this clash. Yet, there are some extenuating circumstances here. Crops failed with the drought of 1856. Brier was not simply making up dramatic stories to gain more support; Brier's family was growing, and the church support and economy were failing. The church books for the treasurer and trustees of the church note that they only paid $100 on his salary for the year, and gave him an IOU of $300. His role as Superintendent of Public Education was not certain as income to him. As two of his three financial supports became wobbly, he lashed out with force to the AHMS. In the next three months the pressure eases. By May his response was softer and warmer. He was focused on spiritual growth and ministry once again.

A dramatic shift of blessing in Brier's life took place. Brayton wrote graceful words of blessing to Brier for his financial assistance and noted that Brier was increasing in his popularity. Was it that Brier had this winsomeness all along, or had he matured? There was a clear transformation taking place; either the ministers were finally opening their eyes to see a new side of him, or Brier was mellowing and working more effectively with his congregation and ministry community.

CHAPTER 30

Signposts on the Frontier: Find Yourself a Bride!

Most men who came to California in the first decade of the Gold Rush came as single men. Being single was good—as the men were tested by fire in the mines and had no time or accommodation for a family. When the mines began to falter, the winds of change began to blow. Whether the men had struck it rich or had become destitute, there was a flurry of men who wanted to settle down and get a bride. Some sent for the girl they had left back home. Others found a bride out west, often the daughter of a nearby farmer.

During his career Brier officiated as pastor for hundreds of weddings. The following list from the county records reflects non-church weddings Brier performed during a two year period. These were registered with the county office, much in the same way as land titles.

May 1, 1855 Crayton Winton to Lidia Buckness by W. W. Brier, Minister of Alameda and Eden Presbyterian Church

- December 25, 1855   John W. Dougherty to Clementina L. Payton
- February 24, 1856   Bradley A. Thomas to Seah Ellen Clark
- February 28, 1856   John W. Carrick to Irene Harwood
- July 17 1856   William Bowers Read to Margaret Johana Harlin
- August 3, 1856   Joel Russell to Caroline Bartlett
- November 16, 1856   Charles F. Martin to Sarah A. Morrison
- December 22, 1856   Frederick Meryre to Hellen Peckkes
- January 15, 1857   Benjamin Murphy to Emily Booth
- January 18, 1857   William Woolsey to Emily Brazee
- March 29, 1855   Nicolas Gadding to Aderlherd Meyer
- February 1, 1857   Henry Clarke to Ann Short

- January 18,1857   John F. Root to Mary M. Culp
- December 18, 1854   Alexander H. Houston to Caroline Luisa Peace
- Sept 30, 1857   Augustus Anderson to Abbey S. Sherburn
- October 27, 1857   Josiah G. Brickell to Bridget Condran
- October 18, 1857   William H. Louther to Maria Huff
- February 19,1858   Lewis Caman to Henrietta Roggans
- March 9, 1858   Edward Lull to Mary Kelley [88]

Church weddings were reserved for church members, and most of these weddings took place during the worship service. The family would add some flowers to the altar that morning, and the ceremony would take place at the end of the Sunday morning worship. The wedding reception would be at a potluck supper to follow. The cost of the wedding was substantially reduced from modern day lavish receptions, and included the whole worshipping community.

If they were not a church family, the wedding could still include the pastor, but would not be welcomed in church on a Sunday morning. Non-church weddings were held in the pastor's study or parlor. Weddings could also take place in a hotel lobby, a garden, or someone's back yard.

Church weddings were equally binding, but there was no requirement that the pastor report the wedding to the county. Being recorded in a pastor's legal record book was sufficient. Pastoral records were often kept as part of a pastor's legal papers, and then handed down to the pastor's family, rather than the church.

Jonathan Mayhew was a church member who elected to have a remarkably unconventional wedding. Jonathan was born in Massachusetts in 1819. He came around Cape Horn to San Francisco in 1849 in the whaling brig *Vesta*. His wife died on the way to California. He bought the land and dock at Beard's Landing from his nephew, Captain Joseph Mayhew, and operated it as Mayhew's Landing. He was a famous as a successful hunter, credited with killing over 6,500 geese for the San Francisco market in the winter of 1854-55. Jonathan once owned the Agriculture Exchange Hotel in Centerville and was an original trustee of the Centerville Presbyterian Church. He was elected Alameda County Supervisor in 1858.

He was successful but still single. On December 26, 1858, Jonathan was out riding in his buggy with Centerville Schoolteacher Miss Everett, to whom he was engaged. They met their friend Reverend W.W. Brier driving in another buggy. The marriage ceremony was performed right then and there, none of the parties alighting from their buggies. [89]

CHAPTER 31

The Baker Family
Mystery and Redemption

The tombstone for Phoebe Baker

Brier's next letter tells the touching story of the personal life of Phoebe and Abijah Baker. Phoebe was a daughter of the large pioneer farming Hawley family and a sister of Clara Patterson. Abijah worked as the bookkeeper for the legendary Patterson ranch. This gives further insight into how one of the Tippecanoe friends, was linked to E.L. Beard in the early years. Abijah Baker was remembered as a successful farmer and businessman in the early years of California. He came to this State in 1852. He was born in Livingston County, New York 21 April, 1821. Living in Lafayette, Indiana, he was engaged in the lumber, wood, and stone business. In 1852 Mr. Baker sold out and came to California; in the spring the following year he began farming at the Mission near San Jose, on rented land. After the wild success of those early years he soon had money enough to buy lands of his own and before long came to be possessor of several hundred acres, a choice ranch, on which he raised large quantities of wheat, barley, and potatoes.[91]

In the early records of the Alameda/Centerville Church, thirty-five-year old Phoebe Baker is listed as a member and regular at church activities. Her sister Clara Patterson was also active in the Centerville Church. But her husband, Abijah was never present. Women were often the predominant worshippers in many church communities, so this did not seem out of place. Abijah had a large farm of his own and worked as the financial manager for his brother-in-law, George Patterson, as a second job. Baker's careful financial ledgers kept the farm prosperous for many years, until Abijah's family crisis plunged him into despair.

Baker was so successful that he soon had enough funds to purchase 5,000 acres just north of Centerville, where he raised wheat, barley, and potatoes. Those were very good years. Records show that he sold 3,000 tons of hay in San Francisco. He was the first man in San Francisco who cut wheat and bailed it without thrashing it first, and sold it as horse feed hay in the city for a handsome sum.

While his farm was such a glowing success, his family was troubled by illness. Two years into their marriage, Phoebe conceived and gave birth to their first child, a boy named Charlie Baker, born November 20, 1857. The child became ill, languished in illness, and then died 11 months later. He was buried in the Centerville church cemetery.

The crop harvest was abundant that year, so Abijah must have stayed on. Abijah and Phoebe were heartbroken, but despair turned hopeful when Phoebe conceived again, and delivered a boy who was named Freddie on March 1, 1859. Then hope against hope, the tragedy struck a second time. Freddie became ill, struggled through the early months of life, and died at 10 months, 19 days old. It must have been unbearable.

It is not only a dark chapter. Brier presented a glorious note in his letter to the AHMS, of how Abijah came to faith. Throughout the next year, his wife Phoebe prayed for him, and had a wonderful confidence that he would give his heart to the Lord. In his declaration of faith to the church, he was baptized with his son, and the water of baptism dripped off his forehead and into the face of his baby boy, as he prayed for the healing and salvation of his second son. It was almost like a double baptism, yet the boy died just weeks later.

This was not the end of grief for Abijah Baker. His wife Phoebe languished, her body growing weaker by the day, and she finally died on October 20, 1861, at the age of thirty-seven years. It could easily be assumed that Phoebe died of a broken heart. Another clue about the tragedy emerges. About a year later, Abijah was taken so ill that he hastily sold his large farm and moved to Europe.

When I studied the tombstone, I wondered what progressive malady afflicted the family. In 2003 I took the Baker family death records to the forensic pathologist at Washington Hospital and inquired what in his professional opinion could have afflicted the family. The doctor quickly dismissed my theory that mercury poisoning in the well could have progressively killed the family over many years. He said the Baker family was probably crippled with the malady of tuberculosis. This slow-spreading, powerful disease would have spread through the whole family and created a series of deaths over three years, and which nearly took the life of Abijah.

It was a sad scenario. In the midst of Abijah Baker's prosperity, his two children died, his wife died, and his health failed. In sickness and sorrow, with his own health broken, he went to Paris in 1867, traveled in Europe for 12 years, and returned to Centerville every few years to check on his financial interests. He erected a white marble pillar monument on the site of the family gravesite. In time, his health fully recovered, he returned to the Bay area. In 1879 he came to San Francisco and invested in city property. And so he returned to the San Francisco Bay Area with a broken heart but a restored physical body.

By the 1880's, rising grain prices led to the escalation of prices for land. Abijah Baker bought 2000 acres in Pleasanton at a price of $150 an acre. He became more of a land speculator, at the same time buying and selling a number of parcels of land in the Hayward and Livermore Valley areas. In 1879 Baker purchased 1,417 acres adjacent to his ranch for $127,509—nearly a "king's ransom" in those days.

A contemporary of Abijah, remembered him in the eulogy at his funeral in 1890, "He is a man of sound business principles, and honorable and upright in all his dealings, and during his long residence on this coast has won many warm friends."[92]

In the things of his world, he seemed to have a golden touch, and was prosperous in whatever he put his hand to. This time, he purchased a large tracts of land near Pleasanton and Livermore, and built a hotel in San Francisco. His name continued to appear in the Centerville church records, until it was clear that he would never settle his life in the area. On July 1, 1886, he began to build a five-story hotel in San Francisco which he named Hotel Pleasanton, with an upstairs apartment where he lived until he died.

Brier's next letter includes this conversion story of this local pioneer family. This is one of the darkest letters he is to write as he serves in California. Brier often claimed that there were special demands upon his appointment and special responsibility of the AHMS to support him.

The Spirit of the Lord is commencing to distill,
like the gentle dew upon the hearts of this people . . .

Brier Letter # 31

May 18th, 1857
Alvarado, Alameda County California
To the Secretaries of the American Home Missionary Society

Dear Brothers,

On the 1st instance, I completed the last quarter of labor under your commission. A kind Providence of God has preserved my life and that of my family. We have performed more than the usual amount of labor. In addition to preaching in the morning and afternoon, in my two churches, nine miles apart, I have preached at night during most of the time, to a congregation of forty in Alvarado, a town which is becoming quite and important station. The interest in the preaching seemed so manifest, that, this week, I am holding a protracted meeting, assisted by Rev. Mr. Pierpont.

The Spirit of the Lord is commencing to distill, like the gentle dew upon the hearts of this people. I held a protracted meeting two weeks in the Alameda Presbyterian Church recently. Christians were greatly revived; yesterday was our communion.

We received into the church on profession of faith one of our principal citizens. (Editor's note—by cross-referencing this in the Session Minutes, this is clearly Abijah Baker, his wife Phoebe, and their son, Charles Baker. The child may have been ill at the time, as the boy died months later, on Dec 8, 1859.) When baptized, he rose from his knees, and took his little boy, and presented him to receive the Seal of God's Covenant. The water fell from his head upon the child's as I pronounced the sacred words of the ordinance.

The wife and mother was a member of the church and recently told me she had spent a whole day in prayer for her husband and knew he would be converted. He was necessarily absent during our protracted meetings, but when he returned he consecrated himself to God. This was a day of great interest to our little Church. Another man, who has been leading a reckless life in California, recently united with the church. He holds on faithful and is much interested in the work. Quite a number are under divine influence. I am much encouraged, and feel that the cloud, which has, so long, hung over the horizon of our California Zion is about to break away and permit the joyous light of *the Holy Ghost beam in upon us—Amen. The Alameda Church is about to make a strong effort to cut loose from its dependence on your Society. The Eden Church (Alvarado) will certainly be compelled to make another application. I have reduced my salary to the lowest cent which will suffice, $1,200.00.*

Yours truly, W.W. Brier [90]

Ps Alameda has raised $320 on its debt of $650.

CHAPTER 32

Brier as Circuit Rider and Exploring Missionary.

Reverend Brier was re-elected superintendent of Schools for a second two-year term, 1857-1858. This was the role he was most comfortable with: traveling, training, and organizing. He was uncomfortable with being stuck in a situation where he was anchored in a rural community where there were insufficient resources to support his family.

He was a pathfinder. The 1857 report of the committee for Home Missions for the New School Presbyterians listed 13 missionaries aided by the committee. Several of these were called *Exploring Missionaries*. By 1861 the list included William Wallace Brier, who was serving as exploring missionary under the Synod of Alta California for the Pacific Coast.

It was in 1858 that his mentor and friend, The Rev. Timothy Dwight Hunt concluded his two years of work as *Exploring Missionary* with the AHMS in California. After leaving his work as chaplain of San Francisco, as pastor of the church, and then as *Exploring Missionary*, he longed for a stable church assignment near his family roots in Wisconsin. He had been in California only nine years, and yet he had supported and encouraged so many of the Presbyterian and Congregational pastors.

During the same years Brier served his second term as County Superintendent of Schools. This worked wonderfully together with his taking over the role from Hunt for the AHMS as *Exploring Missionary*. Brier would first visit the schools to check on teachers, supplies, and other things. Then he would gather local European merchants and families together for a "Sabbath School" which was not simply aimed at children, but an instructional program seeking to train "Sabbath Scholars." He would gather a cluster of men to serve on the founding board of trustees, sometimes meeting at the court or schoolhouse until they could secure a building. Once the school was chartered, Brier would get busy gathering subscriptions (pledges) both for the building of a church and for the support for a new pastor.

As an example, in the spring of 1859 Brier sponsored a two-week protracted meeting in Alvarado that led to a number of conversions. He and other clergy saw this as a small beginning. "I am much encouraged, and feel that the cloud which has, so long, hung over the horizon of our California Zion is about to break away and permit the joyous light of the Holy Ghost to beam in upon us."

The Town of Alvarado

Fifteen miles northwest of the mission there is an unusually beautiful and productive flood plain. The San Leandro Creek, which empties into Lake Chabot, and San Lorenzo Creek meandered through the farmland on its way to the bay. It was subject to overflow and change, particularly following the 1868 great earthquake which split the course in half near Hayward. The valley would include the modern communities of Hayward, Eden, and Castro Valley. In those early days, the land was discovered to be unusually fertile; the climate was unusually agreeable. Warm fog free weather bathed the crops in year round ideal growing conditions. Crops of peas, tomatoes, and rhubarb were planted in the rich black soil.

Alvarado began as a district, flourished as a city, then died as a dream. Most sources paint this town as a gritty community, but one with some promise. There was a county-wide election to determine where to locate the county seat. "*Alvarado was the first county seat, but did not long retain the distinction. The removal occurred in 1854. The first county vote was as follows: Alameda 232, Alvarado 614, San Leandro, 782, Oakland 18, San Lorenzo 220, Hayward, 15. There being no decision at this election, another was held with this result: San Leandro, 1,301, Alvarado 1,067. Previous to 1854 Alvarado was the leading town of the county, with schools, churches, stores, and factories. Union City and Alvarado practically merged into one town. Alvarado was first called New Haven, but was changed to the former in honor of General Alvarado. Dog Corners was a small settlement half way between Centerville and Irvington. Mormon Town was in the hills east of the valley. Red Horner built a hotel at Union City in 1853. It was a wild place then. A newcomer was given his choice of four things to do, as follows: Drink, smoke, gamble, or leave. Nearly all gambled, and it was a common sight to see the eight-sided $50 gold pieces on the tables. In later times Alvarado became famous as the site of the beet sugar factory and as the center of the artesian water supply. In July 1877 Alvarado contained a population of about four hundred. It was a prosperous town before Oakland amounted to much.*" [93]

"Charlotte's Temple" and "Julia's Chapel"

The history of Alvarado Church is a curious one. On the one hand, it seems to be a comedy of errors or, on the other hand, presents an accurate picture of the struggles of planting a church in a pioneer community. Once again, W.W. Brier was linked with his friend and sometime mentor, the Mormon elder John Horner. Horner had often preached in the meeting hall in Union City which he called Brooklyn House. As he had done in Centerville, some fifteen miles away, Rev. Brier was given permission by Horner to begin holding religious services as a Presbyterian clergyman. But there were two different families who had designs to begin their own brand of religion in the area. Mrs. Charlotte Cornell, was a Presbyterian; Mrs. Julia Thompson was a Methodist. They began a Sabbath school in the public school building.

Mrs. Cornell strove to see the establishment of a Presbyterian church in this growing rural community, but Mrs. Thompson was interested in building a Methodist church. Both buildings were completed in 1860, with the Methodist finishing their work a few months earlier. "These religious edifices were for a long time called, "Charlotte's Temple" and "Julia's Chapel." The Rev. Laurentine Hamilton of the First Presbyterian Church of Oakland in May, 1861, preached the founding Sunday sermon in the new Presbyterian Church.

In the fall of 1859, the editors of the *Alameda Herald* were concerned with the competitive building of two churches in the small village and the zeal of the members of each. Yet they neglected having a public schoolhouse. Since it was only five miles from Centerville, it was easy for Brier to get there. On October 5th we find this news editorial on column three.

New Churches

"We notice that the citizens of Alvarado have recently undertaken the construction of two new churches, one of which is nearly completed, and its towering spire is visible for miles around, pointing heavenward, and directing the thoughts of the dwellers of earth, to the author of all things, and the source of all blessings. While congratulating one of the citizens of this place upon these visible evidences of thrift and improvement in his midst, he declined to accept for his town that credit which we were disposed to award, stating as a reason, that the zeal for church buildings had entirely overlooked the school interest of the place, and that while large contributions were made for the erection of houses of public worship, it was totally destitute of a schoolhouse, or any place to hold one. While we cheerfully commend the spirit that actuates the people of Alvarado in the building of churches, we most sincerely regret that the institution, which is the co-laborer of the church, in morality and civilization, as well as the nursery of science and human knowledge, should be so much neglected. We trust we shall soon be able to say of our neighbors at Alvarado, that they have a school-house commensurate with the wants of the children and youth of that town."

Charlotte's Version of the Competition, and the Involvement of Rev. Brier

The story behind this newspaper article is found in a privately published copy, belonging to Mrs. Clara May of Decoto, California. *"Reminiscences of a Private Life. Being a Narrative of a Portion of the Life Experiences of Mrs. Charlotte (Hawley) Cornell"*, New York, 1893. Charlotte reflects on her observations with Rev. Brier and his leadership in the Alvarado Presbyterian Church, later referred to as the Eden Church. Note that she is also related to Clara Hawley Patterson, close family friend of the Briers.

"A little town had sprung up while we were on the farm, about two miles distant from us, and a project was started to make it the county seat. But it proved to be badly situated, being too far from the city, and the site was abandoned, and the county seat located some ten miles below. They left, however, a little river with a bridge over it, having no facilities for removing them. They also left a small courthouse behind. This deserted county seat was called Alvarado, and as we failed on the farm, my husband concluded to try storekeeping again, and accordingly bought the courthouse and fitted it up for a store and dwelling, and started business. But Alvarado was a disorderly place. Many low, tough characters had collected there, and though there were plenty of saloons and similar establishments, there was no church or Sunday school. The nearest church was at Centerville, five miles above. It was of the Presbyterian order, and we had assisted in building it and had united with it. The Pastor's name was Brier. It was the first Presbyterian Church in the valley, and is still there. I felt that I could not live or bring up my children where gambling and horse racing were the favorite Sabbath occupations, and saloon keeping the most flourishing business, but must make an effort to reform the place. So I went to see an old Methodist woman to consult on the subject of starting a Sunday school, and she and her husband agreed to help me if I did so. I then started my son William, (then about fourteen years old), and a little girl named Ada Williams to go and tell all the children they could find that there would be a Sunday School in the old school house the next Sunday morning. When the time came I was surprised to see so many, some twenty-five being present, and this was the beginning of Sunday school in that valley.

This was thirty-five years ago, and it has always been kept up, and was the nucleus of a Presbyterian Church, one of the first in that part of the country.

The history of this little church is interesting. It was built under difficulties such as few have to encounter after the country becomes more settled up and good people are more easily found, willing to help in a good work. Mr. Brier and the Methodist preacher used sometimes to preach in an old shanty schoolhouse, and the Methodist preacher had stated his intention to build a church. We had bidden him God speed and promised to help him as far as we were able, and we were anxious for him to make a beginning. He went about the country to get subscriptions, but had no success, and one day he came into the store entirely discouraged and said, "If they want a church they may build one, for I cannot do it." We felt much disappointed, but did not know what to do. When Mr. Brier heard it, he came to us and said, "If you will go to work and build a Presbyterian Church, I will help you all that I can, and will get five hundred dollars from the Church Erection Fund to pay the last indebtedness." But we said, "Mr. Brier, we have lost most of our means. We cannot give much. What shall we do?" He said, "Do what you can, and trust the Lord for the rest." There was a man named Jones who had a tract of land lying partly in the town. Coming into the store one day, my husband said to him, "We want to build a church, if you will give us the land to build it on."

He asked, "How much do you want?" and we told him "Enough to build a church and parsonage on," and he agreed to give us the land if we could get a release of the mortgage from "Old Murphy." Now Murphy was a rich old settler, living in San Jose, and how to get there was a serious question, in those days, when railroads and stagecoaches had not yet come in fashion. But as soon as it became known what we wanted, one of our neighbors, a member of the Smith family, and a very nice man, came in and volunteered to take us down. My husband being unable to leave the store, the business fell on me, and I went alone with Mr. Smith, to get the release. It was a hot day and the distance to San Jose and back—more than forty miles, over a dusty road. We started early in the morning, and reached there about noon, warm, tired and hungry. But the people were very kind, and gave us a good dinner and a California welcome.

I told the old gentleman my business, and as I had heard that he was a good Christian, I thought he would grant my request. He considered a while and then consented, and the next week my husband had the deed made out and recorded, and today that property, church and all, belongs to the Synod of the Presbyterian Church of San Jose, California.

Now we must see about putting up the building, and we decided to begin by getting up a grand festival, with a capital "F". We were favored in having the use of a large warehouse in which to hold it. The people were delighted with the idea of a Festival. There had never been anything of the kind in that region and they seemed to be ready to do whatever I asked of them, and contribute anything they had. But I was obliged to take the lead and bear the responsibility in everything, and this made it hard for me, especially as they were not religious people, and I was obliged to be very careful to please everybody and prevent petty little jealousies among the women. I tried to make them all feel that the church was to be as much for their benefit as for mine. With the men I argued that it would make the town more respectable and would improve the value of property, and fully realized the force of the Scripture injunction, which teaches us "To be wise as the serpent, but as harmless as the dove."

The warehouse in which the Festival was to be held was a large brick building, and we had it decorated with bunting and evergreens, and lighted by chandeliers brought from the city for the purpose. When lighted up at night the effect was very fine. Money was scarce among the people, and we got but little help in that form, but there were chickens and turkeys in abundance, with a lamb and a young pig, and all the butter, eggs, and cream I wanted. A baker in the town volunteered to do all the baking we wanted done, and the ladies made quantities of cakes, pies and biscuits, as well as bringing in plenty of pickles, preserves and fruit. Indeed, I have never seen so much food in one place in my life. A young man, whom I nursed through a course of Typhus fever, in Oakland, as soon as he heard of our enterprise, sent me all the strawberries I wanted, and a lady went with me to the city where we secured a large stock of books and toys to be sold on commission. We had two tables set, long enough to seat fifty people each. We made lots of splendid ice cream. Everything was in profusion, including our visitors and customers, and such crowds of people came together as had never been seen in the place before, and have never been equaled since. We cleared more than six hundred dollars, and would have done still better but for the scarcity of money among the people, although our charge for admission was only fifty cents.

The next day, as we were cleaning up and disposing of the fragments of the feast in our "banquet hall deserted," a schooner loaded with lumber arrived in the river and made fast to the wharf at the rear of the warehouse, and we were at once delighted and astonished when we were told that it was to build a church! It seemed almost a miracle. We thought that some kind and liberal friends in the city had made us a present, and that the men who accompanied it had come to put up the building. You may imagine the length of our faces when we discovered that the lumber was for a Methodist Church, and they were going to finish it as expeditiously as possible. It appeared that a certain zealous Methodist brother had gone to town, and stirred up the Elders, arguing that they had first right to the place, as they had been the first to "talk about a building!" So some of the rich brethren gave him the lumber and told him to go ahead and build as fast as possible, and they pushed on, and soon had their church finished and dedicated. I think the Methodist minister was a good man, but he was possessed of more denominational zeal than was good for him, and like Saul (before he became St. Paul) thought that he was verily doing God service while pushing matters as he did, for when he was leaving the town, some time after, he came to me and said he "guessed he had made a mistake, and hoped that God would bless and prosper us."

When his church was finished he came to me and said he thought I had better take the Sunday school into the church. I asked him if it was his idea to make a Methodist School. He said, "Why yes, I do not like union schools." I answered, "You can have one of your own, but you cannot take mine there." So I told the children there would be two schools, and they could attend whichever they chose. Every one in the town knew that I had established the school, and had collected books and papers for it from my friends in San Francisco, and they were very indignant, and not a child went to the other school. So I took my little flock into my own house and taught them there.

Then my good brother came to me and proposed to have a union school—the kind he "didn't like"—a short time previous. I consented, with the understanding that my school should go into our church then that was completed.

We concluded to go slowly, but kept up the interest by having little parties and a sewing circle. Our place of meeting was a large room over the store, which had formerly been the courtroom, and we made it so cheerful and pleasant that everybody liked to come. By these means we were making a little money, all the time, and finally commenced our church.

The Alvarado Church, circa 1915, when the original church building was replaced with a larger structure. Photo from Centerville Presbyterian Archives.

It was a hard time, and sometimes it seemed as if everything was against us. Indeed, it required much faith and patience to persevere in our undertaking. But we "prayed on and pressed on", and finally our little church was finished and ready for the furniture. I went to the city alone, and bought carpet hemp for the aisles, ingrain for the chancel, and Brussels, with a handsome sofa and two chairs, for the pulpit, and some fine red plush for the desk. With the assistance of two others, the articles were all put in place, I trimming the pulpit and desk myself, and it all looked lovely. One of the ministers from the city, who inspected it, pronounced it the prettiest country church in California. The church was dedicated in May 1861, the Reverend Dr. Hamilton, of Oakland, preaching the sermon, and Mr. Brier and others assisting in other portions of the dedicatory ceremonies. The house was crowded, and everyone seemed to be delighted. I hardly need say that I was more than delighted—I was humbly thankful that the good Lord had seen fit to make me instrumental in accomplishing the good work, and I felt more than ever like serving and glorifying him for the remainder of my life.

We had enough money subscribed to pay off the balance of our debt, and were happy in the thought of soon being clear of all encumbrances.[94]

CHAPTER 33

Brier as Stated Clerk of the Presbytery of San Jose

1857

Over the years, from 1850-1857, Brier emerged as a significant churchman in the southeast San Francisco Bay Area. First, he was elected as the Stated clerk of the San Jose Presbytery. The two top local roles of the Presbyterian church were stated clerk and moderator of the Presbytery. Brier held both now. Presbyterians have always been passionate about procedures, and each church and Presbytery kept detailed records of the meetings, sacraments, and members. The role of the stated clerk was to be the record keeper of the Presbytery, to review the records of each congregation, and to be the rule enforcer and procedural watchdog of all the congregations.

Becoming the stated clerk was a curious homecoming for Brier, as had begun his Californian ministry with hopeful and confused ministry when he was a guest preacher for Rev. Brayton at San Jose. He continued to live in Centerville, and began his wider ministry throughout the southeast bay and beyond.

This was a complex time in society and ministry as the boundaries of both were being defined in the Presbytery and society. It was also an era when the entire Presbytery consisted of seven delegates who could gather for their deliberations in a pastor's study.

The minute book from Brier's years of leadership is still available at the stated clerk's office of San Jose Presbytery. It is a leather bound lawyer's book, with thick binding stripes and red cover. Inside the front cover is the free-flowing steel fountain pen calligraphy of William Wallace Brier, quoting the resolution of General Assembly, which established the Presbytery of San Jose.

"Five ministers, and three churches, met to form the Presbytery of San Jose, in order to fulfill the mandate of General Assembly, held at Cleveland, on Ohio May 25,

1857 "Overture No 2 being a request from the Presbytery of San Francisco for the divisions of that Presbytery and the erection of New Synod . . . That the Reverend Messrs. Samuel Bell, James Pierpont, William Wallace Brier, Eli Corwin, and Albert White, together with the churches of Oakland, Alameda and Eden be constituted into a new Presbytery to be called the Presbytery of San Jose to hold their first meeting at Sacramento California on Tuesday October 6th, 1857, at 3 o'clock, and to be opened with a sermon by the oldest minister present who is to preside until a moderator be chosen."

The boundaries of this new Presbytery were vast. An imaginary line for its northern border extended from Oakland across the southeast San Francisco Bay to the modern-day city of San Mateo. It then shot south for hundreds of miles along the western Pacific coast to Santa Barbara, and back eastward to the border of Nevada to contain all of the San Joaquin central valley.

As stated clerk, Brier continued to record the Presbytery minute books. In the first few meetings, ministers of the Presbytery are given the title "Bishop." For example, the May 10 meeting of 1859 lists present in the meeting Bishop W.W. Brier, Bishop A.F. White, and Bishop S.B. Bell. This honorary title was later struck down by the General Assembly, which clarified the roles within the church as teaching elder and ruling elder. There were to be no further bishops in the Presbyterian church.

First Meeting of the Presbytery

Being the first convener and Moderator of the Presbytery honored Brier. As the Moderator, he was called upon to lead the meetings, to act as a neutral manager of the business of the churches of the region, and to make certain that accurate records were kept.

"Pursuant to the act of the General Assembly, the Presbytery of San Jose, having assembled at the Sacramento, in the 1st Congregational church, was this day called to order and constituted with prayer by the Rev. W. W. Brier. Sacramento October 8th, 1857. On ballot Rev W. W. Brier was chosen moderator and Rev. E, Corwin temporary Clerk."

Thursday, Oct 8th, 1857

The record continues, "Presbytery assembled according to adjournment at the call of the moderator. Present Bishops Brier (Alvarado), Corwin (San Jose), Bell (Oakland), and Pierpont. (Centerville). The Rev. W. W. Brier preached the introductory discourse from Isaiah 59:17 "And I was clad with zeal as a cloak."

There were a number of interesting actions at that meeting. It was noted that the Synod voted to use the church erection funds to help construct sanctuaries for the congregations of Santa Clara ($400), San Leandro ($600), and Alameda (Centerville—$1000). One topic that concerned the ministers and elders was the lack of pastoral respect and diminished staffing that led pastors to quickly burn out. The solution they saw was to establish a seminary on the western shore, and in true Presbyterian style, they worked to establish a committee. The Standing Committee on Theological Seminary was appointed. Rev's Brier, Scudder, and Wylie and Elder Swezey were commissioned to act to lay plans for a theological seminary on the West Coast.

CHAPTER 34

A Changing Role for Brier

1858

In 1858 the AHMS Society once again had fallen on difficult economic times, and was looking to cut off as many "mature" ministries as they could find. William Wallace Brier was about as mature as they come, having worked for them for eleven continuous years as the founding pastor of five congregations, and now as exploring missionary.

This situation forced Brier to change. Even while constrained to a confined geographical area in the southeast San Francisco Bay, Brier had a unique combination of power and vision, which ignited an explosive growth of the church. He maintained delightful relationships with both Old School and New School pastors and churches.

His travel as the Alameda County Superintendent of Schools helped him feel the pulse of a rapidly changing society. Herein was the opportunity. The California gold rush was over a decade old, and most of the wandering miners had either settled into farming or returned home back east. A stable and growing farming community provided expansive possibilities both for the schooling and for the development of churches. Any growing community within the whistle-stop of a railway or near the crossroads of a stagecoach route would mortgage its soul to establish a courthouse, a schoolhouse, and a church house of significance. These edifices showed that this was a community of substance, and the Presbyterian Church signified a commitment to education and society.

In those days, to be a member of the Presbyterian Church was a sign that you were in the company of the finest people that society had to offer: educated, capitalized, and eager to give to the community. As such, both believers and unbelievers would invest significant sums of money to erect a wonderful church in the center of town; the best their money could buy. But often the passion of the parishioners would lag behind the splendor of the pulpit in the eyes of the local business community.

Supporting a pastor was the different struggle. After all, it cost quite a bit to erect a church, even more to support a pastor. Doing the math is an interesting exercise. If the average chapel could seat sixty parishioners, and it was assumed with the age-old formula that ten percent of the people give eighty percent of the support, then we could assume that ten to twenty families provided the support for the pastor. That meant ten families would need to provide $100 per year. Given the cost of living in those days, the formula clearly fails. No wonder chapel after chapel remained without a pastor, or the installed pastor of the day would be one who had an ulterior motive. Either they had another means of support, or they were in transition in ministry and had a purpose for staying for the year. Then they moved quickly on their way to another promising community.

Other ministers came and went, with many returning to the East Coast after a few years of ministry. Brier had been in California for eight years now, and his family was growing. Elizabeth gave birth to their first son, William Wallace Brier Jr. on August 7, 1858. This was a blessed year, as they now had four girls and a boy. Brier's letter of June 1st brings this painful financial issue to the forefront. He hammers the society for their recent decision to stop sending missionaries to work in California.

"We are here a feeble band, some of us scarred and scathed"

Brier Letter #32
Alameda County, Alvarado,

June 1st, 1858

To the Secretaries of the Home Mission Society,

Dear Brethren,

At our last joint meeting is Sonora, I was appointed to the Commission of correspondence with your society, to represent our destitution and implore aid. But, what more can I say? We are here a feeble band, some of us scarred and scathed. For myself I would ask, if I can obtain nothing more, the prayers of God's people; which have prevailed so mightily for this land, that we may have the power of the Holy Spirit sent down upon us also.

But dear brethren, can you send a few men of strong heart? We ask not for those who seek peace or honor: good places are always easily filled: but we ask for men of faith, who will take up the cross, and bear the burden and heat of the day. Who can go out into the center of a vast moral waste, and single handed lay the foundations of churches on bare ground; men who can work in planting seed that which others shall reap; who are willing to bear a load of toil, which will crush out the very oil of their spirits to be scattered upon the turbid waters of wordiness and ungodliness?

O has not God, in your great revival, given to some men a strong faith sufficient for these things? We need men also to take the places of those, who have been on guard, at this outpost of Zion for so many years. "Ministers are returning," say you, "and why demand more to be sent at an expense so great?" We cannot make the churches understand this, We answer this is an important station, on this great battlefield of Zion. Here the conflict is fierce; it is not wonderful if some should retire, should fall back upon the main body, with their shield shattered by the "fiery darts of the wicked" but shall those of us who stand firm be left to fight alone? Shall no new recruits be sent to our aid?

I write in behalf of the Presbytery of San Jose. We need at least two men to occupy places not hither occupied. All the Southern portion of our state has no one of our bodies to hold up the standard of the cross: and very few of other denominations. Do the churches feel an interest in foreign missions?

We are training men from every land either to reverence our religion or despise it. What can a missionary do in a Chinese city where there are thousands of returned California China-men to represent their people as a drunken, selfish, profane, cruel, devilish, race? And yet this is just what will be done in every heathen land, unless the gospel is here preached. It is worth infinitely more to Christ, to maintain the institutions of religion here, than it is to maintain them in New England. The aggressive movements of his Kingdom have always been westward. Westward the star of Christ's empire has found its way. It has traveled with emigration alone and we may send it on from these shores with the thousands who come hither for gold to the place from which it started.

The sentiments acquired by China-men here is about the revolutionizing power of that great Kingdom. I would not have the church do less to plant the gospel amid the darkness of heathen lands; but it appears to me to be one part of that work to raise up here a missionary making State, to exhibit what Christian society is, before the 50,000 heathen among us, that they may convey the impression to every land and be co-laborers with the missionaries. All these considerations are brought together with the manifest destiny of this coast. But it will not do to expect that when men are here on the ground, they can get support without aid. I know of very few such places. Even the one, which I occupy, is not independent. During the past year I have not permitted my churches to apply for aid, but they have complained bitterly of it. I could not consistently ask you for money.

Indeed I have always, as you know endeavored to save your society expenses on my account. I have done extra work as Superintendent of Public Schools in this county and thus kept along. The churches are now out of debt but are behind in my salary $900 on the last two years, $500 on the last. Our crops look very badly and were entirely dependant upon a farming community. I know not what to do. I have been on the point of leaving, and indeed have often turned my eyes back toward the Atlantic shores. I am persuaded that my particular field of labor has been set before you in the wrong light.

Our people are exceedingly poor and very much scattered. I preach at three different places, traveling 18 miles each Sabbath, and yet these three congregations, taken together would not make more than 130 or 140 people. Thus I am toiling in the belief that after I am dead there will here a number of strong churches. You must not be astonished that we sometimes feel like going back to the fatherland to see dear friends (and how dear) and lean upon the bosom of some warm-hearted church. That some fall back in this conflict is not wonderful. In California I have received some hundreds of dollars less than a bare living from all sources, for my ministerial labor, and we have been very economical. Others have fared no better. We would not lead you to believe that there are places here eager to support men, but that there are desolations which may be made to blossom as the rose. I should be glad to hear from you and to know whether you could grant two or three hundred dollars to the Eden Church if applied for. The Alameda church raises their proportion of my salary by deducting what I receive for services in the common school cause, which is a field of usefulness.

Yours truly,
W.W. Brier[95]

Brier tells the AHMS society that the Centerville church permitted him to be Superintendent of Schools by subtracting the amount of his public salary from his church salary. There were several factors that led Brier to allow this strategy. Perhaps the writing was already on the wall with the faint message of a coming church split. The New School Presbyterian ministers were feeling increasingly uncomfortable with the support and direction of the AHMS. Brier may have realized that both the congregations of Centerville and Alvarado were reliant upon him for discounted ministerial services, and they would never fully grow up unless he were to leave. This split role in tent-making as county superintendent was a half step out the door.

It is also interesting that his remarks regarding the Chinese seem abrasive or even racist in our modern day. We do not know if he was simply reporting on the issues they wanted to hear about, or if he really held these views. "What can a missionary do in a Chinese city where there are thousands of returned California China-men to represent their people as a drunken, selfish, profane, cruel, devilish race? And yet this is just what will be done in every heathen land, unless the gospel is here preached."

He is defending the need to reach the Chinese with the gospel while they are in California so that when they return to China they may have a good report of the Chinese who remain behind.

CHAPTER 35

Brier's Second Term as Superintendent of Schools

April 24, 1858

Life in Centerville continued to be difficult for the Brier family. William Wallace had given the church six years of good leadership and was finally able to construct a chapel, but the congregation was still unable to support a pastor on their own. The crops were established, but the boom and bust of crop prices made it difficult to support a pastor. So he began looking for a secondary income to support him. It is interesting to look at the financial ledgers of local farmer and orchardist Joseph Shinn who notes his contributions both to the church and to Mr. Brier. There is a note that he paid $15.50 on November 4th, 1857. Then the ledger for 1858 mentions that he paid $10.00 on January 12th to the church for his yearly tithe, and on April 25th, he paid to Mr. Brier $20.00. It seems that his gift to the church is a yearly gift, whereas the twenty dollars is an assessment for the schools, based upon farm size and income.

Brier was elected to a second term as superintendent of schools in April of 1858. But the schools were without adequate instructors. On July 21, 1859 W. W. Brier, county superintendent, appointed as trustees Messrs. C.L. Fitch, James Millikingon, and Dr. Henry Gibbons, who, the majority favoring the appointment of a male teacher, engaged W. W. Holder, who occupied the position until January 9,1859, when he was removed and M. A. Lynde substituted.

Funds were low because of the recession. In order to pay the teachers salary, Brier proposed to establish tuition rates as follows: Children under ten years of age, one dollar per month; under fourteen years, one dollar and fifty cents: over fourteen, two dollars.

The First Alameda County Bond Issue

Brier was thrust into traveling extensively from the Sacramento delta to San Jose. Schools were being formed privately, some in homes, and he wanted to strengthen their support. Settlers wanted civilized schools, a building, and then a teacher. Only unmarried women would do for teachers. If they married, they were asked to resign, because it was considered dishonorable for a woman not to care for her husband and children as a first priority. Brier led a movement to increase school funding. The following year the trustees held an election to decide whether the taxpayers of the district were willing to be taxed two thousand dollars for the purpose of building a new schoolhouse spread across the 6,000 residents in the East Bay. Thirty-three votes were cast at this election, of which thirteen were in favor of the tax and twenty against it. Not satisfied with the result, a second election was held, August 4, 1860, to levy a tax of eighteen hundred dollars. This time twenty-eight people voted; sixteen for, and twelve against the tax levy. This was good enough to pass. The assessment roll of the town at that time added up to one hundred thousand dollars, making the rate of taxation one dollar and eighty cents on each one hundred dollars of assets owned.

On June 10, 1861, the county school board voted to support Brier's recommendation as they appointed a teacher, Miss Eliza Webb. To afford the extra expense they added a tax on non-residents of the city or county of two dollars per month. This tax targeted non-land owners who had children in schools.

Shifting Ethnic Tides at Mount Eden

Mt. Eden is located five miles north of Brier's home in Centerville. The Eden Township is largely the flat tide lands and marsh on the eastern side of the San Francisco Bay and also includes the fertile farm lands and moderate foothills that wrap over toward the valleys of Pleasanton. The township was only a mile north from Alvarado, where Brier was already working, and he began to notice significant growth of the region. It was a slice of the region that was bounded on the north by the Oakland hills rising above the backwash of Brooklyn Township, to the south by the flat plains of Washington Township and the golden hills east toward the Pleasanton Township.

The expansion into the Eden Township was the next most likely place for Brier to begin a church. It represented a number of new ventures for him. Having begun preaching at Alvarado, this might be understood as being a good neighbor, and he was gaining both church support and financial support from the Alvarado church, which would round out his salary needs by the gift from the AHMS Society. But the move to expand his ministry five miles north into Eden was a sign of both restlessness and a gift to see the needs of a growing farming township through the eyes of faith.

Brier urged the elders to decide to plant a church in that area; they responded by sending a few elders to begin a church in that community in 1857. Things started out well, but there were problems along the way. Brier could not read the signs of change which would soon come to the area. Just months after constructing a church and chartering the congregation, a social transition began to sweep through the East Bay community, moving from pioneer farms to settled communities.

Alongside that transition came a variety of changes in population, identity, and name. Churches would spring up with fresh immigration, and wilt in the summer sun of change. Communities would change their names as the county courthouse was moved from community to community, and with it a number of people and businesses would move.

Farm families who built the church were soon overrun by new immigrants, a people who Brier wrote were "loud, aggressive, rude, and had a hard time learning the English language." They were Germans! With this alarming shift, the church of Alvarado began to dwindle and die as the church leaders failed to adapt their ministry to appeal to the German immigrants that were taking over the vast farming area in Alvarado. Many of these tight knit German families, who recently were settled in the Castro Valley hillsides, now spread throughout the Eden Valley. Farms were downsizing, and the large wheat farms were being subdivided into smaller forty-acre tracts planted in sugar beets. Union City was the site of the first beet sugar mill in the United States, and they were eager for immigrant families to become steady suppliers of mature beets.

German families of that area tended to be either Catholic, or German Lutheran. While they were strongly Christian, they were culturally resistant to becoming Presbyterian. The Alvarado church had many families of English and Scottish descent and did not take easily to the social customs of these Germans.

One of Brier's letters offered to move the church building three miles to the north, suggesting the sale of the property and the relocation of the church to a new location in a more "Protestant community." But there was a subtle racism at work here. The real issue beneath the surface of the debate was the concern about the numbers of German and also Portuguese immigrants, the latter being more distant both in language and in culture. Besides this, they were Catholic and were highly resistive to dialogue about their faith. The early pioneer missionaries called the Catholics empty formalists, papists, and Romans. What concerned them were the infrequent attendance at church functions and their aggressive farming practices.

Presbyterian churches were deeply affected by these population movements, and with them the church name would change. At the gathering of Presbytery in 1859, a pressing item on the agenda was the change of name for the Eden Presbyterian Church to the First Presbyterian Church of Alvarado. The name change from Eden to Alvarado was an effort to keep the church alive, identifiable, and growing. Many of the members of the Eden Church had moved to the Alvarado Church in Union City, and then a decade later they would move further south to the congregation at Centerville.

In November of 1855, Brier wrote of his frustration with the waning of the congregation due to the transition of the population in the area, "You may easily see that but little would be raised for the support of a minister in a community whether all the people were giving liberally to build a house of worship. In this congregation no effort has been made. In Eden many of my supporters have sold out to Germans and left. Where, last spring, I had the best congregation, where they had built a church without my aid and agreed to raise $500 towards my support, there is now a very small congregation. Germans have settled all round the church, which are Catholic and rely on formalities and speak the English language very imperfectly. I fear that it will be necessary to move the (church)house three miles to get away from them."[96]

There was no getting around the transition, and perhaps then the congregation would dwindle and die.

Brier Letter # 33

"I feel like giving up the battle"

February 2nd, 1857

To the Secretaries of the American Home Missionary Society.

Dear Brothers

I received your commission in November, but as the time had passed I omitted to make a report.

I have labored in this field regularly during the past six months having had better health that when I came to California. There is nothing interesting to report, but many discouragements. The steamer of the 5th February will carry away a member of my Eden congregation who has been my main stay there, R. Mac Doule. He was converted about two years ago, and has been a very active Christian. Another, who had also been converted here, has gone up to the Father.

I feel like giving up the battle. We build up churches only to have the choicest stones swept away by emigration. When a man acquires wealth he goes back to the States to enjoy it. The Alameda church has also lost one of it's chief supporters. Mr. Beard, who was a very wealthy man failed three years ago and has recently gone to the mines with his family. Others have come in who increase the number of the members of the churches, but they are commencing in a new country to acquire a competency. Christians here are poor: why I cannot tell. It may be that it is necessary for the Lord to withhold wealth in order to keep them in the way of life.

You say that you had hoped the people would have assumed my support. I also heed such a hope. I have urged them to the duty as well as Mr. Hunt, and the result is that I have received about $4500 in the last ten years from them. They acknowledge their duty, and say, "hold on a little longer and we shall be able to pay". One man wished to give me his note, so that he could sign his subscription had been paid. The tax assessor came today and took a list of my property. He asked what money I had.

"None", was the answer. "What notes are outstanding in your accounts?" I responded, "Nothing, but subscriptions to my salary." He closed his book, and politely bowed himself out, for one of the subscriptions he had made himself; he thought them not worth taxing.

I see nothing to hope for until another crop comes in; and should it be as the last years, our people will be driven to bankruptcy. Not long since I called a meeting of the Alameda Church and told them if they did not do better I should leave them on the 18th of May. They expressed "great regret" at such a resolution and determined to exert themselves.

But if I should leave I know of no place where I could do as much good as I am doing here, in the entire States, and I believe but few men could do as well as I am doing. My congregation in the Alameda (Centerville) church is better than at any former period and fills the house.

At Eden it is about the same. There it will be necessary to remove the church three miles or build a new one. The Germans have taken the settlement where it moves. I applied to Mr. Hunt for relief and he promised to make up the $200, which was applied for and not granted. I received $40 of it last week. I went down to draw some more, found that there was no agent in the City and was compelled to wear the same coat which has covered my back for sixteen months. I am not fond of telling hard stories, but I have spent $700, which I had left from my business operations when I was out of health and receiving no salary.

I could write the "Shady Side" of ministerial life in California which would throw all Eastern shadows in to the deepest midnight. What do you think of one of your missionaries having lived, with his family, on potatoes for three days, and another reduced to squash? If the credit system did not prevail to an alarming degree, starvation would have cut off half of the ministry of this State of California.

I do not say these things to extort from the A.H.M.S. But to let you know that we do not live like princes, I am ready to go any place at any time. I had serious thoughts of returning to back east if you will give your consent.

I have labored and suffered a thousand deaths in this country, and am ready to labor on, but not to starve. I have made money at business and can do it again, but I believe it is neither the will of the Lord nor your will that I should divide my time with the world. Will you send what pleases you?

Your Truly, W. W. Brier

At this point, Brier appealed to all their compassion and mercy. His family was starving. This seemed to be the worst time of his life. He was wrestling with what to do with his ministry calling. He felt betrayed by the Mission Society, and betrayed by God. Brier wrote, "What do you think of one of your missionaries having lived, with his family, on potatoes for three days and another reduced to squash? If the credit of the system did not prevail to an alarming degree, starvation would have cut off half of the ministry of this state."

Once again Brier went over the top in his desire to communicate his desperation to the New York board of the AHMS. He was truth telling about the economic state of affairs, but he left out the assumption the AHMS had for providing adequate support for the pastors. One additional dimension of the problem was that the newly birthed congregations had no historic pattern of stewardship, and no established discipline of generous giving. In the frontier society, families had less discretionary funds to give to the church, and were literally plowing money into the building of homes and infrastructure.

Brier was hard to understand. In his letters he could be a beast. His victimization and manipulation drove his supervisors crazy. In person, if you got him into a corner and he felt powerless, he would get agitated, forceful, and bombastic.

Yet when the road was rocky and challenging, there was no better leader. He could carve a smooth pathway to plant the church in the wilderness. If there was no clear way to get the job done, Brier would find the simplest way to perform it.

In the rough-hewn pulpits of the west, he was powerful as a preacher and frequently revealed eloquence in language and practical application that kept him in high demand as a preacher.

He was always calling for change. Others had been successful in raw mining communities, but they had not been successful in agricultural communities. This was the specialty that Brier brought to the task of church planting. He had an inner compass for the simplicity and complexity of the community in transition. He knew the pastor would have to obtain multiple levels of competency and support. Through strategic alliances with people of many denominations, he would forge a creative energy in the community for the church and for the cause of the Kingdom of God!

Brier Letter # 34

Alvarado, Alameda County May 1, 1859

We the undersigned wish to hereby apply to the American Home Missionary Society for aid in supporting Rev. W. W. Brier, pastor of the Alameda and Eden Presbyterian Churches.

Said Pastor preaches at Centerville, Eden, and Alvarado each Sabbath. Besides (preaching) near the Post Office at Alvarado I have worked at building the Alameda (Centerville) church which has 44 members, and average attendance is 81 or so.

The Eden Church has 10 members; average attendance is 20. This congregation had run down on account of a large depopulation, Germans taking the place of the American, but at Alvarado the interest has greatly increased. The growth of the Alameda Church there has built a neat church of 26x46 feet and hence needs aid.

We are attempting to raise a salary of $1200 for the year and from our peculiar situation and building enterprise but are only able to pay $600.

The Eden Church will probably be the Alvarado branch of the Alameda Presbyterian Church soon, and the congregation there will probably be increased. It is now from 50 to 60 in number. We would represent that the pastor of these churches has (for two years) received a portion of his living acting as Superintendent of Public Schools in this county, which is now cut off. We would first represent that during that time he devoted his entire time to the ministry, and secondly gave his time to the school administration.

With the aide of $600, which is herein prayed for, we hope to be strengthened and encouraged to place our financial affairs as a church on a more solid foundation.

All of which is instigating your involvement.

Signed,
A. A. Saunders
S. A. Willey
J. H. Warren.

CHAPTER 36

Brier's friend George Patterson:
Farm Prices, Recession, and Church Planting.

The fluctuations of the economy could make or break a local congregation, as the resources of the members swelled and shrank. Briers forty-acre farm was five years old at this time, the fruit trees were beginning to bear a crop, and his 20 acres of dry range crops were providing a steady income for his family and freedom for him to travel and support churches that were in financial crisis.

Brier had a neighbor, George Patterson who attended the church on occasion. Patterson was a regional giant in farming, but was struggling to find his place in the society and church of the day. Patterson seemed to be cut out of the same cloth as E. L. Beard, and was in the cluster of Indiana pioneers that settled in California.

They had both been bitten by the gold rush fever and had organized themselves to take advantage of it. Patterson had joined a group of twenty Tippecanoe settlers who formed a stock company in 1849 and ordered supplies delivered to California before they sailed to Texas and rode horses overland to California. Patterson arrived in August 1849. There must have been joy when they reached San Francisco and found the supplies they had ordered. The company then dissolved partnership, divided their goods, and Mr. Patterson, with four others, went to the American River, where he engaged in mining with considerable success.

He was a risk taker like Beard. Patterson quickly saw the mines were controlled by the lawyers and large companies, and the true riches were not in the hills but found in the rich earth of the California farm fields. On January 1, 1851, Patterson came to Alameda County and in the effort to regain his health took a job at Beard's ranch near Mission San Jose. Patterson began to purchase land in the county until he owned over three thousand acres devoted to the cultivation of grain and vegetables.

Although Patterson was legendary in his connections with the farming community, he was not highly visible in Centerville Presbyterian Church life with his wife Clara. In his book on George Patterson, Keith Kennedy reaches this conclusion about Patterson, "It is unclear whether Patterson knew Brier before they came to Alameda County, but they both worked with Beard on his lands, and Patterson soon purchased considerable acreage in the Alvarado plains near Brier. Both his grandparents were Protestant, but we have no direct evidence of his religious beliefs. Just as family friendships and work relationships were used in earlier chapters to reconstruct the Patterson past; perhaps these can be used also to discover a profile of his religion. A network of his friends and acquaintances forms evidence that strongly suggest he was a Presbyterian. W.W. Brier, a Presbyterian clergyman, and a schoolteacher arrived from Indiana in 1852, and just as Patterson had E.L.Beard as an early patron, so also did Brier."

Beard had encouraged Brier to come to Alameda County and help him establish the first public school. Patterson no doubt knew Brier through Beard, and all three shared the common Hoosier heritage. Brier's first students included Clara's (Mrs. Patterson) older sister, and all the Hawley children were raised in the Presbyterian church, which was started by Brier in June, 1953, in Centerville, a few miles from the Patterson farm.[97]

Not only was the Centerville Church near Patterson's farm, but Brier's home was closer to the Patterson homestead and farm. In addition to being his pastor, Brier was a farmer, and he took farming strategies into the church. William Wallace Brier was a life long farmer, but as a farmer he was better at being a planter, not a harvester. In the planting of a lush orchard, Brier left much of the day-to-day work in the hands of his workers, many of them Chinese laborers. Overall decisions were his, but his traveling ministry always kept him on the road and on the move.

CHAPTER 37

Transitions in Ministry
Founding of 1st Church of Brooklyn,
in East Oakland

1859

In 1859 Brier's friend, Rev. Bell, had developed a growing Presbyterian congregation in the city of Oakland. He convinced Brier of the need to work on the southeast side of Lake Merritt in order to plant a new church, effectively the second Presbyterian Church in Oakland, in a more diverse neighborhood. Brier was determined to begin work in the newly formed Oakland tough neighborhood, which was unincorporated and referred to by many names: Clinton, Brooklyn, East Oakland, and Lake Merritt. Those who were working class primarily formed the small village. The city was known for its rough and tumble citizens, with frequent lynching and public drunkenness.

Dr. Edward Wicher, in his definitive history, *The Presbyterian Church in California*, notes, *"We begin with the Brooklyn Church, which is now a downtown church in the city of Oakland, faced with all the perplexing problems of a district from which the older families are removing to the desirable new residential suburbs. But in the early sixties it was a village of a few hundred inhabitants, known by the Mexicans as San Antonio Embarcadero, and having the additional American name of Clinton, cut off from Oakland by the marshy estuary, which is now Lake Merritt, and having a reputation for whiskey drinking and insecurity of life and property. Not far from the place where the church afterwards stood was the bullpen, where there was a large amphitheater in which on Sunday mornings the populace would gather to see bulls and bears fight. No one believed that a church could live in this place. It was a very unpromising field.*

But here the Reverend W. W. Brier, the vigorous Synodical missionary of the New School, determined to start a church, holding the first meeting of which we have record on

April 16, 1859, when he gathered a group of five men "To be known as the Trustees of the First Presbyterian Church of Brooklyn, and to receive and hold in trust all property which may be acquired by the said Board." Mr. Brier being a minister of the San Jose Presbytery, this church became connected with that body. There was in the community a Mr. A. G. Webster, who was a godly man, and who was the first person to try to hold religious services there. He fitted up the old school house after a primitive fashion and sent out invitations to different ministers to come and preach.

Just then there appeared the Reverend George Pierson, a returned missionary from the Micronesian Islands, who was detained in San Francisco harbor by the illness of his wife, who undertook the pastoral care of this needy field. He organized the church on February 16,1861, and dedicated the first building on the first Sabbath of the following May. He was a man of rare devotion and power, and from the very outset of this ministry worked without the aid of missionary money. Even the men who ridiculed the project of the church respected him. The proprietor of a circus one-day came to him and offered to give him a show for the benefit of his church. The offer was graciously declined.

Mrs. A. H. Hamilton, one of the few original members of the church, has supplied some significant reminiscences of those days. Among these she tells us: "The morning on which we went across from Clintonside to the dedication of the church, a lady walking with us, looking at the beautiful sight of the new church, and the people gathering, said: "This is a very different sight from what I saw as I looked across there a Sunday morning a year or eighteen months ago, and saw two human bodies hanging from limbs of one of those oak trees, on the other side of the street in front of the church.""

From the outset this church has been blessed with the spirit of evangelism and missionary zeal. The neighborhood soon outlived its earlier qualities of roughness, and became one of the most desirable residential districts of Oakland. Who can say whom for the presence of Brooklyn Church in the community was the cause of the change? But in the cities of California no population is permanent: and Brooklyn church is engaged in a new struggle for existence of a kind which the last generation could not have foreseen."

Brier was becoming an expert at the task of launching and organizing a new church development. With this latest success under his belt, he was feeling called to a much wider ministry of church planting, but he first needed to clarify his ties with the two churches where he was the installed pastor. Neither the Centerville Church nor the Eden congregation had paid him his part time salary for years.

Brier felt the call to the wider ministry, and as he presented his decision to the Presbytery, they were alarmed that he had not been paid for his labors completely by either congregation. The Presbytery committee discussed with Brier the options before them, the committee returned in the afternoon and moved the following.

"Resolved that in view of the mutual understanding between Rev W. W. Brier and the Alameda Church in Centerville, and the Eden Presbyterian Church fully and satisfactorily made known to this body, and in view to this body, and in view of the fact that he is about to enter on a wider field of usefulness, his partial relation to these churches ought to be and is hereby dissolved. Presbytery comes to their result with the express understanding that these churches shall settle their arrears in salary to Mr. Brier's satisfaction, it would also express its confidence in Brother Brier as a minister and a man, and recommend him to the church of our faith as a talented preacher and a faithful pastor, presbytery would too express its sympathy with the churches in Eden and Centerville in their bereavement, and pray the Lord of the Harvest to send to them speedily a faithful pastor, who shall go in, and out before them, and break unto them the bread of life."

This note is strangely pastoral to both the church and the pastor. It is compassionate regarding the loss of the pastor and the financial struggles of the church to support the pastor. Both churches continued for the next decade, to pay Brier the salary he had not been paid during his eight years of service. This was a matter of honor for them to show this support to him spiritually and physically.

Rev. Brier could have forgiven the money, but instead he allowed the congregation to pay so they could grow in ministry and be responsible in their support of a pastor for the future. In looking through details about his income for those years, it became evident that he eventually gave the same amount of money away to other churches in need, and became a self-supporting missionary.

In Brier's next letter, we see the continual call for more workers, as if more staffing sent from the east could usher in the Kingdom of God. He attempts to hook interest by requiring recruits who are hale and hearty with "strong hearts," "men of faith, who will bear the burden and heat of the day." Perhaps this is because of his own readiness. Later in the letter he confides that he has reached his limit and is both discouraged and demoralized. He wrote, "Our crops look very badly as we are entirely a farming community. I do not know what to do, have been to the point of leaving, and indeed have often turned my ears back to the Atlantic states."

"What I did was only to plant the grain of mustard seed."

Brier Letter # 35
Alvarado
September 1st, 1860

To the Secretaries of the AMHS

Dear Brethren

I have labored according to the requirements of my commission, but postponed my quarterly report. Since you paid one third of the year had passed; and again I have had in contemplation a change of fields of labor at this time. I have been here since 1852 *preaching for the people, and receiving very little more than half enough to pay for my bread. Exclusively of aid from your society I have only received $50.00 per month since January 1856 and less before.*

The people have been very poor. In 1853 nearly every man in the valley has run ruinously in debt. The years since have been dry, and farmers made very little. This year is better—nevertheless, I have come to the deliberate conclusion that some other minister can do more good here and I must move to another place. As I look back over the ten years spent in California, I am despondent. Care and toil has commenced to silver my head and furrow my cheeks, and yes how little has been done? At Marysville, indeed the church, which I planted, is perhaps the strongest New School Presbyterian in the State, and has always been self-supporting; but other brethren have devoted years of toil upon it. What I did was only to plant the grain of mustard seed. Yet when I look at the fortunes of other men and what they have done, I am ready to say that the service of the Lord is not useless and am willing to try ten years more of the same self denying toil if the Lord wills it, with not greater results, for he will bring out his own glory in his own time. I even rejoice in what God has permitted me to do here, when I compare it with my expectations. I came to this place with shattered health, thinking my work on earth completed.

A kind friend (May the Holy Spirit yet lead him to the cross, and his reward be eternal life) {Ed note: This is Brier's code about his friend, E. L. Beard} invited me to his house. From a beginning of a congregation of a dozen there has grown up three churches with houses of worship, two of them paid for and the other nearly so, worth $7,000.00. These congregations are not in a situation of self-support. Indeed it is probable that in the field of my labors, two ministers will be required, taking a little wider range. At Alvarado a church building worth $3000.00 has been erected and a church organized within the year. It is probably that the $200 now due will be all which I will call for on the commission which you were so kind as to grant me. If I shall be able to return the other $200 I trust that it will find some better investment in the work of the Lord. Pray for us on these shores for our faith is sorely tried. When I consider the years gone by, and all the gloom of this sinful land, I bless God that any of us have been able to stand so long it is only by grace, grace!

Please send the $200 as soon as you funds will permit. If I move I will need it soon.

Yours in the Gospel,
W. W. Brier

Brier expressed his hurt and frustration in the enduring work, by writing how the work had taken its toll on his body and soul. "I am despondent. Care and toil has commenced to silver my head and furrow my cheeks, and yet how little has been done. Pray for us on these shores, for our faith is sorely tried."

Listen carefully to this letter and you can hear the despondency of Rev. Brier. He was depressed by the repeated cycle of neglect of his ministry by both the AHM Society and by the people within the local congregations he serves. He makes it sound as if he were suicidal. He has been magnificent in his analysis of the country, advocated on behalf of the causes of education, and worked tirelessly to establish churches. And yet, there was a bone weary fatigue within his soul.

Indeed he was weary, and he was hopeful too! He speaks humbly of seed planting for the church to grow in the future. Surrender and despondency were not his only options. At the same time the doors were opening to him to ongoing leadership within the New School movement. He has preached the opening sermon at the New School Presbytery, widely published in The *Pacific* newspaper, but also opened himself to new ministry with both the Old School and New School Presbyterians.

What he lacked in income, he made up for in the status of his leadership. He was already engaged as stated clerk of the Presbytery, a job without pay but with significant status. In 1860 his name was dropped from the annual report of the AHMS roles. His name never appears in their national newsletter, and subsequent ministers within the congregations he founded are not considered "ministry partners" either. It was a new beginning for him, and into this freedom he breathes new life.

CHAPTER 38

Presbyterians as the Middle Way

W.W. Brier was invited to preach at the 1860 opening of the Synod of Alta California. It was a bold sermon, with the purpose of defending the New School separation, yet is just two years before the reunion of the Old School and the New School. The Alta Synod of California just got large enough to have their own meetings, although they were held concurrently with the Congregational Church Synod.

This sermon was a cautious defense of the separation of the two Presbyterian denominations as New School / Old School. While Brier's remarks follow the party line in God's ordained reasons for fragmenting denominations, it also had many nuances of reconciliation and tolerance for strategies of ministry. He established a novel theme in his sermon that positions the Presbyterian form of government as the middle way between other styles of church leadership. For example, he offered that Presbyterians were the middle way between the extremes of Papist rule and one-man one-vote Congregationalism.

The sermon created a big splash for the Synod and was both published commercially and featured in the newspaper The *Pacific*. The actual sermon was twelve pages long when printed as a booklet. Although five hundred copies were printed, only a few survive today. It also launched Brier in his publishing venture, later named W. W. Brier and Sons. This started the process of the Brier family operating a firm in San Francisco as a religious book publishing and printing house for the next twenty years. Included here is a brief selection from the sermon.

1860

The Opening Sermon of the Synod of Alta, California

Preached by the Moderator, William Wallace Brier
At the Howard Street Presbyterian Church

Nehemiah 3:28 "Every One Over Against His House"

This language describes the manner in which the priests worked upon the walls of Jerusalem, when Nehemiah built them in "troubled times." Tribes, orders and families had a portion of the work assigned, best suited to their several capacities and positions; and thus all was completed speedily and harmoniously. Each one built the part opposite his house— that in which he felt the deepest interest—it being a direct protection, and yet rejoiced in the work of his neighbor, as important in the common enterprise.

This is a good example for the various denominations and ministers of the Christian religion, who are called to build the walls of Zion in our land, and "in these troubled times." Every one over against his house.

What is this Church?

We are a part of the great Presbyterian family, possessing a government which gives to the individual churches all the life and vigor derived from an independent, self-controlling existence; while it secures the strength of uniting in one the separate parts. Each part contributes to the strength of the whole, while the whole wends back life-pulsation to the parts. The perfection of the organism in each community or congregation awakens a family-like life, love and unity; while the relations in Presbyteries and Synods furnish a system of courts and legislative bodies, calculated to promote purity of doctrine, justice and harmony of government, and present a more extended object of affection and interest to the entire membership.

There are three leading types of Church polity: on one extreme is Episcopacy; on the other, independence, between these stands Presbyterianism, uniting the Excellencies of both. Pure Episcopacy has great strength in government; the clergy hold the scepter of absolute monarchy, but the people are prone to commit the keeping of their consciences, as well as church matters, to their spiritual guides according to the natural desires of the human heart. This weakens the vitalizing power of the gospel. On the other extreme stands independence, or the separate existence of congregations. This develops activity in a high degree, but is attended with great danger of becoming radical and corrupt in doctrine and practice. Restless spirits have opened to them a field in which to propagate themselves. The ministry must either rule with an absolute sway, or yield to be over-borne and driven out in disgrace.

Between these two extremes, we find a variety of systems. There is limited Episcopacy and limited Congregationalism; but, mid-way, stands Presbyterianism, which is neither the one nor the other, but a mingling of the two. Presbytery has Episcopal power, but it is an Episcopacy modified by the individual churches—one-half its numbers, the direct lay representatives of the churches, the other half the Bishops or Pastors. The churches are free to choose their own officers and manage their internal affairs as congregations, only limited by a constitution establishing the superintendence of this republican Episcopacy, which preserves purity of doctrine, justice and order.

It is a remarkable fact, that the General Assembly of our Church, in America, came into existence in the same year with the Constitution and Confederacy of the United States; both being the union of pre-existing elements of freedom seeking greater strength; both the product of the experiences of previous ages. A striking similarity exists between the judicial and legislative functions of these two great republics—on formed for the promotion of civil liberty and power, the other for religious liberty and good order.

The sermon goes further on this theme.

My brethren of the various Christian denominations here represented, build every one over against your own house; perfect your organism; inspire confidence in each department; bring to view all you can for your people to love as their own; make them feel that they have a home, and a work, and a joy differing from others. Nevertheless let us remember that, although these different forms are expedient for the cause yet we are all laboring on the same wall. If we each build faithfully our own part, we may soon be permitted to see Zion's bulwarks strong, and all nations coming within her sacred precincts. The prophets of God point to this age and even this decade of years as the period in which anti-Christ shall fall and the Holy Spirit will be poured out like floods on thirsty lands. The signs of the times speak the same language. Even now the temporal dominions of the Pope crumble and disappear; and never in the history of the church has there been a more marked fulfillment of the promise, "Ask and ye shall receive," than that which has been vouchsafed to Zion during the past few years. It entered the heart of the Lord's people to pray for the Spirit to fall upon all flesh, and to send the word of life to every family of earth, and lo, at once the windows of heaven are opened and showers of Divine grace descend all around the globe. It is God's set time to favor Zion; Jerusalem will soon be free from the tread of the infidel; the river Euphrates dried up, and the way prepared for the kings of the East to come and worship in her holy hill.

When the telegraph shall span the earth, and thoughts and acts, new born in the great and good nations run like light to every habitation of man; the dispensation of mind be established, then shall the Holy Ghost be sent forth according to the words of the prophets.

There are a few notable observations on this opening sermon. In this part of the sermon he creates a clear rationale for separation from the Old School, but there are conciliatory notes throughout the sermon. It is clear that he is raising a flag of separation for others to follow, but he is not closing the door completely.

Just as his sermon suggests civility, he was trying to play a middle road. This was a historic moment for the Presbyterian Church, and for the religious community on the California frontier. Brier had worked for years as a go between from the New School to the Old School Assembly. He had been frequently recognized as a guest at the Old School meetings of Presbytery, and had even worked with the moderator to hold the Old School and New School Presbytery meetings in the same city, on the same week so that they could attend each other's meetings and network.

Some pastors saw the significant differences between the two branches of the church: others saw them as incidental. Perhaps in the rugged assignment of the frontier, the clergy would set aside their differences in order to share together in the face of the changing society and ministry. In most cases, there were not competing churches within close proximity, as if these were a gentleman's agreement not to duplicate energies on competing Presbyterians.

Gilroy

Brier experienced a new-found freedom in not having a permanent church assignment. His fellow ministers began to instruct him to visit churches in need, with the hope that he could get the church back on track. First, they drew his attention to the troubled church in Gilroy. After a short beginning with two brief pastorates, the church was once again vacant. Presbytery minutes record, "On motion Rev W.W. Brier was instructed to visit the church at Gilroy, preach and administer the sacrament and report to the State of religion among them at our next meeting." March 20, 1861

CHAPTER 39

The Next Chapter of His Life: Exploring Missionary

1860

The Pacific
Thursday Morning, October 30, 1860

Red Bluff, Rev. W. W. Brier, will preach next Sabbath at Red Bluff, and if any opening presents itself, will at once make arrangements for a permanent occupancy of the field. We hope every encouragement will be given him there, and that his services will be received with an appreciative and hearty welcome.

Brier selected Red Bluff as the first church he would cultivate following his appointment as Exploring Missionary. Why Red Bluff? Brier's knowledge of this city came from his early days exploring around Marysville some ten years earlier. This town is north from Marysville, and perhaps he was aware of its growth from ongoing reports from the pastors at Marysville who followed him. Settlements reached out like arms in all directions from the Sacramento River. In the 1850's the village was considered insignificant, too far removed from the mining activity along the trails toward the golden hills near Auburn. But as the first years of gold frenzy began to fade, the true gold was to be found in feeding the burgeoning population of California, and Red Bluff became a significant community.

Although he would travel extensively over the next 25 years, Brier would keep his home base in Centerville and continue working the farm.

He would travel to cities that needed a Presbyterian church. First on his list was Red Bluff. In order to get there he would ride in a carriage to the city of Benecia and join a river boat steamer for a three-and-a-half-hour boat ride to Sacramento. After a brief stop in Sacramento, he would steam another two hours up the river to reach the final bend in the river near the city of Red Bluff. It was at the base of these red rock cliffs that Brier would get off the steamer and walk nearby to the town of Red Bluff.

He was not the first preacher in town, as the newspapers of the day observed that there were many attempts to minister to the community. *"Prior to the establishment of the organized churches in Tehama County the spiritual needs of the people were met by ministers and priests traveling through the Sacramento Valley."* But he was there to pull a church together, to organize a faith community, and to make it stick. Brier sought contacts that knew a Presbyterian in these new towns. The pattern was common. A church member would attend the nearest community with a Presbyterian Church, introduce himself or herself as a resident of the nearby city, and express an interest in starting a church there. The pastor would pass on that request to the Presbytery Committee on Church Extension. This town would then become a preaching point until an exploring missionary from the Synod could be sent there to assess the viability of the church. Pastors like W.W. Brier would visit for a week or two, preach at a variety of homes, meet with town leaders, and see if they could circulate the subscription papers to support a pastor or build a church structure.

The Pacific newspaper, Nov 8, 1860, quotes a local unidentified newspaper:

Red Bluff—From the Independent, published in Red Bluff, we notice that the people have very favorably received Rev. W. W. Brier. Quite an interest has been awakened for the erection of a church building, toward which a thousand dollars have been subscribed and a lot donate, and his mission likely to succeed.

The first meeting of eleven interested Christian men and women was held in the old brick schoolhouse on the Tehama County court house grounds on November 4, 1860. The minutes of the November 9 church board note that the Red Bluff congregation was chartered:

Rev W. W. Brier, assisted by Watson Chalmers examined into the Christian character of each one signing the foregoing request, and were convinced that all are truly devoted to the service of God. Mrs. Mary Off and Miss Margaret G. Orr united on profession of faith. Mrs. Elizabeth Chalmers by letter from the United Presbyterian Church of Scotland; the others signed after examination as to their former church First Constitutional Presbyterian Church of Red Bluff. Elected as an elder was Watson Chalmers, who was chosen to that office by vote of the Church freely given. W. W. Brier

In the first two years worship services were held at various sites, including the schoolhouse, the courthouse, and out-of-doors. During these first years of the church Reverend J. McLaughlin was the minister until he resigned in 1863 to conduct a young ladies' private school. Under Reverend Mc Laughlin's leadership, eleven new members were added to the congregation.

1861

Brier visited Red Bluff a number of times in 1860 for support and supervision. He already had two new communities identified for church planting in San Leandro and Alameda Following the organizing of the church, he traveled further north to the Russian River coastland, and then returned through the Napa Valley to explore church planting sites. After he returned home to Centerville, he wrote a letter outlining his trip.

Brier Letter # 36
Alvarado, Alameda County, California.

January 1st, 1861

To the Secretaries of the American Missionary Society.

Dear Brethren,

When I reported September 1st it was my thought that the remaining $200.00 for the last third of the year would be relinquished: but it appears that I am again reporting(without any pay). Part of the last four months I spent as the commissioner called for in the labors with the churches here, but most of the time has been employed in general missionary work, which the California agency has approved.

During this time I have assisted Brother Pierson who is doing a noble work at Brooklyn. I have also spent two Sabbaths at San Leandro and Alameda, important places in this county where a minister would be aided, if possible, in planting the gospel.

I also visited Red Bluff, an organized church of 11 members, raised a subscription of $4,500.00 to erect a house of worship. Herewith please find a description of the place published in the "Pacific". During next summer this church will be in a condition to call and support a minister without aid.

I have also visited the Russian River country, occupied by Brother J. Pierpont. At the request of your agency, my object was to decide its comparative importance as a "Home Missionary field". I have to report that Brother Pierpont lives in the midst of a vast fertile territory, large as the state of Rhode Island. All religions appear to have "pitched in" to take possession of what is or is to be in this modern "Promised Land". At Healdsburg there are eight ministers to about 500 inhabitants. They preach and do other things not, necessary to mention. The people are proof. The valley appears to be to these denominations what Kentucky was to the Indian tribes of North America before the whites disturbed them, a common hunting and battleground.

This region is unsurpassed from beauty of scenery and healthfulness of Climate. It consists of wide level gravely plains covered with scattering oak timber; rich bottoms, alluvial deposits of the stream and a commingling of hills and vales. This last is characteristic above Healdsburg. On a few hundred acres are found miniature mountains with springs of water, timber and charming valleys. These little mountains are perfect models of the great ones, which rise in grandeur, are far away on each side of the basin of the Russian River.

This is a little world in itself. Our Brother Pierpont is laboring at several points of importance, much as a large majority of our missionaries are in the Great West. If Taylor's theory is correct, that the gospel is only promoted by the vicarious sufferings of its promulgators, then our brother is eminent in the work. My heart was praised while witnessing the poverty and desolation of this situation. Strange that man can endure what appears to be his lot, a sick wife confined to bed most of the day with incipient consumption, three little children to care for. All the cooking to do, trembling lest your society should refuse the only means of a living, and yet conscience bound not to turn aside from the ministry devoted to the work in California, willing to go to any place.

Since my visit I have taken myself to (reading) the book of Job to learn the ways of God to his servants. Brother Pierpont should not be deserted in his time of trial. I pray that the light of your countenances as well as God's face may be upon him.

That field would not be deserted. I trust that our brother has sown much good seed. The inhabitants are changing for the better. Will you be pleased to send a draft for $200.00 this is all, which I will receive for four months labor?

Yours truly,
W. W. Brier

CHAPTER 40

The Civil War
Signposts on the Frontier:
The Church Must Be Patriotic!

1861

As the Civil War broke out a deep pain struck the hearts of Presbyterians. The division of the church was no longer Old School and New School theologies or ministry strategies; it immediately became North and South, Union or states rights. As the winds of war swirled into the church, a debate erupted over the display of flags in the church.

Before 1853 no flags were allowed in church. Then came the Civil War, and with the war came tensions in the western states regarding loyalty to the North and the South. Both New School and Old School Presbyterian pastors continued to relate to one another as "holy half-brothers," and some five years later the churches reunited. But as the conflict intensified, a division emerged surrounding the moral stance against slavery and its linkage with loyalty to the Union. The Union flag became identified with the moral cause of opposing slavery.

One of Brier's friends was the Old School Presbyterian pastor, Rev. William Anderson Scott, who served as the pastor of the Calvary Presbyterian Church in San Francisco. (It was then located on Union Square where the Saint Francis Hotel is today.) Although they were collegial, Scott and Brier often argued over theology and ministry strategy. A particular controversy arose: should churches demonstrate their loyalty to the Union by displaying flags from the front of the church building on Sundays? Church members felt that since this was a free country the church should show its gratitude for its freedom by being loyal to the Union.

Pastor Scott held a different position. Scott was a southerner, and had been the pastor of the First Presbyterian Church of Baton Rough, Louisiana. As a southerner, he was offended by the thought of displaying the flag on the front of the Calvary Church and chaffed at the theological thought of the church being a temple for nationalism. He wrote, "Shall the church continue this theme, and sing the Star Spangled Banner in the midst of Communion? No! National expressions should be removed from the house of the Lord entirely!" Although Scott's loyal Christian principles and theology were on the right track, his position got him into deep trouble and ended his ministry in California. On Sunday, September 22, 1861 a crowd gathered in front of the church to defy the pastors' order that they not raise the Union flag. The crowd outside in the street swelled in size, became unruly, and threatened to kill Scott and his family over their "Southern loyalties." The crowd hung not only the flag, but also hung a mock effigy of the minister from the street lamppost.

Rev. Scott was not swayed by the crowd and made his way to the church, passing through the center of the crowd, and continued to hold worship services in a packed church. The following day, heeding the advice of his elders and local civic leaders, Scott and his family left the church and sailed out of the bay on the first ship to Europe.

Many of the New School churches eventually found a way to display the Union Flag from the front of the church building. Following the war the flag was moved into the narthex, and then moved up near the pulpit. Some worshippers felt uncomfortable with this display, and years later the balance was struck when the Christian flag was added to the lectern side of the chancel.

From Stewart Chapel at SFTS.

William Anderson Scott, founder of San Francisco Theological Seminary, is pictured in the top triangle along with the founding date, 1871

The bottom triangle shows the Golden Gate Bridge and Mount Tamalpias representing the location of the Seminary. The medallion shows: (top left) City College of San Francisco which Dr. Scott helped to found in 1859 and in which the Seminary's first classes were held: (top right) the first building owned by the Seminary at 121 Haight Street from 1877 to 1891: (bottom left) a steamship smokestack with the dollar sign, a reminder of the work of Captain Dollar who endowed the Chairs of New Testament Interpretation and Christian Social Ethics; (bottom right) the oil derrick, symbolic of the wealth of Mary Stewart who contributed the funds for building this chapel bearing the name, Stewart Memorial Chapel.

CHAPTER 41

A Healing Invitation to Santa Cruz

In Brier's role as coordinator of the AHMS, he founded churches that were either Presbyterian or Congregational. He seemed ready to go in any direction to plant them—north, south, east, west—any way the relationship networks would take them. One example was in Santa Cruz, which was only 35 miles from Centerville. William traveled to the church where his brother first preached in 1850. In 1850 the population of Santa Cruz was only 650: *"It was the only settlement in the region that could be called a town, however there were about 20 ranchos in the surrounding country, each with its little center of life. The port, though not very satisfactory, served for the surrounding country."*

There was significant history for the Brier family in Santa Cruz, which linked again the two brothers who departed from Indiana on their way to minister in California. Rev. James Brier, his wife Juliet, and their three young sons arrived in Santa Cruz in 1850. The story loops back to the departure of the Brier brothers from Indiana two years earlier. In the *History of Santa Cruz County* (1888) James was listed as their first full-time minister after the erection of the first Protestant church building in the town at Mission and Green streets. James Brier and his family had an experience comparable to that of the Donner Party lost with other parties in a great desert that Juliet named the anguished land, "Death Valley," facing slow death from thirst, exposure, and starvation. From late December, 1849, to early February, 1850, they had plodded across the Mojave Desert trying to reach the coast. No one in the Brier or Jayhawker parties was ever the same after enduring this harrowing crossing.

Dr. Robert Glass Cleveland in his book, *"Wilderness to Empire,"* remarked about the Briers: *"Probably the most heroic role in the drama of the Death Valley party was played by Mrs. Juliet Brier, wife of Rev. James W. Brier and mother of three small boys, the oldest of whom was nine. The sheer physical endurance of the tiny woman, who weighed less than a hundred pounds was amazing: faith and self sacrifice made her life a daily benediction: her courage in that land of hunger and thirst and awful silence proved an unfailing inspiration."*

In another connection the story shows that *"she put two of the tired children, begging for water and whimpering for food, into rawhide bags slung over the back of an ox while she led the third little boy or carried him on her back over the rough desolate trail."*

They were saved, arriving at a rancho in Santa Clarita. The Briers had heard from other Methodists that the next boomtown in California would be near the Plaza Mission in Los Angeles. They quickly departed and spent the next twenty years starting Methodist churches in Southern California, before they made their way to San Jose, then moved to Santa Cruz in 1852. It was clear they were casting about for a stable community to begin a church.

Once in Santa Cruz, they realized they were already legendary for their role in surviving the Jayhawker Party incident. James Brier used that notoriety for his benefit, and it brought many people into the church. But he was also known as a serious-minded, harsh pastor with a temper that exceeded that of his brother, William Wallace. James rarely stayed long in a church community. In Santa Cruz, he stayed for one year and planted a Methodist church. While there, one of their young children died, and was buried in one of the oldest cemeteries in Santa Cruz.

From Santa Cruz, they moved on to the mining region of Grass Valley and switched to the Congregational denomination. He founded Congregational churches in Grass Valley, and finally purchased a farm in Lodi where he was known to have preached on regular occasion until his death.

In the meantime, the Congregational Church reached out to the Presbytery of San Jose for their chartering. Santa Cruz church records recall, *"The following request was made to Rev's W.W. Brier and Rev. J. S. Zelie, who came to Santa Cruz at the request of this new Church of Christ: We, the undersigned, professing Christians, desiring the ordinances of God's House, do request you to organize us into a Church of Jesus Christ, to be known as the First Congregational Church of Santa Cruz, with power to determine our ecclesiastical relation and Covenant."*

"The public services at which this new church was formally recognized and its organization completed were held Sunday, September 13, 1857, in the Methodist Church located on Mission Street. In the morning Rev. W.W. Brier preached from the text found in John 16:7 and the members were organized into a church as agreed upon at the meeting of July 26."[98]

Here is the classic example of the mixture of denominations on the western frontier. Often the church denominational style was not the issue in whether a congregation was chartered one way of another. Immigrant communities would sometimes find their way to settle in one particular community and would want a church like the one they had back home.

Watsonville

Brier's leadership was frequently absolutely brilliant. His eyes danced with excitement as he surveyed the burgeoning farming community and breathed in the productivity of the crops and the vast untapped potential for planting a church community. The hills to the southwest, beyond the Salinas River, held the rich farming valley of Salinas, Watsonville, and Gilroy. He had already been exploring this area on his trips south from San Jose for the past few years by horseback, stagecoach, and buggy.

Sometimes his leadership was ordinary and cumbersome. In his stubbornness he would not ever give up on a congregation. He had a pastoral heart for the weak, the struggling, and would go to great lengths to breathe life into any faltering congregation. In the case of Watsonville he was there from 1860 to 1863 and again from 1865 to 1866. He came back to reorganize the congregation in 1864, which means he took in new members, re-chartered with new elders and trustees, and registered new documents with the county clerk.

The record of the church says that Rev. Mr. Brier came in April, 1864, reorganized the church, and put it on a firmer basis. The trustees agreed to rent the pews for $600.00, which helped them secure a pastor on a long term basis.

First Presbyterian Church of Watsonville
Watsonville Historical Society

The Fiftieth Anniversary of First Presbyterian Church, Watsonville 1860-1910, written by Rev. Edwin Hays, pastor at the time, notes that, *Rev. Woods organized the church, December 2, 1860, Rev. W.W. Brier; the Superintendent of Home Missions from the Synod of Alta California New School reorganized the church on April 14th, 1864. In those early years the church embodied the Christian family's daily life including not only their spiritual well-being, but more often than not, their social and community life as well. These dedicated and spirited people now wanted a church building of their own and began collecting monies under the driving and dedicated leadership of Sarah Trafton Hatch. If there was another nickel or dime to be found to add to the meager funds: Sarah was the one who could do it.*

By January of 1863 enough money had been raised to purchase a lot on East Third (Beach) street for $150 from Jesse Carr. Local man, Alex Chalmers, was hired to design and construct the new building—the first in Watsonville for the Presbyterian denomination.

In September they were back again meeting at Scott's Hall while the new church was being painted and money was still being raised to pay the bill. Serving as Pastor at this time was the Reverend P.G. Buchanan who was to serve until 1865. He preached his farewell sermon on July 30, 1865 after which he and his family returned to the East. The Rev. W.W. Brier became pastor for a short time until H.S. Huntington came in 1866—the same year that a new bell was hung over the church building. It weighed over 600 pounds and was purchased in San Francisco for $300.00. [99]

CHAPTER 42

Nevada

1861

Brier's Nevada work began in Carson City, because it was recognized to be the place where the capitol was going to be located.

Thirty years later, *The History of Nevada* reflects on those initial historic days and notes that not all efforts were successful. *This was the initial movement to plant Presbyterianism in the State. The Rev. W. W. Brier is at the present time a resident of Centerville, Alameda County, California. He organized the churches at a later date at Virginia and Austin. The work of building of the Presbyterian Church in Nevada has been expensive, and not as a whole successful. The History* continues that, *"Today there are only four church buildings in the State under the control of the denomination—at Carson City, Virginia, Elko and Eureka. All the congregations occupying them are self-sustaining except the one at Elko. At other places societies have been organized, but they are now practically extinct. The growth of all has been extremely slow—barely perceptible. For a long course of years they seem stationary or declining. Church organization as an experiment or an expedient may have been carried too far. Previous to June 14. 1870, the Presbyterian Churches of the State of Nevada belonged to Presbytery called Sierra Nevada, and the Presbytery belonged to a Synod called Alta California.*

A Nevada Style of Church Planting.

W.W. Brier's Nevada style of assembling a church fell into a new shorter time frame. Ordinarily it took Brier six months to organize a church, but following his experience at Red Bluff, he discovered he could do it with a two week visit. He would do a great deal of advance work to make it happen. Brier would collect names of potential members of the church from friends and church members, and following his arrival in town would call them together in the home of a prominent member of the community. They would then pledge to spread word that a preaching post would be established in the courthouse, the local school building, or on occasion in another church. An advertisement would be listed in the local newspaper, announcing the worship services of the coming weeks. Through this networking the nucleus of a church would emerge.

Carson City, Nevada

The capital was the most balanced population of any city in Nevada. In 1860 the population was 714 people; 547 male, and 167 female. The vocational statistics in 1860 for Carson City reveal that there were 7 hotels, 3 restaurants, 10 saloons, 32 stores, 6 barbers, 46 teamsters, 5 doctors, and 5 livery stables. Into this lively context, Brier came to found a church.

"*The Reverend W.W. Brier, Exploring Agent of the Assembly Committee of Home Missions, visited the Territory of Nevada in his official capacity in the spring of 1861. He preached in Carson City and called a public meeting at the Stone Schoolhouse to be held on the 19th day of May, for the election of a board of trustees for the purpose of procuring a site. They were committed to erecting a house of worship for the use and benefit of a church to be in connection with the Constitutional General Assembly of the Presbyterian Church of the United States.*

On the morning of the second day of June 1861, the following request was presented to the Rev. Mr. Brier. "We, the undersigned, desiring the ordinances of God's house, do hereby request you to organize us into a Church of Jesus Christ to be known by the name of The First Presbyterian Church in Carson City, and to be placed by you under the care of the Presbytery of Sierra Nevada, and of the Synod of Alta California."

The church records in Brier's handwriting that proud day in this manner,

"*After public service at 11:00 o'clock a.m. a conference meeting was scheduled for those joining in the above request for 3 o'clock in the afternoon. A full examination of Christian experience was entered into; from which it appeared that all the persons mentioned except Mrs. N. G. Boyd had been members of various evangelical churches. It was decided to approve the qualification of all the others and agree to unite in church fellowship. After the sermon at 7:30 o'clock p.m. the usual obligations and covenant were publicly assented to by the persons above named, whereupon they were, by solemn prayer and proclamation, constituted a church of Christ under the title specified. Signed, W. W. Brier.*" [100]

The Clemens Family, Mark Twain, and William Brier

Presbyterian Churches were often built through the hard working and influential members of society. Sometimes referred to as the high church tradition, Presbyterians are often a magnet to draw a collection of the leaders of any community. In Carson City, Brier linked up with the newly appointed Secretary of State, Orion Clemens. The Clemens family was from Missouri, and Orion's mother was a devout Presbyterian.

Orion loved the Presbyterian tradition of democratic orderliness, and vowed to attend a Presbyterian Church out west. Orion's brother Samuel rebelled against all traditions, and spent his life wrestling with organized religion.

Orion came to the role in an unusual manner. He met Edward C. Bates, as they were stumping Missouri for the Abraham Lincoln, and when Lincoln won, Bates became Attorney General in Lincoln's cabinet. When Nevada was organized as a Territory Bates secured Orion's appointment as Secretary of State for Nevada. In the first month that the Overland stage ran from St. Joseph Missouri, to Carson City, Orion and his brother Samuel Clemens came to Nevada.

In one of his first acts in office Orion called his brother Samuel, and appointed as private secretary. The new private Secretary's job was to organize chaos. There was no place for the Constitutional Convention to meet: no stove, no desks or chairs, no paper, pens, or pencils—and all were in short supply. And of course the brother took the mining fever. Neither of the brothers was a good businessman. But Orion was so honest and efficient in his public life that the newspapers began to refer to "Governor Clemens".

Orion Clemens and Molly Clemens
Photo courtesy of Nevada Historical Society

Orion's wife Molly and daughter Jennie arrived in Carson City. The Clemens built a comfortable home. Molly quite enjoyed being the First Lady of Nevada. She entertained well. Since his secretarial duties were not challenging enough, Samuel Clemens took a second job, and began using his pen name, Mark Twain. Mark had become a reporter on the Territorial Enterprise, Nevada's leading paper.

Jennie Clemens
Photo courtesy of Nevada Historical Society

There was a forth Clemens, Jennie, only child or Orion and Molly. Any child was an attraction in the bachelor populated Western states, and Jennie was especially so. Both her parents were deeply religious. Orion became treasurer of the First Presbyterian Church, and Molly was active in all its affairs. Brier made repeated visits to Nevada, and always stopped to visit with the stated clerk, and friend, Orion Clemens.

Jennie, like many other children of that early day had a short life. Before she was nine she died of spotted fever. She had been saving her pennies to buy a Bible for her church. When this became known, friends bought a handsome pulpit Bible (which is in the church today). It has the inscription: Presented to First Presbyterian Church, Carson City, Nevada. A memorial of Miss Jennie Clemens, died February, 1864.

Signposts of the Frontier: You Gamble!

A unique part of the Wild West was the openness of gambling in society. Pastors like W. W. Brier frequently would condemn open gambling. But the state of Nevada presented an unusual problem with gambling, as it was licensed, promoted, and was the cause of many a miner's ruin. The religious papers frequently discussed this social evil. Note Brier's entry from the *Occident* newspaper, which he wrote in Austin, in January, 1869

"You bet!"—With a peculiar jerking accent on both the little words, is now on the Pacific Coast, and especially in Nevada, a pet provincialism.

Such betting is big business here! Everybody bets. It has become an important ingredient in social life: a canker which has already eaten deeply into the vitals of society; a practice which fearfully assisting to undermine confidence between man and man, and largely helping to obliterate all moral distinction between mine and thine.

Is there any remedy against this widespread and still increasing canker of money gambling? Shall we, however, as Christians, become content with imbecile complaints and inactive hopelessness, as our secular journals seem to do? Thanks be to God, there is a remedy, one only, for this and all other maladies which debase our race—a cure sure and perfect: the true Gospel leaven. These sinners must be born again ere they leave off their betting. If we who preach had but faith as a grain of mustard seed, this mountain would soon become a plain before the onward movements of Christ's Kingdom. Yet is not this devil cast out, save by a prayer and fasting."

Virginia City, Nevada

It was time for Brier to keep moving. He kept his ear to the ground, consulted local leaders about the best city to work in next. He was interested to know where the next movements of miners would lead and where the speculators might found a village that would support a church. The consensus was that the next significant town would be Virginia City, some fifteen miles away, high up in the canyon on a mountaintop overlooking Carson City. It would take an hour by buggy up a rugged canyon before the roadway would drop into the town of Virginia City. You can imagine that to the Indiana preacher, Brier found the sights of this hillside town confounding to the eye and imagination. Carved into the hillside nearly two thousand feet above Carson City was the rough and tumble industrial town that was trying to exploit the gold and silver in a speculative search. Throughout the northeast valley, mining factories were sprinkled about, poking mine shafts thousands of feet into the earth. Man-made mountains of tailing piles scraped from inside the mines spewed like tan volcanic ash from the earth's floor. The hillsides were dusted with scrappy sagebrush and random ponderosa pine among rust yellow boulders.

Street scene in the Virginia City hills.
Nevada Historical Society

The city was a sight to be seen. Virginia City was predominantly male. By 1860 the town had a population of 2,337: there were 2,198 men, and 139 women. The town reveals an interesting picture from examining the directories of businesses and resident professionals. There were 10 hotels, 6 restaurants, 42 saloons, 41 supply stores, 68 mining companies, 17 blacksmiths, 14 boot makers, 9 doctors, 1 dentist, 2 school teachers, 16 bankers. A main street gouged through the middle of the hillside, filled with brothels, saloons, bathhouses, hotels, banks, and newspaper offices. Two blocks south, the Episcopalians were building an imposing brick church, and the Catholics were erecting a cathedral and tower to serve the growing Irish Catholic community of miners. To the south of town, the Fourth Street school soared like a capital building at the edge of the towns Virginia City and Gold Hill.

One block up the hillside stood the hall of justice. Lawyers outnumbered doctors as they fought to perfect the mining claims and rights of the numerous companies who surveyed the rich land. Further up the hillside were the growing number of Victorian homes, looking down on the rough and tumble world of C Street and the boarding houses and mining camps of the valley floor below.

Throughout the day, the miners would crawl like worms from the earth, broken and quivering in the light, only to drown in liquor at the local watering hole. They emerged from the mines with the sweet smell of sweat, extruded whiskey, blasting cap sulfur, and a gritty mixture of mining silt. The men wasted their free hours at the bathhouses, the brothels, and saloons along C Street. Miners were paid four dollars a day, and although the work was extremely dangerous, it was the best mining labor pay in the world—if they were able to save any of it.

Brier found some friends in Virginia City. Two members of his Centerville congregation were working there. First, his good friend and farming mentor, E.L. Beard had moved to Virginia City. Beard had overextended his purchase of land, and was ruined by the crash of produce prices. He moved to the mines for one last gamble to make his fortunes.

A second friend had moved directly to Virginia City. The son of Niles farmer Joseph Shinn, Charles Howard Shinn, had landed a job as a reporter with *Virginia City Telegraph*. Years later, after he had relocated in the Niles area near Centerville, he would write his recollections of those rough and tumble communities, entitled, *A Life in the Mines*. Brier had purchased fruit stock from his father, Joseph Shinn and had been involved with the Shinn family as they were members of the Centerville church. The family would move back and forth from the Niles Congregational Church to Centerville dependent upon how often Mrs. Shinn would argue with the local pastor.

Another Virginia City connection was Brier's growing friendship with Orion Clemens, and his brother, Samuel Clemens, who was reporting for the *Territorial Express* under the name Mark Twain. There were a number of comments in Twain's correspondence related to his church attendance with Brier's friend, Rev. Walsworth of San Francisco. Samuel was known to attend church with his brother Orion when they were at their home in San Francisco. He regularly visited the Presbyterian Church in Virginia City as well, as noted by his comments regarding the Rev. Palmers health in his book, *Roughing It.*

1862

Brier worked hard and fast in planting congregations, and in moving on. It rang true in Nevada as he landed in Carson City, then jumped north to Virginia City.

From The Territorial Express

The First Presbyterian Church of Virginia City is formed.
On September 14, 1862, W. W. Brier met with those interested in forming a Presbyterian Church on the Comstock, and met again with a larger group on September 21, 1862.

In a history of the church written in 1876 there is a record of the early activities and challenges of the church.

September 14, 1862

We the undersigned, desiring the ordinances of God's House according to the Presbyterian forms and usage's, do hereby request you, Rev. W.W. Brier to organize us into a Church of Jesus Christ to be known by the name of "The First Presbyterian Church of Virginia City" and to be connected with the Presbytery of Sierra Nevada, of the Synod of Alta California.

Rev. W.W. Brier, who was then the Secretary of Missions, labored in Virginia City only a few weeks, and then left the congregation with no one to care for it, except as the Rev. Dr. White, then of Carson City, now of Los Angeles, found opportunity to leave his own charge and run up to Virginia City. This neglect was cruel, though no particular person was to be blamed for it, because the best opportunity to secure one of the strongest organizations, and the noblest edifices, and the largest amount of funds, for Presbyterianism on the Pacific Coast was allowed to bypass the city.[101]

Brier recruited a man just out of Seminary to be the founding pastor. There was some delay, as he had to finish school, and make his way across the country to the rustic state of Nevada.

The history continues, "Some months later, the Rev. D. H. Palmer, graduate of Auburn Theological Seminary and being sent by the Home Mission Board, arrived in Virginia City on the 10th of September 1863, preached on Sabbath the 13th, and left in the middle of November, 1864.

The Christian Church has a hard road to travel in this wild, wealthy, and wicked City. There are at least four hundred prostitutes and two hundred saloons and gambling is licensed! The wealthy men are divided between the Roman Catholics and the Infidels.

Mr. James G. Fair was born of Presbyterian parents in the north of Ireland but is a low coarse atheist."[102]

This comment by historians of the church was significant because Mr. James Fair was one of the wealthiest beneficiaries of the Comstock mining boom. What the history of Virginia City laments is that although he had a Presbyterian childhood, he had no interest in the gospel. He could have endowed the church in Virginia City so as to makes the congregation self-sufficient.

Creative Funding for Church Building Projects and Stock Market Speculation

Establishing a church sometimes entailed creative church fundraising. In the claim staking and speculation of the frontier, the Virginia City Presbyterian Church needed to raise money for a church lot and for construction of a building. They went about it in an unusual manner. "In 1864, the trustees received inside information from a friend in the mining business. They invested the little money they had in the treasury in shares of local mining stock. When the mine struck silver, the stock soared, and in a few weeks they had made several hundred dollars. With these profits, they bought four lots on C Street and plans were made for a church building."

The Virginia City Church
Photo by Ron Weeks, First Presbyterian
Church of Virginia City

The January 1, 1867, edition of the *Territorial Enterprise* newspaper carried a few paragraphs about the opening of the church.

The Presbyterian Church Dedication

The New Presbyterian Church on South C. Street was dedicated with all the usual appropriate and interesting corum populo. The dedication sermon text being from Luke was very able, interesting, and instructive effort. The singing by the unrivaled choir belonging to the church, assisted by the choral society, was particularly extra ordinary. A collection was not taken up and $500.00 in cash was raised by subscription in a very short time, so that now the church is entirely out of debt.

True to his calling, Brier left Virginia City a few weeks after the organization of the church. His friend, Rev. A. F. White, took over as the pastor and worked as the only installed Presbyterian pastor in the Nevada Territory.

The Presbyterian Newspaper, the *Occident*, notes this transition.

From the Occident

Soon after Virginia was built as a city, a New School Presbyterian Church was organized and grew strong, becoming the only self-sustaining congregation in Nevada: having, also, a neat and commodious house of worship free from debt. For the last year the interest of the church has seemingly waned. A number of members and families have removed to White Pine and other new mining regions. During the past summer they have had neither pastor nor any regular preaching.

CHAPTER 43

Moving Over the Hill

Gold Hill, Nevada

It was remarkable to see the visionary work of Brier and other church pioneers, as they had their ear to the ground to listen to the movements of the miners, and respond in time to plant a congregation. The city of Gold Hill was literally over the hill, just one mile south of Virginia City, and it had 10,000 residents at its high point. It was on the edge of the canyon with jutting fantail piles of peach and rust colored rock tailings. The excavation began to reveal the white chalky gypsum and tan anthills of mining tailings of the Crown Point Mellon Mine and the Yellow Jacket Mine. Mark Twain, the stringer reporter for the *Territorial Express*, was often seen eating and drinking at the Gold Hill hotel and saloon built in the 1860's.

Gold Hill held the hopes and prayers of miners who had missed the bonanzas of Virginia City. Just over the hill from the local school, mining companies began testing shafts for the potential of gold. When they burrowed into the hillside, they discovered three new quartz veins which proved to have promise for silver and gold. Swarms of miners boiled over the hill and went to work on exhuming the bowels of the earth to expose the ore. Where there was gold, there was the promise of people and the prayers of the faithful to begin a new church. Rev. Brier moved over the hill, and began services there.

The *Pacific Newspaper* notes this golden opportunity.

August 16, 1863

This is a commercial metropolis of Nevada. Located against the side of an arid and barren mountain, its position must have been as un-attractive as possible. The skill and energy, however, of our people, especially in city building, surmount any and every obstacle. Within the last decade without the assistance from farming, manufacturing, commerce, or timber within sight, all this has been accomplished. In connection with Gold Hill, which is a suburb, the place numbers about seven thousand people. As a structure, it presents all the elements of substantial greatness belonging to a modern city—fireproof buildings, water, gas, etc. The key to this being is that the city rests upon the most productive silver lode in the world.

Many speculated Gold Hill was the next big boomtown where the silver would never end. Although Brier organized a church here, the town began to fail and flounder, and nearly fold. A visitor to Gold Hill today discovers only sixty residents in this community, twelve houses, a stone hotel, and no visible church.

1862
Austin, Nevada

Main street in Austin
Photo courtesy of Nevada Historical Society.

In the spring of 1862 a man walking through a canyon discovered a quartz vein of rock bearing gold. The gold rush in Austin began that year, motivating claim owners to build a road, and advertise the sale of claims and home lots in the area. It was strategic timing. Austin held the central path of the rails and trails to three other crucial gold strikes in Hamilton, Tuscaroro, Eureka, and several smaller towns scattered in the foothills.

Situated on the line of the telegraphs and the overland stage, the Reese River was relatively easy to reach. The rush continued through the spring of 1863. The arrivals at the new camp of Austin lived in stone huts with cloth or canvas roofs, tents, and a sprinkling of log houses.[103]

Austin had its Pony Express station and a maintenance point on the transcontinental telegraph line, two hotels, and a post office. Yet the church would not aggressively grow, as the city was stagnated by the drifting claims. The potential mineral wealth in the mining district was great, but it did not have the luster of the wealth of Virginia City.

In 1864 land lots for homebuilding were selling for as much as $8,000 in gold. In a few more months, 366 houses had been built. The boom continued, and by 1867 there were 6,000 claims, several public schools, and at least one private school. The Methodist Church was the first to land in Austin in 1864; the Presbyterians came later. Brier did the exploring work, saw the potential here, and quickly assigned a pastor to take care of fully establishing the congregation. The church struggled to get on its feet, first needing to locate a building to meet in. The Methodists were kind enough to open their fine building and jointly use it with the Presbyterians for the first five years. Yet the church would not aggressively grow, as the city was stagnated by the drifting mining claims.

Against this backdrop we find that Brier was already hard at work. Here is how local historians remember the event. *On January 3, 1864, Brier organized the new Austin Presbyterian Church by accepting into the Nevada Presbytery a 45 member group of worshippers gathering at Landers County Courthouse. The continued existence of Reverend Brier's Virginia City and Austin Churches depended absolutely upon a sustained prosperity of the silver mines along the Comstock lode and on Lander Hills in those two cities: when the mines began failing, so did they. By 1870, the Austin Presbyterian body (which never did succeed in building a church, although several abortive attempts were made) was assigned to the Sacramento Presbytery, but it never afterward made any reports to that Presbytery. In 1873, the Austin Church organization was finally broken up, never to be renewed.* [104]

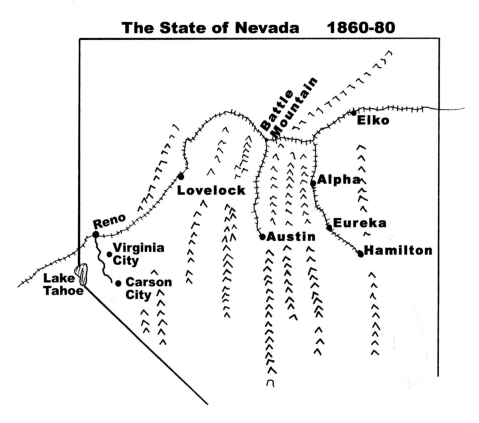

Map of Nevada

CHAPTER 44

Placerville
Transitioning and Strengthening

1863

There were several seasons when Brier was organizing one church while he was temporary pastor at one or two congregations. This is evident in his overlapping role in Placerville and his exploring work in Nevada. In 1863, Brier served at Placerville for nine months.

In March of 1853, Rev. James Pierpont was assigned to the newly growing community of Placerville. The First Presbyterian Church of Placerville, was organized May 1st 1853 under his ministry. But the financial support was not sufficient, so he resigned to accept a temporary supply position in Brier's home church, Centerville.

Like any struggling mining town congregation, the turnover of ministers was significant. Brier was pulpit supply preacher for three months in the spring of 1861, and he returned as stated supply pastor from August, 1863, until March, 1864.

"*The church was organized on May 1st, 1853, under the leadership of Rev. James Pierpont, a missionary of the American Home Missionary Society. He began to labor for the founding a church for about two months. In 1861 he left, and the pulpit became vacant, and Rev. Brier was called as temporary supply for three months.*

The Rev J. H. Mc Monagle became the stated supply from January 1st, 1861, until August 1863, when he relinquished the pulpit on account of ill health. Then an old friend came back to help them out. The organizing pastor, The Rev. W. W. Brier, succeeded and served as stated supply from March, 1864, until April 30, 1865"

This was a convenient assignment, as Brier would preach monthly in Placerville, then continue up the rail lines to visit the churches in Nevada. Thus he created a new definition of "circuit rider" as pastor and minister.

1864
The Presbyterian Church of San Leandro

When Brier would return home to the Centerville family farm, he was still restless. He had interests in planting churches in broader areas of Alameda County. He had worked to establish a church in Mount Eden, which failed and needed to be combined with Alvarado. Then he dreamed of a better church-planting target in the village of San Leandro, some six miles to the west.

Here again was the relational connection. The first recorded session meeting was in the home of Emerson Crane, who was the husband of Mrs. Lucy Crane, one of the charter members of the church in San Leandro. Rev. Brier had been stuck in Panama with Emerson Crane, and nurtured their friendship when they both stayed with Elias Lyman Beard at the Mission San Jose, fourteen years earlier.

In 1852 the population began to swell. The boat landings at the mouth of the bay were later called Eden Landing and became the site of heavy freighting of farm produce to the city of San Francisco. Farmers in that region planted crops of potatoes and grain.

Portuguese immigrants came to the vicinity in the early years, investing in farming and chicken production. The 1856 county seat was located in San Leandro. It was in the 1870's that industrial development came with the Sweepstake Plow factory and other light rural manufacturing that followed. It is no surprise that a school was founded in Hayward in 1855 while Brier was County Superintendent of Schools. The March 20, 1861, minutes of Presbytery remember, "In the matter of the Eden church it was resolved that the Rev W. W. Brier and G. Pierson be appointed to look after its affairs and report at the next meeting, also in regard to the interest of Christ's cause in San Leandro . . ."

The San Leandro church history remembers the founding pastor this way:

"On August 25, 1864, a twenty nine year old missionary by the name of Reverend James McKinley Alexander began preaching in San Leandro and San Lorenzo. He had gone around the Horn from his birthplace, the Hawaiian Islands, to attend Williams College in Willamstown, Massachusetts. He then completed his theological studies at Union Seminary, New York City and at Princeton. His personal account of his first preaching is given in his journal."[105]

Alexander was a lifelong friend of Brier and preached at Brier's funeral. Of those early years, in San Leandro, he wrote: "I began labor in San Leandro in 1864, I think in June. On the previous Sunday, Rev. W.W. Brier, the Missionary of San Jose Presbytery, had preached in the County Court House, then located in San Leandro, and secured the consent of the people to Presbyterian services, to be conducted by myself, with a view to a future organization of a Presbyterian Church. With consent of the County Supervisor, Mr. Robert R. Farrelly, and the County Sheriff, I held meetings in the Court House until the earthquake destroyed it. The joint church of San Leandro and San Lorenzo was organized with twenty members February 11, 1866."[106]

Both San Leandro, and San Lorenzo were within a few minutes' buggy ride of the area where the church was to be located. A notice was sent out to residents of both communities to meet in the court house at 11:00 on February 11, 1866. There were fourteen members, and they voted to call the church "The San Leandro and San Lorenzo Church."

The church members met alternately in the courthouse and the Methodist Church until they had an opportunity to build their own congregation. The earthquake of 1868 destroyed the courthouse, which forced the county political leaders to move the courthouse to the city of Oakland. This meant that the community of San Leandro would not boom with growth but would become a beautiful family farm town. This was the community that held the Presbyterian Church of San Leandro and San Lorenzo.

1865
Chartering of the Church on Alameda Island.

Writing a church history is difficult. Churches sometimes lose records of the early elders and pastors of their congregations. Brier and other leaders were involved in exploring, in establishing a preaching point in Alameda Island, or in being the stated supply pastor, but the records of the congregation do not reflect this, as local histories often begin with the first "installed pastor" or founding pastor. Add to this the confusion that Brier was the founding pastor of Alameda Presbyterian Church (in Centerville) which later changed its name as Alameda Island was a growing community within the north bay and was often confused with the namesake in Centerville near San Jose. In the same manner, Mission San Jose was often mistaken for the city of San Jose, some fifteen miles to the southwest.[107]

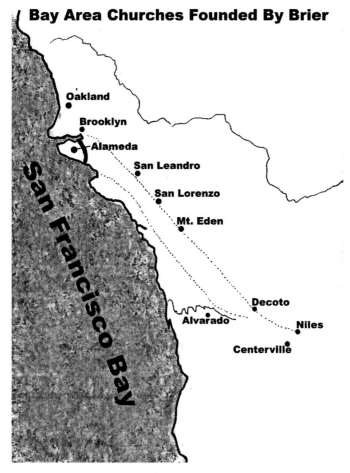

Bay Area Churches Founded By Brier

Oakland

Brooklyn

Alameda

San Leandro

San Lorenzo

Mt. Eden

Decoto

Alvarado

Niles

Centerville

San Francisco Bay

Map of East Bay

The minutes of Presbytery record the event this way:

"The Presbytery of San Jose, having been duly petitioned, sent a committee to organize the First Presbyterian Church of Alameda on November 5, 1865, with twelve charter members, consisting of ten by letter and two on profession of faith. The records show that the twelve original members of the new congregations presented a Communion Service set to the church. Regular services were held in the schoolhouse and in the homes of the members. The pulpit was supplied by visiting ministers in the Bay area until 1866 when the Rev. F. L. Nash arrived as a missionary from the Presbyterian Board of Home Missions. The Rev. Nash served as supply until he was installed as the first Pastor in 1867, continued with the church until 1869, when he accepted a pastorate in Sacramento."

Dr. Edward Wicher, in *The Presbyterian Church in California 1848-1900*, notes: "The church began in 1864 with an afternoon service given by the Reverend George Pierson of Brooklyn, who labored here for six months, and who was followed by the Reverend W. W. Brier, who organized the church on November 5, 1865, with twelve members. Its story has been one of steady, intermittent growth. And so effectively has it covered the needs of the city of Alameda, that a second church has never been seriously undertaken. November 5, 1865"[108]

The local church history recalls a different sequence of events: "The history of the church began with the organization of a Presbyterian Society on September 25th, 1864. At the time Protestants of Alameda were worshipping with Methodists in the first church building erected in Alameda in May 1854 at Jackson and Mound Streets. By the fall of 1865 the local Presbyterians had decided to have a home of their own, and they purchased property for the construction of a church building of their own."

CHAPTER 44

The Presbyterian Church in Gilroy

1866

Gilroy was expanding with burgeoning farms. Farm owners planted neat crop rows in fertile fields that stretched out in every direction. The farmers from the east were astounded, as fields were so fertile the crops could be replanted and harvested twice a year! Powerful farm families were breaking up the valleys into sixty and one hundred eighty-acre plots. But the story does not begin there. In May through August of 1860, Brier's ministry to the church in Gilroy is linked with his trips to Watsonville, and Salinas. It served as an example of how he strengthened, nurtured, and lead several congregations at the same time. He did the initial scouting of the area in the Salinas valley and then brought his good friend Rev. A. F. White back from Virginia City to gather the church together to be chartered. In the same period of time, Brier was traveling north to Red Bluff to charter a church. The results were encouraging.

The Presbyterian Church in Gilroy began by a petition that was presented to the Rev. A. F. White, on September 5, 1860. "We the undersigned believing that a Presbyterian Church of your order would greatly advance the cause of truth in our community and be of the highest spiritual good, to ourselves, our families, and our neighborhood generally, earnestly ask you, without delay to take such measures as are consistent with the rules of your Church." Signed by Asa Ferguson, Nils Eliza Ferguson, Horace Wilson, W. Furlong, Dorson Wilson, William Eames, Mrs. Eliza Wilson, Mrs. L. Wilson, Rodney Eschenberg, Joseph Johnson, and Joseph Rico.

"Very quickly, the full function of the church was developed, with a Sabbath School beginning and the starting of a weekly prayer meeting on Tuesday evening. The Rev. Mr. Hamilton of San Jose added leadership while the church got off the ground in the early months. They built a house of worship, and the Rev. A. F. White began to meet with them. By November 1860, the congregation negotiated to have Rev. A. F. White come every other Sunday morning for worship.

By 1862 the congregation, called the Rev. John Edwards as stated supply pastor, with Communion served in January, April, July, and October. Through the next years, the Session minutes were full of transfers in and out of the congregation with the turbulence of the times, as farming in the Salinas valley was attempting to be stabilized.

In 1866, the Rev. John Edwards is released from the church to work in organizing the church in Visalia. The lack of pastoral leadership presented an opportunity for Brier to come again and minister to them during the transition. On October 2, 1866, the elders extended an invitation for the Rev. W. W. Brier to come and preach." Brier arrived on January 1, 1867, to supply the pulpit "as a missionary from the Presbytery of San Jose preaching once a month."

Here is an example of what those visits would look like. On Saturday, May 4, 1867, after two days of travel, the Rev. Brier arrived to deliver a preparatory lecture for communion. In those days, a Saturday lecture was given to prepare the members of the church for communion. It was a powerful opportunity to examine your heart, to repent of misdeeds in preparing for communion. When members attended these services, they were issued a "communion token," a round coin like a token, or a piece of paper with the pastor's permission to receive the elements. It was a sign that they had prepared their heart for the Lord's Table. This token would be presented prior to taking communion on Sunday morning. Pastors would also use the issuing of tokens as a vehicle of outreach, going from farm to farm, asking families if they were prepared to be present at the Lord's Table. It gave them a reason to make pastoral and evangelistic visits and to broaden the base of the church. Often during these visits the pastor would go with a farm family to the neighboring farm, and visit newly arrived families.

Church records recount, "The next day, May 5th, the communion of the Lord's Supper was administered by Rev. W.W. Brier. After services, session met to present new members who were ready to join the Gilroy Presbyterian Church."

Rev. Brier continued his visits, in between new exploring work at Livermore, Pleasanton, and Milpitas. The Gilroy session records note services held by Brier in February, March, and April. In March they paid Rev. W.W. Brier $194. On May 30, 1868, Brier notified them that he would preach his final sermon to them on August 23, 1868, and he would assign Rev. J.M. McLaughlin to begin preaching. This was not the end of their friendship or the challenges in keeping the church going. Due to a shift in the population of the area, it seemed more appropriate for them to relocate the church. The church was moved from Old Gilroy to New Gilroy and on August 26, 1870, the trustees moved the property of the church in Old Gilroy (San Ysidro).

Brier's friend, Rev. A. M. Steward, had taken over as pastor, but there was an abrasive way about him that had a negative effect upon the membership. In May of 1873, the church giving began to decline steadily.

Pastoral leadership moved quickly through the years. Rev. DeWitt was briefly appointed. Then Rev. L Drumell served until 1878 when the Rev. A. F. White was asked to return and fill the pulpit. In 1879 Rev. Oviatt was presented as a candidate for pastor, and on May 25, 1880, the commission of Rev. W.W. Brier who preached the installation sermon installed him as pastor. But he only lasted briefly. W.W. Brier filled the pulpit for the year 1882 and 1883; June 24, 1883, Rev. Brier preached and served the sacrament of the Lord's Supper.

CHAPTER 45

Brier's Friendship with Rev. A.F. White

William Wallace Brier in 1866 (age 45)
Photo courtesy of Doug Kinney

One pastor who followed Brier's career for many years was his favorite school friend from his Indiana days at Wabash College, Albert Frank White. Albert White was two years ahead of Brier, but they participated in the same debate societies, and attended the Crawfordsville Center Church together. Albert White went on to Lane Seminary, and they overlapped in Cincinnati for one year. Following his graduation, he served as pastor to the Presbyterian Church in Brier's boyhood town of Attica, Indiana. After two successful years there he was recruited by Brier to work with the AHMS in Indiana.

Brier wrote to his friend, A. F. White, and recruited him to come to California, and encouraged the AHMS to fund his ministry. White arrived in 1854, and his initial California assignment was to Redwood City. The planting of a church there was not easy, and there was considerable discussion in letters between Rev. S. H. Willey and the AHMS regarding the subsidy they were giving White and his wife to keep the ministry afloat.

In his role as mentor, informal "bishop" and friend, Brier linked White with the church in Carson City. When he saw the church faltering after the first pastor suddenly left, Brier assigned him to Virginia City. The Reverend A. F. White was well-loved in Western Nevada, not only by his own congregation, throughout the entire Carson City valley. Following in Brier's footsteps, he was elected in 1864 as the new State of Nevada's first Superintendent of Public Instruction. Brier later recruited White to pastor the church he organized in Nevada. White was Nevada Superintendent of Schools in Ormsby County, 1862-1863, and was appointed Superintendent of Public Instruction in Carson City from 1863-1866. Education and pastoring were not his only skills. He was appointed State Mineralogist by Governor Blasdel, 1869, and served as Trustee of the Continental Silver Mining Company in the White Pine district.

The Virginia City church expressed their love for Rev. White, by setting up a pastoral housing fund to help him buy a house. He was able to cash out the house some years later with a large stake of equity. He then transferred to the church in San Leandro still close to the Brier family, where he pastored for 14 years from 1876-1890. Following San Leandro he went to pastor in Los Angeles, and Santa Monica. He died January 17, 1899, and was buried in Gilroy.

It is touching is to see that friendships from the early days of ministry would last across many years of ministry and the immense trials of life. Brier and White stuck together, and their paths crossed frequently.

CHAPTER 46

Theological Boundaries and The Hamilton Controversy

1868

The year 1868 contained an extremely painful chapter in Brier's life as he entered into a prolonged public theological battle with his longtime friend and colleague, the Rev. Laurentine Hamilton. Brier felt as though it was a personal betrayal when Hamilton challenged the orthodoxy of the church through his denial of the theology of heaven.

Their friendship had been cultivated through 16 years of working side-by-side in church and society in the East Bay of San Francisco. Just two years after Brier arrived at Centerville, and a few months after he had taken over as Alameda superintendent of schools, Hamilton arrived from the East Coast and took over as the Superintendent of the San Jose schools. The problems facing both districts were immense, and Brier regularly consulted with Rev. Hamilton during his trips throughout San Jose Presbytery. Rev. Hamilton was appointed to be the pastor of the Presbyterian Church of San Jose. With so much in common, the two pastors became close friends. They shared freely about their school districts, their congregations, and their dreams. Hamilton served as Superintendent of San Jose's schools but achieved more far-reaching fame from something unrelated to preaching and teaching. Hamilton was already legendary in the city of San Jose, as the mountain overlooking the town was named after him. "On September 1, 1861, he accompanied a college friend, William H. Brewer and his U.S. Geological Survey party on the first recorded ascent of a high peak in the Diablo Range. Professor William H. Brewer of Yale College, in charge of the party, named the peak 'Mt. Hamilton.'" [109]

Bronze bust of Rev. Hamilton, at the James Lick Observatory on top of Mount
Hamilton.
Photo by author.

By December of 1864 Rev. Hamilton had already served for 12 fine years of ministry
in San Jose when he was called as pastor of the First Presbyterian Church of Oakland. The
city of San Jose honored him further by naming 'Hamilton Avenue' in his honor.

This move to Oakland brought Brier and Hamilton even closer. Brier had always
been competitive with the Oakland church, as his home congregation in Centerville
was meeting a year before Oakland was chartered as a congregation.

Sometime in 1867 rumors began to circulate among the ministers that the
congregation of the Oakland church had been stirred by a controversial sermon Rev.
Hamilton delivered, in which it seemed he was questioning the reality of heaven, hell,
and the nature of faith in determining the destiny of our lives.

The rumors began to intensify, and Presbytery called a series of meetings so the
ministers of Presbytery could understand and challenge Hamilton's orthodoxy in these
matters of faith.

At the Presbytery meeting in April of 1868, Brier took up the matter and asked
Hamilton to deliver the controversial sermon to them. Hamilton deferred, saying he
was not ready. He was invited to preach the sermon and explain his views at the next
meeting of the Presbytery.

Two months passed before the Presbytery would gather to hear the troublesome sermon in person. Hamilton came to the podium, and delivered it with eloquence and wit, but the members were not impressed. Brier felt it was as though his friend had changed. It was near to a personal betrayal.

In proper Presbyterian style, after hearing the sermon, they composed a committee to further discuss their reactions with Rev. Hamilton. "On motion Rev. W. W. Brier and J. Wylie, and F.L. Nash were appointed as the committee to confer with Brother Hamilton on the subject and the discourse he has read and the remarks made." After their conversation with Hamilton, the committee returned a report of deep concern to the Presbytery ministers.

Rev. W.W. Brier, the chair of committee, thundered the report to the gathered assembly. "The committee finds that the Rev. L. Hamilton sermon on Matt 25:46 read before Presbytery contains teaching, in the judgment of this body contrary to the Word of God and the standards of our church, and we further ban him from leadership in the church."

Hamilton listened to his good friend William Brier, and looked around at his colleagues in disbelief. He was furious that he had been so deeply misunderstood. In the pain of rejection, he wanted to lash out, yet he did not recant, and he did not cease from these controversial teachings. If anything, the questioning of his theological orthodoxy simply hardened his position and alienated him from the Presbytery.

Some voices in Presbytery were not satisfied with this censure, and in the months between this meeting and the next gathering of ministers, there was considerable political maneuvering by elders and pastors alike. When the Presbytery gathered for their next meeting, they asked him to review his theology again. The newspapers picked up the story and printed transcripts of his beliefs in the papers. This intensified the concern of Presbytery further, as their actions of investigation and discipline became the tabloid news of the day.

Three months passed, and there were further speculations about the extreme action of Presbytery. The questions continued. Did they have the right to remove him from his pulpit? Had his conclusions crossed the boundary of theological orthodoxy? Was his argument true to the Bible? This time the Presbytery gathered at Hamilton's home church in Oakland. Rev. Hamilton appeared again to present a written statement of his views and read the theological paper to Presbytery. There was a stir of excitement as he walked down from the pulpit and out of the church. Presbytery re-appointed the committee to review the matter a second time. Again, it was led by Rev W.W. Brier. The committee of three adjourned into the pastor's study to review the sermon and his theological paper. They were shocked to read Rev. Hamilton's clear denunciation of the existence of a state of being following death which was referred to as hell. He further noted that a loving God would not create a place so repulsive and that we must assume that salvation was in the plan of God for all the people of the earth. The report written by Rev. Brier was modified and did not directly remove Hamilton from ministry, but it rebuked his false teaching. Presbytery minutes recount,

"Resolved, That the paper presented by Rev. Hamilton to this Presbytery on the subject of the Future Punishment and Probation after Death contains doctrines contrary to the Word of God and our Confession of faith, and to doctrines of vital importance to the salvation of men."

The public controversy continued to spread to many papers. It is not known what Rev. Hamilton said to his congregation on Sunday morning, but a loyal group of supporters took up the defense of their pastor and reviled the condemnation of Hamilton in the newspapers. They represented the view that a group of narrow-minded preachers without Christian love were jealous of his ministry and were persecuting him. A printed tract was distributed by a member of the Oakland church to rail against this decision by the Presbytery.

The editor refers to Brier's stubbornness in considering the issues, and suggested that the other members of the committee were more open to the teaching of Rev. Hamilton. "One member of this Committee remained true to his convictions of right and duty. The other members of the Committee of three, by way of explanation for this strange conduct, stated in public as the reason for the substitute motion 'that other members of the Presbytery were not satisfied with the first report.'"

"A committee appointed by a religious body, and under the most solemn obligations to report conscientiously, bring in a second resolution which declares most unmistakably that their first resolution was false, because, as they themselves confess, "They wanted something the Presbytery could endorse." Some willful members of the Presbytery would not yield to them, and so, to make their action nearly unanimous, they yielded their conviction of the right."

Brier had won the battle but lost a friend. And the battle did not end quietly with the verdict of the Presbytery. Throughout the Bay Area many people witnessed this destructive fight, and Reverend Brier became the lightning rod of contempt in many letters to the editors of local newspapers. In particular, The *Oakland News* published an exchange of letters between a local community leader, Mr. Emerson, and Reverend Brier that were intense and personal.

For nearly two weeks, the Oakland papers were full of reports, charges, and countercharges. The *Oakland News* was owned and published by a member of the Oakland Presbyterian Church, a man who was highly sympathetic with Rev. Hamilton. The *Daily Democrat* was more neutral, and while it initially supported Brier, its editors then came to criticize the behavior of both men.

The *Daily Democrat*, on Friday Evening, March 9, 1869, recorded

The Emerson/ Brier Correspondence.

The News has another letter from Emerson. Emerson made the attack; Brier answered, and charged replication, which we hope, is the final charge in this most undignified and unchristian warfare of words. Political security is bad enough, and is contemptible when it descends to personality, but when men, assuming to be the proponents of religious differences, so burden their arguments with personal abuse and fill the space, supposed to be allotted to discussion of principles, with such venomous vituperation, they appear in a most scandalous light, and the sight of their productions is painful to even those practicing the doctrines which the pretend to support. It seems somewhat unfortunate that both the Presbytery and the Independent Presbyterian Church, have no power to appoint their own champions rather than have their cases plead by gentlemen who so forget the great lesson of Charity uncalculated by all churches, and who, heading their articles with "Speak the Truth and Lie Not," wind up by mildly calling each other liars and accuse Church organizations with intended theft. Both these religious bodies may well pray "Save us from our friends."

We hope the following from the Transcript (newspaper)of this morning, contains a typographical error, otherwise the Rev. Mr. Brier is entitled to the sincere sympathies of this community, Christian or secular.

We have said before, that in our opinion, Mr. Brier has been very wrongfully and outrageously assaulted by certain of the newspapers, some of which could hardly discriminate between the Thirty-nine Articles and a pack of cards. Because of his physical and mental stricture, which is somewhat of the Bonerges order, Mr. Brier has been somewhat more conspicuous than the others, but we are told that he is sustained by the other members of the Presbytery, from the venerable Dr. Sessions down to the most juvenile ecclesiastic in that celebrated council."

This second newspaper article appeared three days later, full of satire meant to shame Brier for leading the charge against Hamilton.

Printed in the *Daily Democrat*, on Friday Evening March 12, 1869

"Brother Brier, through the columns of the (Oakland Daily) News, sends, hurtling, another ecclesiastical bomb-shell after the audacious layman D. E. Emerson, and with a refreshing awareness of temper, and a pious tone, of evangelical conciliation, thus discourseth his erring brother: "I do not wonder that you speak falsely, then you believe that truth is falsehood and falsehood truth. I am not astonished that you rage over your defeat in an unholy war against a Presbytery. To charge home your double dealing and low trickery, is to you falsehood and wickedness."

"This is genial, gentle, scholarly, polished, and in spirit, breathless something of, "Love your enemies—pray for those who despiteful use and persecute you, and love your neighbor as yourself." We hope to have much more of the same sort, for the public are not quite nauseated."

Under all this scrutiny of Presbytery and the media, Rev. Hamilton decided to withdraw from the church and the Presbytery. Finally, without admitting any false teaching, Rev. Hamilton left the church, and a number of members followed him in forming the "Independent Presbyterian Church of Oakland." His friendships with other pastors were severed, and the Presbytery held a number of special meetings to try to prevent him from using the name "Presbyterian" in the name of his congregation, until they discovered there was no legal control over the name.

Hamilton pastored the congregation for thirteen years before they changed the name to the "Unitarian Church of Oakland." This change organized the first Unitarian church in the Bay Area.

There is a sad and glorious story of the ending of Laurentine Hamilton's life and ministry. On Easter Sunday, April 9, 1882, while preaching on a text from Matthew 5:17, *"I am come,"* he collapsed and died in the pulpit.

CHAPTER 47

Signposts on the Frontier:
Entering California, 3% Christian!

As the years went on, Brier was active in giving away his life in supporting churches, physically and financially. This fact was noted in this report from the Presbytery. "The Rev. W. W. Brier had contributed $235.00 of his personal money to the Committee on Home Missions. And under expenditures it reports that he was given a salary of $450.00 and traveling expenses of $22.75."

To get a picture of the growing size of the work of Presbyterians in the Bay Area, the Synod minutes record there were 15 Presbyterian churches (5 churches in San Francisco Presbytery and 10 churches in San Jose Presbytery). There were twelve ministers in the Bay Area, and 956 members in the churches.

It is easy to think today that in the early days of California people were more responsive to the message of the gospel, or that churches were formed easily and naturally. But the depressive laments of the pastors through letters to the American Home Mission Society have proved that there is momentous hard work involved in planting a church and even more work in keeping that church alive and growing. There was some surprising news in the estimates of the number of people who name themselves as Christians, compared to the fewer number of people who were in churches on any given Sunday morning.

"The masses of the people of the State are still untouched by the Gospel. We have endeavored, from the limited knowledge we have been able to obtain on the subject, to arrive at a reasonable estimate of three per cent of the population of the State who hear the preaching of the Word from Sabbath to Sabbath. Our investigations have led us to conclude that eight per cent will include our entire church going population.

Perhaps three percent will include all the Protestant Church membership on the Coast. We will not pretend to say how many of this three percent, are active Christians, and what proportion are zealous Christians." [110]

This three percent figure is a prime example of the struggle in the life of the local church and the Centerville Church. Early founding families often stayed in the area but a few years and then moved on to pursue farming or mining ventures in other communites.

After numerous misunderstandings, the following letter included a message of reconciliation with Rev. Brier. Rev. Brayton noted this in an 1869 letter to his supervisor when he tells a story of how Brier helped him in finding a new ministry site. Rev. Brayton, wrote to the AHMS,

"By a remarkable leading of Providence, I visited this place with Rev. W.W. Brier, and found the people without a spiritual guide. We preached four evenings in Martinez and its vicinity, and on the following Sabbath, I remained at Martinez, and preached morning and evening too. I preached morning and evening to audiences of fifty or sixty. After the morning services, the congregation re-examined me and organized a meeting, at which a formal paper was drawn up and signed by those present, inviting me to settle in Martinez and minister to them in holy things."

Reunion of Old School and New School Presbyterian Denominations.

Brier was a participant in the historic mending of a broken church when he was commissioned the Presbytery to go to Pittsburg, Pennsylvania, for the vote on reunion. The reunion between the two Presbyterian communities was a long time coming, as a beautiful way opened to heal the wounds that had split the denomination. Local ministers and churches had grown closer together through the pressures of working in rough and tumble California. The division over slavery between the New School and the Old School Presbyterians was resolved through the conclusion of the Civil War. In May, 1869, Presbyterian General Assemblies (both Old School and New School) met in Pittsburgh after almost 30 years of conflict and separation. They celebrated a "Reunion Jubilee" and the renewed Presbyterian Church in the United States of America. The celebration lasted for the week of General Assembly. Brier was there as a delegate from the San Jose Presbytery. His participation was a fitting tribute for him, since he had worked to build so many bridges between Old School and New School pastors. Rev. William Strong, moderator of the Assembly proclaimed at the end of the re-union voting, *"Now no person should say: 'I'm an Old School Presbyterian' or 'I'm a New School Presbyterian.' Now we must all say we are members of the 'Presbyterian Church in the United States of America.'"*

1870

The church had grown significantly in western soil, and Brier's family also continued to grow. Lizzie was 20, Mary was 18, Caroline 14, William 12, and Louise 8. Brier's wife, Elizabeth, began involving herself in broader work of the church, appearing on the program for the Women's Presbyterial Mission Society of the Bay Area, the ladies' group formed to advocate for Presbyterian missions.

There are some interesting demographics that put the church growth in perspective. The total population of Alameda County in 1870 was 14,382, of which 7,332 were born in California. There were 1,722 who had come from New York, 1,265 were Irish, and 1,292 were German.

CHAPTER 48

Brier's Curious Legacy in Nevada

During this chapter of his ministry in the West, Brier worked at planting the Presbyterian Church throughout Nevada. His work was commemorated in a curious stained glass window. In Steward Chapel at San Francisco Theological Seminary, there is a window dedicated to Brier that is two feet narrow and four feet tall. The Brier window allows him to take his place among the early pioneers of the Presbyterian Church. The seminary guide to the windows describes the design of the windows as written by Clifford Merrill Drury. He describes unseen events in Brier's involvement in Nevada.

The Brier window at SFTS.
Stewart Chapel, SFTS Library.

Professor Drury's comments on the images on the window:

The top section of this window is devoted to the work in Nevada, with the Reverend William Wallace Brier as the chief figure. He is shown in the central medallion at the railroad junction at Elko, Nevada, with the four sagebrush lots, which he was given so that a church might be built there. Although his work was mainly in Nevada, his headquarters were at the church in Centerville, California, shown behind him.

The top medallion shows the map of the state of Nevada with the date 1864 indicating that this is the Battle-Born State . . . and the dates 1861 and 1862 to indicate the founding of the first two churches in Nevada at Carson City and Virginia City. Brier traveled extensively, always preaching to the people at every opportunity.

The circuit rider, the wagon wheel, and the pulpit shown in three other medallions symbolize this. In addition to his missionary duties, Brier also served as the first financial Agent of the San Francisco Theological Seminary and was active in raising the initial funds in 1872. The ledger book commemorates this.

The curious thing about this beautiful window is that Brier is celebrated for the work he did in Nevada, which was actually a very small part of his life-long ministry. Drury, as the Professor of History and designer of the windows, has written three articles for the California Historical Society about Brier in Marysville and one regarding his ministry in Centerville, which has numerous references to him in other settings. In this window, he celebrates a few of Brier's unseen and unsung efforts in Nevada.

As the decade-long gold rush in the "Mother Lode" of California began to falter, the timing was perfect for a boom in Nevada. Some mines were already stripped of their gold veins, while large industrial mining interests now controlled the remaining gold. Lawyers swarmed to fight over the claims. The whisper that there were great undiscovered resources in Nevada sent hoards of miners scrambling over the Donner Pass.

Brier took his role as exploring agent seriously, and he spent a great deal of time organizing churches in Nevada. He was not always the first Presbyterian presence in the community. In some cases, there had already been visits made by Presbyterian pastors at a variety of preaching points.

But it was not an easy time to minister and was a difficult time to plant churches. The early Nevada church history, *Sagebrush and Steeples,* notes, "The pioneer ministers did not come to gain material wealth. Had they been worldly-minded they might have been rich. The pioneer ministers saw the rougher side of life. They had few comforts. They were glad to have a board shanty to live in and a tent for a place of worship. These men and their associates not only founded churches, but every one of them was an earnest advocate of a system of public education. They sought not their own, but only the highest welfare of their communities. Nevada might lose all its mineral wealth and not encounter any such loss as it would were the initial work of the pioneer ministers absolutely stricken out. They stood in their places not only for religion, but for education, law, justice, for temperance, honest industry, and for eternal principles of right to lay at the foundations of the State."[111]

A street view of Elko
Photo courtesy of Nevada Historical Society

Elko, Nevada
May 26, 1870

Brier went to the mining districts of Elko to explore the new area the railroad lines were reaching. Elko had 45 saloons and several houses of prostitution before it was six months old. But a respectable investor soon erected the fine Depot Hotel with 80 rooms and a dining room that would seat more than a 100 persons. One of the early amenities was an opera house. By some accounts there were 4,000 people in the town before that first anniversary was observed. Soon it had a flour mill, several gold refining furnaces, and two weekly newspapers.[112]

Elko had its periodic experiences with mining excitement. The geologists revealed oil shale beds thought to be coal, located not far away. A flurry of prospecting and gold and silver production occurred about 50 miles northwest in Tuscarora in the mid 1870's, but these development were much more modest than at White Pine.

It is interesting that Elko church history has little record of Brier being involved. In the Stewart Chapel at San Francisco Theological Seminary, there is a stained glass window of Brier to celebrate his ministry in Elko.

Once again, looking at Brier's "Nevada Style" of church planting easily solves the mystery. Travel was much improved from Centerville to Elko, with the completion of a rail line. By leaving his home at 9:00 A. M. he could arrive the next night at 6:00 p.m., covering the 634 miles in 33 hours. Brier visited Elko twice in the summer of 1869. The long trips began to wear on him, he agreed to assign Henry Otis Whitney, a Yale graduate, to begin the work on establishing the church in Elko. Due to the harsh winter that year, he developed complications from tuburculosis, and died March 2nd, 1870. He was 29 years old. Through contacts he made at the national General Assembly, Brier was told of the Rev. John Brown, a recent graduate of Princeton who was from Scotland. Brier recruited him to come to Nevada, and his cross-cultural experience in Elko was strange indeed.

The *History of Nevada* recounts the difficulty of ministry in those early 1880's pioneer days in Nevada. "*In 1870 the Rev. John Brown, then a graduate fresh from the Glasgow University, Scotland, arrived at Elko to take charge of an organization of Presbyterians just formed there*

During his first week in Elko, Mr. Brown spent his time prospecting, not for silver, but for proper material to build a Presbyterian Church. He was convinced that it was there, if he could only get it mined and separated from its surroundings. The railroad Company gave him four nice lots, so, when he stood up to preach on the second Sabbath, he told his hearers that they were going to build a church, and that right away. He invited his congregation to meet him next morning to clear away the sagebrush. They obeyed the summons, though there was not a dollar with which to begin operations, and $2,500 at least would be required. In the crowd was a character known as "Parson Cook". He could drink his whiskey straight, could hunt Indians, make bricks, build houses, or exhort the "boys" on the street from the top of a dry-goods box. This rough and shaggy pioneer rose and declared that the church had to be built: and if he was pledged a benefit night—that is an occasion to exhort and take up a collection when the church was built—he would give the bricks and build the foundation. It was unanimously agreed to accept his offer, and to proclaim the "parson" the best fellow in the entire town. He was as good as his word, and when the church was completed he got his benefit service."[113]

The Elko church was incorporated December 24, 1870, and a church building was erected on the corner of 6th and Pine street. There is one lasting legacy that had Brier's fingerprints clearly upon it. Brier reached out to one of his own mentors, Rev. Henry Ward Beecher, and asked him to sponsor the purchase of the organ for the Elko church. When the church was built, the church organ was donated by Henry Ward Beecher. It was just like Brier to reach out to friends and mentors back east, and to spin a vision for how they could share in building up the Kingdom of God in the west.

Brier's hunt for gold continued that year, but it was not the metallic sort. He was on the trail of the gold-crazed mines and families, eager to plant churches throughout the state. He began exploring other potential gold mines the following year at Hamilton, Nevada.

Main street in Hamilton
Photo courtesy of the Nevada Historical Society

Hamilton, Nevada

Brier's work in Elko continued as he encouraged and trained Rev. Brown. As he made his visits, he would explore for the next church planting bonanza. After discovery of rich silver lodes on Treasure Hill late in 1867, the newly-formed White Pine district needed a town with a desirable location. In May, 1868, a promoter named Hamilton laid out a town site near a campground which was dubbed "Cave City" because the earliest settlers first sought shelter in a number of caves. The first business established was a saloon. Beginning that June the sensational stampede to White Pine created the fastest and most intense mining rush since the gold rush in California. Brier founded the church here, but it quickly faded.

Southwest of Eureka, at an elevation of 8,000 feet in the White Pine mountains, prospectors found another silver vein in the fall of 1865. As in the case of Eureka, full development of the district did not begin until three year later. When systematic work began in 1868, there was wild speculation and wasteful exploitation far in excess of anything that happened in Eureka. The prosperity of Hamilton and its neighbor, Treasure City, lasted from 1869 to 1871. After that, the towns and the White Pine district declined rapidly, because the ore veins did not extend very far downward.

Yet while it lasted, the White Pine boom provoked some of the greatest investment opportunities in the far west; the excitement became known as "White Pine fever." Within a few months, prospectors filed thousands of claims with the county recorder, and about 170 companies were created, many of them listed on the San Francisco Stock Exchange, with a capitalization of nearly a quarter billion dollars.

At the height of the boom in 1870, the official census showed that Hamilton had nearly 4,000 people and Treasure City nearly 2,000, but local booster newspapers characteristically claimed five times that number. The Nevada legislature responded to the rush in the usual manner in 1869 by creating a new county named "White Pine."

CHAPTER 49

Brier as Regional Leader: Moderator of the Presbytery of Sacramento, Moderator of Pacific Synod

1871

William Wallace Brier in 1871 (age 50)

Longevity is often the vindicator of history. Brier had been on the field nineteen years. Of all the early ministers in California, he had stayed the longest, and had outlasted Blakeslee, Douglas, and Hunt, who all returned to their homes on the East Coast. To show the breadth of his ministry contacts and influence, the 1871 denominational roles listed W.W. Brier as a Minister from San Jose Presbytery, Moderator of the Presbytery of Sacramento, Moderator of the Pacific Synod, and also as the secretary to the Synod Committee on Home Missions.

Over the years, he became skilled at working the procedures of the church. He had been on the field nineteen years, and had matured significantly. On April 25, 1871 the Presbytery met in Centerville, and Brier wrote in the Presbytery minutes,

"The reports coming in various fields presented at this April meeting of Presbytery will seem of an encouraging character. Although many and great are the discouragement's under which the Christian brethren are laboring, yet a general tone of hopefulness pervades the tidings from all quarters.

With no marked revival of interest prevailing in any of the churches, yet in all there have been during the past year, accession to the number of believing Christians. Peculiar circumstances have placed some of the churches in especially trying position. Financially many are very weak, so much so as to cripple their energies and retard their possible growth. The whole region embraced in this body is passing through a state of great trial and depression arising from two seasons of drought. The prospect before most of the churches is one of struggle, yet we trust even this which seems worse than death, will eventually through God's blessing for a higher life."

During the Spring of 1872, Brier took charge of the First Presbyterian Church of Salinas, as it was in disarray following the departure of its founding pastor. He personally invested hundreds of dollars to support the church, and reached out through his contacts to secure a new pastor for the congregation. Although there was only a six month gap between the departure of the former pastor, and the arrival of the new, Brier did significant work to set the congregation on a new footing. Brier recruited Dr. McCormick from the east and he served over fifty years in the pastorate in Salinas, which became a denominational record of longevity and fruitfulness.

CHAPTER 50

Mentoring in Livermore

As the East Bay of San Francisco was settled, there were opportunities over the inland hills for ranchers and farmers as they sought open range land to support the growing populations. Just beyond Niles Canyon, vast hillsides were golden brown, and the ravines were dotted with ash, buckeye, and oak trees. Many eastern sides of the hills were lush forests. The hill valleys from Sunol to Stockton were brilliant green in spring, golden brown in the summer. Many pioneers saw this land as rich for farming, grazing cattle, and they scrambled to obtain the clear title to it.

His enthusiasm as a missionary brought Brier from his home in Centerville to the Livermore Valley at least twice monthly in the years 1866-1873. It was a long ride by horseback but was made easier when the railroad passed through.

William Wallace Brier may have already visited Laddsville on one of his many trips to the gold fields and was steadily eyeing it as a potential site to organize a church. The new pastor in Centerville, the Rev. Seymore, had already preached in Laddsville a few times. This was well and good. Brier began making trips to Laddsville in the summer of 1866, preaching and making contacts with merchants and schoolteachers. The *Occident* of May 23, 1868, reports the following from a correspondent of the Amador Presbytery who writes as follows from Amador Valley: The *Occident*

The Rev. W. W. Brier, of the Presbyterian Church, has maintained a regular monthly appointment in this valley for the last two summers. Aside from his appointment (which embraces a morning and afternoon service at two different points) there has been no regular means of grace in the valley.

Most of the lands have been brought into cultivation within the last three years, which accounts for this sad state of things. Consequently everything is new. A Sunday school was organized on the Sabbath of our visit, which promises very favorably for usefulness and success.

On the Sabbath of our visit, we heard the Rev. Mr. Brier preach a truly evangelical sermon, to the edification of the people, and the comfort of the Christian.

Local history fills out this detail further, *the first Protestant sermon in Livermore Valley was in May, 1866, preached by Reverend B. N. Seymour, a Presbyterian minister from Centerville. After preaching a few times, Mr. Seymour discontinued his visits. The Reverend William Wallace Brier, a Presbyterian minister, began regular services once a month in June or July of that year and also organized the first Sabbath School. In 1867, a Methodist brother included this place in his circuit, and until the organization of the First Presbyterian Church in Livermore, the Presbyterians and Methodists alternated their religious services."[114]*

The early town grew a cluster of hotels and houses, followed by stores, livery stables, blacksmith shops, schools, and churches. The census figures of the city celebrated its change of name to Livermore in 1869, stating there were 75 people in town.

While visiting Livermore, Brier met a young man named Charles Anthony, and sensed his giftedness and calling into pastoral ministry. He decided to sponsor him, bring him under care of the Presbytery, and move him onward to gain seminary training.

Charles enrolled in the College of California and graduated in 1870. In those days, any respectable New School pastor went back east to Princeton to gain a good theological training. Brier requested Anthony to go to Princeton, but the Presbytery said no, "decidedly," insisting that "we must raise up an indigenous ministry for the Pacific coast." [115] He noted the results, that "I was therefore turned over to the Pacific Theological Seminary for nearly two years while a class was being prepared for me." He joined three students to form the first class at the San Francisco Theological Seminary. Anthony complained to his pastor at First Church in Oakland, Daniel Poor, soon to be the first professor of church history and polity at SFTS. Rev. Poor responded "with a comical mixture of commiseration and amusement in his round, beaming face, 'It can't be helped, my dear brother: we must sacrifice you to found a seminary.'"[116]

Brier continued to mentor Anthony and secured a parttime job for him teaching Sunday School classes at the First Presbyterian Church of Oakland. Briers' inquiry to Daniel Poor regarding money for the seminary encouraged the elders of the church to donate a house to the seminary. This donation became the first gift to the fund that Brier secured, which had a value of $5,000. The intrigue over Anthony's training must have frustrated Brier, as there were many levels to the resistance by the the Old School pastors when they saw their first student being shaped in the ways of the New School movement, and being trained in the seminary. They had not yet completed the plans to begin their own seminary. It was interesting that Charles Anthony was in the first graduating class.

"*On February 12, 1871, there was organized by the Reverend W.W. Brier the Presbyterian Church of Livermore, which was then a town in an upland valley of wheat. Today the fruit crowds the wheat. The church has had no unusual growth at any time, but it has steadily held upon its way, ministering to the community, and, like scores of undistinguished churches, standing to the glory of God and shedding light and life over a whole countryside. The value of the work of all such churches, country churches, and small town churches is invaluable.*"[17]

The memory of this great event is recounted in the local newspaper, the *Livermore Mid-winter Herald,* January 25, 1896

"*Rev. W.W. Brier, a home missionary came to the Livermore Valley in February 1871, and organized the Presbyterian Church. The church edifice was built in December 1873, and formally dedicated, amidst universal rejoicing, on the 26th of July, 1874, the Rev. C. W. Anthony being at that time the minister in charge.*"

The congregation moved to the seminary school building, which was managed by W.B. Kingsbury, and regular services were held until February 1, 1873. The college was too far from the village of Laddsville for the community to attend regularly, so they temporarily moved to the city mercantile Exchange Hall, where they met until July 26, 1874.

During that time Charles Anthony preached several times. Brier makes note of the transition in his letter to the *Occident.*

The Occident April 10, 1872
Livermore: the Church and School.

On last Sabbath, I visited and preached in this field, which has been committed to me for some years past. The growth of the country has been slow but sure, so also the church. There is now a promise of abundant crops of wheat, and, I trust, a harvest for better. The town is growing rapidly. The people have resolved to build a Presbyterian Church this spring: they are united in this. By a unanimous vote on the Sabbath, the church and congregation invited Charles Anthony, who will soon graduate from our San Francisco Theological Seminary, to settle among them as their minister. They expect to secure a salary of $1,200 for him, if he accepts.

The Collegiate Institute, after a long struggle, has been founded on a sure basis—its own merits. It has twenty-one boarding pupils, and about twenty-five day scholars. It richly deserves and needs ten more to fill up the rooms. Mrs. Kingsbury is a graduate of the

University of Michigan, a fine scholar, and an excellent teacher. She has charge of the
schoolroom and is aided by the very best teachers in music and other departments.

W.W. Brier

The Livermore church would ultimately benefit from the transformation of the neighborhood. Once the rail line was contracted to run through the valley, close to Laddsville, it was a sure sign that a church would bloom like a flower in a fertile field.

The Occident March 4, 1872
Livermore Valley

On the Central Pacific Railroad, forty miles from San Francisco and nearly five hundred feet above the level of the sea, you find yourself in the center of the level country, surrounded by green hills. The valley contains about sixty square miles of excellent wheat land, which will, this year, yield five hundred thousand sacks of grain. This climate is good, a little warmer than the San Jose valley, the air dryer. For two years the crops have almost failed, as in other parts of the State. Now the people are full of hope.

At Livermore town, there is a preaching once in two weeks by a Presbyterian minister, a small church organization. Preaching is the school—room of the Institute. A Church building is much needed, as the congregation is large, even meeting a half-mile from town, and in the secluded place. The people feel too poor to build now. Three lots have been donated by William M. Mendenhall for a Presbyterian Church and Parsonage.[118]

A great day had come to pass, when Charles Anthony graduated, and came to pastor his hometown church.

The Occident, May 22, 1873

Livermore—Rev. C. W. Anthony a licentiate of the Presbytery of San Francisco, who recently graduated with very high honors from our Theological Seminary, has accepted an invitation to supply the congregations at Livermore and Pleasanton, and will immediately enter upon the duties of his charge.

Pastor Anthony began his work on June 1, 1873. During his ministry the church was able to build a wonderful church. Local fundraising was successful, added to by support from the national church erection fund.

It took nine months of his pastoral leadership to strengthen the congregation, before they were ready to build the church structure. The first challenge was to raise money for the building project.

As a fundraising strategy for the new building, the church held a community festival on April 21, 1874. They gathered local talent for the program including singing and music from Mrs. Kingsbury's class. The event raised twenty-five dollars beyond all expenses to support the church building fund. All was well until a rare windstorm blew through the hills and damaged the progress of the building. Pastor Anthony filed this letter to clarify the extent of the storm damage.

The *Occident*
Livermore
January 17, 1874

A report was found placed in the papers that the new Presbyterian Church was completely destroyed by the gale, which raged here Thursday the 14th. Such a report causes anxiety to our friends and I hasten to correct it. The truth is although, the foundation of the church has been laid, and well laid, a small portion of the frame was up and blown down in the storm. The damage was but a few dollars and a little delay. The builders are responsible men, and the prospects of the rebuilding soon are quite good. There is every indication of a fruitful season to come. Sowing of grain has gone forward with every indication— every one full of hope. Many new residents are coming in. Now is the time to lay the foundation for effective Christian work in what must be a long and prosperous community. While railroad interests prosper, we trust that God will not suffer his church here to languish.

Pastor Anthony

"*Total cost was three thousand five hundred dollars. The dedication service was held on July 26, 1874, by Rev. Dr. Scott of St. John Church of San Francisco, preaching the sermon, and he was assisted by Rev. W.W. Brier.*"

From The *Occident* dated July 29, 1874
New Church Dedication

Surely we may regard the Sunday the 26th, the dedication day of the First Protestant Church in this place as a memorable day for Livermore. Our new church completed and nicely furnished is a great joy to us. Rev. Dr, Scott and Rev W.W. Brier were present with

us. Dr. Scott delivered eloquence and impressive discourse appropriate to the occasion
after he offered the dedication prayer. A large and attentive congregation was present.
No attempt was made at begging for money.

The church began to take root and flourish. Through this effort, Brier began to have a vision for the payment of cash for the buildings of the church, so the congregations could fully support the salaries of the pastors.

CHAPTER 51

Brier as Fundraiser for the Presbytery

1872

Early in the New School movement, Brier became the leader in promoting good stewardship in the local church to support the structural growth of the Presbyterian Church. You might say that this was a first. He was the first stewardship committee chair in the Presbytery. While most congregations were struggling to pay the pastors, Brier saw the higher calling for faithful members of paying off church debts, and endowing the institutions of the seminary and beyond. To secure funding for the churches in the region that were in need of money, Brier began soliciting for a Memorial Fund, which was a capital campaign to help a variety of church projects in the Presbyterian Church in the 1860's.

This fundraising task became the central calling for Brier's life for some time, as he recognized and asked to be a leader in writing and preaching on this subject over the next few years. He began the campaign with a editorial column in The *Occident*, in which he elegantly illustrated the importance of this campaign.

December 14, 1870
Ministers and the Memorial Fund

When an army is about to fight the decisive battle of a war, the officers of each regiment lead their soldiers with daring and enthusiasm.

We may safely say, that, to raise the "Five Million Offerings" will affect the final victory over every struggling thought of division and difference in the Presbyterian Church. When men are successful in a common understanding, they are united and good-humored, when unsuccessful, they are distracted and cast the blame one upon the other.

> *Let the minister preach on the subject, talk, and organize a system of giving, which shall reach every person in the congregation, and then lead off in a noble donation from his hard-earned income.*
>
> *When the work is done, well done, lay the gift on the altar of prayer, and claim the promise of God, and see if He will not "open the windows of heaven and pour you out a blessing that there shall not be room enough to receive it."*

W. W. Brier

In this notice he trumpets the cause of raising more money for the memorial fund. The efforts would start slowly, with only a few churches on board. But the campaign was effectively prepared for the rebound in the economy. The first subscribers to the fund had designated the appeal for external giving. Nationally, it was concluded that with the economic slump, the campaign might not be successful. The motion was made to shift the strategy so congregations could include in the memorial gifts to their local congregation to support the capital needs of their church. This seemed to open the floodgates of heaven, as people caught a vision for both giving to their local church, and with it a portion to the national church. The blessing of this was that many of the projects which were designed to be nationally funded were now successfully gathered at the local level

A reporter for The *Occident* mentions the impact Brier had on the congregation in San Jose as he preached there for three consecutive Sundays

The *Occident*, Thursday, October 31· 1872

When the Memorial Volume was issued, one of the agents, Rev. Mr. Cain, disposed of some twenty copies (of the book) in this congregation in the course of a day or two. This revealed a good degree of interest on the subject of reunion, and urged well for a (donation to the) Memorial Contribution. But the winter rains still lagged behind: prospects were far from cheering; and businessmen were in some anxiety and doubt about the future.

In the meantime, Rev. Mr. Brier had prepared a sermon on the subject of the Memorial Fund, which he came up and delivered, on a Sabbath morning, with encouraging effect. The people were evidently disposed to do something for the Fund.

The subject was followed up by the pastor on two successive Sabbaths, in a sermon from Nehemiah 4:6, "For the people had a mind to work," and another from 1 Corinthians 16:1,2 expounding and enforcing the Biblical mode of giving: meanwhile the trustees, aided by a gentleman of the church, had devised and brought forward a plan for raising the money, which was explained to the congregation. As this is the feature of greatest practical interest, it will not be improper to explain it here. There was a debt of more *than $500 resting on the church, incurred chiefly in repairing the damage done to the building by the memorable earthquake of 1867. There were other items of estimated expenditure, raising up over $2,000.00, the whole sum to be raised being in exact numbers, $7,200. This was divided into 300 shares of $24 each payable weekly, in installments of four bits a week, or in any other way most convenient for personal and self denial. They had just succeeded in clearing it (the debt) off, and had barely time to breath easy, when it was so severely shaken by an earthquake as to require several thousand dollars for repairs, leaving them again in debt. This has now at length been provided for, and it has a prosperous future before it. It (the church) is steadily increasing in number and influence, had a large and growing congregation, and a very flourishing Sunday school. Still we are unprofitable servants: we have done which is our duty to do, no more and indeed not as much.*

CHAPTER 52

Mentoring Thomas Frazer

Thomas Frazer was the Synodical Missionary of the Synod of the Pacific for the years 1868-1883. These years coincided with William Brier's work for the Synod as Church Organizer. Brier had already been organizing churches for 18 years on the West Coast before Frazer's arrival.

When Frazer arrived, he first went to serve in Santa Rosa, and began traveling through Northern California. Brier met with him early in his career at the Synod meetings in 1869 and shared with Thomas what he could about the church planting efforts in the community.

They were very different individuals. Frazer was slight in build and thin but was unstoppable in his travels. He traveled more miles on horseback than any other Presbyterian Church planter in the country. Although different in temperament from Brier, they shared a common passion which connected their hearts.

Rev. Frazer spent the first six years based in Santa Rosa and traveled from there. Similar in focus and energies with W.W. Brier. He enjoyed the luxury of not having a family to attend to in California and was able to travel widely.

Here is an example of their teamwork, from the newspaper, The *Occident*.

March 23, 1871
The Calvary Presbyterian Church

"On next Sabbath, at the morning service, Rev. Mr. Brier will officiate, and in the evening, Rev. Mr. Fraser, as Dr. Scott goes to Bodega Corners, Sonoma County, to dedicate the new Presbyterian Church."

This was a significant event, as Dr. Frazer and Brier were jointly in charge of church planting on the West Coast, but also for the issue of working together to raise awareness of the expanding nature of the church. Brier made efforts to reach out and encourage Frazer as a younger church planter as he tried to build connections between the New School and Old School Assemblies. They served together on the Presbytery of San Francisco committee on boundaries and also on the Synod committee of church extension to strategize about the next challenges of the frontier. There is an additional stained glass window featuring Thomas Frazer."

The Frazer window.
Stewart Chapel, SFTS Library

The guidebook notes: "Thomas Frazer is shown with a map of California with churches on it to indicate the locations where he founded them. Around the map are the names of four other states where he worked—Oregon, Washington, Nevada, and Arizona.

The books and chair in the top square represent the Robert L. Stuart Chair of Systematic Theology, which he held at San Francisco Theological Seminary.

The bottom triangle shows the First Presbyterian Church of Los Angeles, which he founded.

The medallions show the variety of places in which he held services—a courthouse, a home of a pioneer, a schoolhouse, and a town hall."

He was a young but experienced man. Thomas Fraser graduated in 1845 and accepted for his first challenge the missionary life in Wisconsin. He served there six years, organizing twelve churches before being called by the Old School Assembly to be the Pacific Synodical Exploring Missionary on the West Coast, in 1868.

Half of his salary was to be provided by the Presbyterian church board; the remainder to be raised "on the field" from churches in California and Oregon.

Bringing Presbyterians together, Frazer himself wrote, "I saw at once the necessity of thorough exploration and gave myself to the business, and traveled incessantly. Each year I covered everywhere from 1200 to 1500 miles a month at enormous expense which for two years consumed my entire salary."

He was known for his energy and enthusiasm about his work. He traveled from northern borders of Washington State to the southern borders in the Mexico region. Although he is credited with chartering 125 churches, he was not successful in assigning a pastoral leader to many of those churches. Fewer than fifty of those congregations survive today.

CHAPTER 53

Milpitas

As in most of Brier's congregations, a new church began with a significant friendship. This friendship began in Panama. In 1850 Brier was stranded for six weeks in Panama and while there, became fast friends with Joseph Weller. Unlike most of Brier's friends, Weller was not an Indiana Hoosier. Together, they waited for a steamer to bring them to San Francisco. The wait ended when they were placed on the ship *Columbus,* fresh from her first trip to San Francisco. Weller and Brier sailed together and arrived in San Francisco on August 7, 1850. Shortly after his arrival, Brier lost track of his new friend.

A sketch of Joseph Weller.
Sketch from Pioneers of Santa Clara County

Weller pressed ahead to the mines at Colomy in El Dorado County. In the following spring, he suffered from the effects of the fever, came south to Santa Clara County, and located on the Charles Weber Ranch. He returned again to the mines in Mariposa and took two loads of produce with him. These sold quickly at a fantastic profit. On his return to San Jose, he acquired fifty acres of land from James Murphy, farmed it for two years, and then on May 1, 1853 moved to Milpitas Township, to a farm which originally had four hundred acres. He had an orchard, and also raised hay, grain, and stock. He is credited with naming the area Milpitas to represent the many gardens growing in the area. He donated a corner of his property for the Presbyterian Church which he helped Brier found in 1871.

Rev. Brier connected easily with him shortly after his arrival. As he commuted the fifteen miles from his house to the churches of the San Jose Presbytery, he had a natural opportunity to travel through Milpitas and visit with Weller. Milpitas was then only a collection of ranches and a small village, remembered by the German immigrant Jacob Pfeifle as "a thriving village of two adobe saloons and a blacksmith shop." The road through town had a toll booth that charged a five dollar toll to the miners with wagons who were leaving San Jose and heading northeast past Mission San Jose, up through the pass to the southern mines. But the dynamics of the town changed in 1869, when the first train from Sacramento came to town on its way to San Jose, which connected with the transcontinental rail line. A year later the population of the township surrounding the village skyrocketed to a total 645 residents.

Weller was well connected and well respected. In 1855 he organized the Milpitas school district and was appointed a trustee. He also filled the office of Justice of the Peace from 1856 to 1878. In 1878 he was elected to represent the county in the Constitutional convention.

A sketch that shows the Weller Farm and the proximity of the church.
From the Archives of the San Jose Mercury News, now held at the
California History Room, San Jose Public Library.

In *the History of Santa Clara County*, he is remembered fondly. "His duties in life have not been in their nature brilliant or prominent, but they have been such as to require the most solid and useful of the civic virtues, courage, integrity, justice, and steady, indomitable energy. Possessed of genial disposition, and a firm Christian faith, he acts by his own honest convictions in the fear of God, and is ever ready to assist all that is good and repress all that is wrong, or hinders the general prosperity of his fellow men."[119]

The minutes of the church remember the official chartering of the church this way: In the first entry from October 14, 1871. The people of Calaveras Valley and Milpitas met in the school house of the former place and presented the following paper:

"We, the undersigned, desiring the ordinances of God's House, do hereby request Rev. W. W. Brier to organize us into a church of Christ, to be known by the name of the "First Presbyterian Church of Milpitas Township" which shall be placed under the care of the Presbytery of San Jose. Names: Janet Buick, Mary Carrick, Mary Sherman, Leonard Hayden, Joseph Merritt, Charlotte S, Campbell, Joseph R. Weller, Lydia Valpey, Marion W. Weller, Stella Merritt, Lizzie Hayden, John Adair, John Patton, Hester Patton, Marion Carrick."

After a sermon by Rev. S. P. Webber, the above named persons were examined and declared to be fit persons for members of the Presbyterian Church. Six presented letters from Presbyterian churches and one from a Methodist church; eight were examined as to their faith and Christian experience.

Each one was received by a unanimous vote after being examined in their faith by W. W. Brier and S. P. Webber. Then the following day after a Sermon, *The First Presbyterian Church of Milpitas Township* was organized. As usual W. W. Brier, the Home Missionary, officiated at the celebration.

The *Occident* reports on this by including a note from Brier. "Fifteen persons united in the organization, eight on profession of faith and seven by letter—six of the latter from Presbyterian churches and one from the Methodist Episcopal. Two elders were ordained. Preparatory meetings were held on Friday night and Saturday. Rev. L.P. Webber, of Anaheim, assisted in the organization and by preaching. It was a time of religious interest among the people, and there is broad prospect of an increase in members soon. The church has two preaching places."

Church planting was always difficult work. Starting the church does not mean that it will gain its own source of water to nurture the roots. In the 1870's a strong shift in farming was taking place like the transformation that took place in the Eden Valley some years earlier. The large grain fields were being broken up into smaller truck gardens or row crop fields. New immigrants from Germany and Portugal were arriving to own and often tend to labor intensive but very lucrative crops. What was good for farming and for the development of a diverse community was not good for the growth of a young Presbyterian Church. What started out as a promising church plant in 1871, languished as the number of English European immigrants moving into the area slowed to a crawl. Most of the new families were Roman Catholic.

Brier is listed as pastor of Milpitas for eight years. He led the church through those difficult years of transition. Viewing the statistical ebb and flow of the congregation over those years reveals a portrait of a struggling church in a small community. In the General Assembly statistical report, Brier is listed as stated supply pastor to Milpitas beginning in 1874. There were 100 Sabbath scholars. But there was a drop the following year, 1875, as the report listed 60 Sabbath scholars and only 18 members of the church. By 1876, there were 30 Sabbath scholars, but a gain of one new member, bringing the church to 19 members. Brier is also listed as Exploring Agent of the Synod. In 1877 they lost one, down to 18 members and 30 Sabbath Scholars; 16 members were reported in 1878. By 1879 Milpitas reported three members lost, three members gained. In 1880 there were 14 members, a net loss of two; in 1881 there were still 14 members. The last year he was listed as pastor of Milpitas was in 1882, with 17 members reported and 40 Sabbath scholars.

CHAPTER 54

Growing Old Gracefully: Brier's Last Sermon Before the Synod

In 1872 the Synod nominated Brier to preach the opening sermon to the gathered delegates. The sermon in its entirety was published in The *Occident* at the request of the Synod. This means that they thought it was one of his finest sermons, delivered to speak to a significant issue of the day, and it should be widely distributed. It also reflected his love for raising money. Like his sermon to the New School Assembly in 1860, his theme was once again the distinction of denominationalism, while stressing the importance of Christian unity. It may have struck a cord in the hearts of others as a point of unity, yet it supported the need for Presbyterians to have a unique ministry and calling in the context of that unity.

There are some interesting images and facts in this sermon. It is a victory sermon on the occasion of the closing of the campaign for the Memorial Fund, which Brier has been so passionate about in his years of service. He notes that from a goal of five million, the final result was over eight million dollars contributed, spurred on by the opening of the campaign to local projects to benefit the local church.

But what emerges so clearly from his sermon is the ongoing passion to plant churches.

Sermon
Preached before the Synod of the Pacific, at Gilroy,
by the Moderator, Rev. W.W. Brier,
October 1, 1872

"Work, for I am with you, saith the Lord of Hosts." Haggai 11:4

This text was addressed to the people, sent by Cyrus the Great to rebuild Jerusalem and the Temple. What is the work presented to us as a denomination?

I do not mean to ask what we have to do—that others branches of the Church are not doing: but what we have to do in our own ways, which sister denominations are doing in their ways?

The General Assembly, and our present constitution and form of Church courts took their beginning in the same year the constitution of States was adopted. The government of the Presbyterian Church and our civil government are very nearly alike; both are popular with the American people.

The National Government, rent asunder for a time, and again cemented together more firmly, is dearer to the people: so our Church rent into two parts and again united, stands forth in greater strength and is more beloved and honored. We have a complete government, a written liberal constitution, a system of doctrines to which the best educated in all denominations assent, and a well defined set of church Boards to carry forward, in all its branches, the general work of extending Christ's kingdom. These instrumentalities are the growth of ages. We should study to make them more and more effective, each year.

They are our own, the hands with which we work. Each year would add greatly to their strength, and our knowledge of what is accomplished should be a constant and increasing joy.

Giving as a means of grace, is no new theory. If we would prove all its blessedness, we must give in such channels as will enable us to follow up and see what is accomplished. This may be done by contributing to our own Boards, and reading our own periodicals to see the result in the land and the world.

If we scatter our benefactions and never know what they accomplish, we shall have very little comfort or grace from giving. The boy, who went to the monthly concert of prayer to hear what the small dime he contributed to Foreign Missions had accomplished, illustrated a principle of human nature to which all should take heed.

The result of the Memorial Fund of our Church illustrated the same thing on a grand scale.

The resolution to raise $5,000,000 as a special offering of gratitude for the union of the two branches of the church, was passed at the time of the union. At the end of six months only $1,900 had been raised. It was then published that objects in your home church might receive memorial gifts. This raised enthusiasm. The people saw what was to be done with the money. $8,000,000 was contributed in the remaining period, of which $2,000,000 were for general objects, but objects in which the donors were especially interested, and they contributed all with which they were acquainted.

All should know what the Church is doing. To secure this end, every family in our congregations should have our Foreign Missionary Journal and the Presbyterian Monthly, and all in California, The Occident.

We should work to establish new churches. Institutions live, men die.

A church may be small, like a grain of mustard-seed at first, but it will grow. Some here present whom yet feel young, planted the first churches in this State and have seen them grow great. Howard Church, of San Francisco, began with ten members, six of whom had not received their letters at the time of the organizations.

So, most of our churches began small. When God's people are united together in a community they begin to work. There are many places where churches should be planted on this coast. One wise man said, "A man should not claim to be a gentleman who has never planted a tree to beautify the earth," How much more truly may it be said that a man should not claim to be a minister who has not planted a church.

There is no room now for slow movements! We must get up and work, make every edge cut, show practical earnest effort, meet activity with activity, and above all, seek the strong arm of the Almighty to be with us and make our work effective

His conclusion comes twelve paragraphs later:

Seedtime and growth are long compared with harvest-time. If we go fourth here in the van of the westward, surging movement of the heavenly kingdom, and fight manfully, our Great Captain will give us the reward in His own time. If not in this life, we shall see from the battlements of heaven the last triumphs of His kingdom, and shout glory with our comrades in the war. I hope to live, however, to see the Church moved with one mighty impulse, to redeem the race from the dominion of sin: to see armies of young men and women offering themselves to the work, and hundreds of millions of money laid at the Savior's feet.

In the time of our rebellion, the North was not stirred up to action when seventy-five men were called for. When it was published that a half-million men and hundreds of millions of dollars were needed to put down the rebellion, the heart of the nation was touched. Multitudes of the best blood of the land offered themselves. When the Church wakes up to the consciousness that its work is to go forth for the speedy conversion of the world, shall it not be true.

The Annual Report of General Assembly lists Brier as the stated supply pastor in Livermore, with 9 members and 65 children in Sabbath School. It also lists him as the Stated Supply pastor of Milpitas, which has 15 members, and 61 Sabbath Scholars.

CHAPTER 55

Fundraising for San Francisco
Theological Seminary

During the 1860's Brier continued his role as bridge builder with the Old School network of pastors and regularly attended their Presbytery meetings. Both Old and New School Presbyterian pastors numbered just over thirty. Brier was passionate about education and had promoted several overtures to the Presbyteries regarding the launching of a seminary for the West Coast. There were many leaders calling for the establishment of a seminary, including Dr. William Anderson Scott, Sylvester Woodbridge, and William Alexander of the Old School branch. Brier emerged as the champion for the New School branch and offered this enabling motion to the Synod Assembly in July of 1870. Here is the press report for The *Pacific Newspaper*, regarding Brier's ongoing work to fund the seminary's launch.

The undersigned members of the joint committee appointed at the joint meeting held last year with the Synod of Alta California, to take into consideration.

That in view of the rapidly increasing wants of this coast, needing an increase of the ministry keeping pace with the rapid growth of the population: in view of the vital importance of purity of doctrine: and of a ministry thoroughly imbued with a knowledge of the doctrines of our own Church: in view of the prospect of an early union of the two branches of the Church and the fact that one of the chief causes of the original dissention was the introduction into the ministry of our church of large numbers of ministers not trained in our own Seminaries, or under our own ministry: and lastly, in view of the fact that there are many young men within our bounds, who might be turned into the ministry, were facilities for obtaining theological education properly provided: in view of these, and other weighty considerations, it appears that the importance of the early establishment of a Presbyterian Theological Seminary without our bounds can hardly be overstated.

W. W. Brier
P. V. Veeder

It took two years before the dream became a reality. The organizing board of the seminary designated Brier to lead the cause to raise funds on the West Coast, and they appointed Dr. Cunningham to do the fundraising on the East Coast.

The *Occident* notes Brier's launching of the campaign.

Endowment of the San Francisco Theological Seminary

The work commenced in earnest this month. Dr. Cunningham is to put forth all his energy in the eastern cities. The General Financial Agent, Rev. W. W. Brier, has commenced operations on this coast. His intention is to give every member of our churches and congregations an opportunity to subscribe and have his or her name and subscriptions preserved in a book in the archives of the Seminary. This will show to all generations that have founded it. We hope every one will desire to take part in the noble work of laying the foundation of an institution which is to be great and do more than any one thing to add power and glory to our civilization. The work commenced in the Central Church; it was a noble beginning. It is a church recently very small, now not large except in heart, soul and every good work. With the burden of building their own immense church tabernacle, yet, on last Sabbath the congregation subscribed over four thousand dollars towards the endowment of the Seminary. That church has no fear of causing religion to appear secular by raising money in church for a good cause. They seem to feel that God listens to the jingle of coin cast into His treasury, as to songs of paradise. Should all the congregations of the coast respond with equal promptness and liberality, according to their ability, Agent Brier would have a short and pleasant work to perform.

When the San Francisco Theological Seminary was established in October 1871, Brier was one of its enthusiastic supporters. But he continued to have a challenge in being accepted fully as a New School Presbyterian pastor even after the reunion of the two churches. "On Tuesday, October 3, 1871, Scott, as chair of the synod's committee on education, made a verbal report urging the necessity of organizing a seminary. During Scott's report, Alexander was called on to present his memorial (gift). Finally the memorial (gift) from San Francisco Presbytery was presented."

Brier proposed a balanced group of ministers, and he would be the fifth vote on the committee. It seemed to be either a wise or innocent choice but was perceived by the Old School ministers as a dangerous precedent. Rev. Alexander decided to fight the proposal, and in the fight Brier was wounded by the political intrigue. The leaders of the Old School misunderstood the way Brier was recruiting leadership to the funding campaign.

The records of this decision are conflicted, as they reflect some turmoil regarding both the activity and formation of this committee. Brier's track record in raising monies for the Presbytery was already legendary.

There is an explanation in the report of the San Francisco Theological Seminary. "W. W. Brier, the agent of the school on this coast, has not attempted much in the way of raising funds here, thinking it best to defer pushing the matter until it is ascertained what our success would be at the East." [120] His term on the board expired, but he was appointed to a new three-year term on the executive board of directors of the Seminary.

It seems that he was embroiled in the ongoing politics between Old School and New School pastors, and had excluded Rev. Alexander from the committee. Rev. Alexander had a specific plan on how to raise the funds, which he had been vocal about. Perhaps Brier excluded him because of the difference in their plans. It may also have been that Alexander had been forcefully critical of New School Presbyterian pastors and had challenged their theological orthodoxy.

"The moderator was W. W. Brier, a former New School Minister on indefinite leave, who had, however, agitated even before reunion for a Presbyterian mission board separate from the American Home Mission Society, the old joint Presbyterian and Congregationalist Mission board. After a little hesitation, the next day Brier was authorized to appoint a committee to deal with the memorials. He appointed four ministers—including Scott—one from each presbytery. Alexander with his plan was pointedly excluded, apparently because of his open criticism of the orthodoxy of former New School members. "As I had the plan in my pocket," Alexander later recalled, "the committee might have been embarrassed, had not some one moved that I should be added to the committee, which was done by a vote of the Synod. All then was plain sailing." Together with Alexander, the Synod, controlled by Old School interests, added Coon and Hemme to the committee, giving the signatories to Alexander's memorial, a majority."[121]

In *The History of San Francisco Theological Seminary*, Hadsel and Coote conclude that the tension over control of the seminary continued between Old School pastors who thought the New School was not completely orthodox in theology. [122]

While Brier was momentarily caught up in the intrigue of the politics between the Old School and New School, it did not damage his role on the board nor derail his friendship with Dr. Alexander. In the years to come, Dr. Alexander would become the pastor of the Centerville Church where Brier and his family attended when he was not traveling. Dr. Alexander would preach the sermon at Brier's funeral some years later.

Brier continued his efforts in raising money for the memorial fund for San Francisco Theological Seminary. Brier wrote in The *Pacific* in 1872,

"It is proposed to endow the San Francisco Theological Seminary at once. This can and must be done. Dr. Cunningham is in the East to plead its cause. To succeed he must be able to say that California is giving liberally. We want $300,000.00. We must have, now, at least $60,000. Can this not be raised before Thanksgiving Day as an offering to God for his blessings this fruitful year?

Will all the ministers in the small churches make an effort to have each member of the congregation subscribe according to ability, to this great work to be paid on or before January 1ˢᵗ, 1875. Brethren, you can do this and save the expense of travel and time. Send us the results soon.

Let us hear a booming report from all parts of the coast at once. The sound will reach New York. Read the subscriptions yourselves. If you will do this we shall surely hear an answer from the heavy ordinance of our great churches in the east. The rich men of San Francisco will do nobly and the poor also.

For our Zion's sake keep not silence in this matter. Come up to the help of the Lord just now, when it will do most good.

W. W. Brier

Brier seemed to have good connections with the business community throughout the East and South Bay, and seemed adept at raising money for the church erection fund. Yet, the results of this appeal were most discouraging.[123]

July 1st, 1872 The Occident

Subscriptions to the San Francisco Theological Seminary

Last Sabbath, Mr. Brier presented the claims of this worthy institution in the Hayes Valley Presbyterian Church of this city. A subscription amounting to $527 was taken in the church, very liberal for that congregation. One of the Elders said in relation to it: "It did us good, it was worth a thousand dollars to that church to do this thing." It always helps a church to give to outside objects.

Dr. Alexander noted that after Brier became the seminary's first financial agent in March, 1872, "at first he reported good success, but as the misunderstanding between him and the Board soon emerged, he gave up his agency, and very little was realized."

The exact nature of the difficulties is not explained, but it may not be coincidental that the first two New School appointments by the seminary quickly failed to work out. Brier served as fundraising agent for only a few months, though he remained on the board for many years. Brier's replacement as financial agent was Thomas Cunningham, a former "Old Schooler," and he reported great success until the crash of 1873, the first truly modern depression, spoiled his effort.

Brier must have restored his faith and commitment to raising funds, because he did not slip away into obscurity. He redoubled his efforts to reach out to the congregations of the Presbytery, as is reflected in The *Occident*, which includes a report on his sermon preached at the Howard Presbyterian Church.

December 5, 1872

Rev. W. W. Brier preached in the morning in behalf of the San Francisco Theological Seminary. His discourse was based upon the words, "For you have the poor with you always, and whenever you will, you may do them good: but you do not always have me." Mr. Brier made a strong appeal in behalf of the cause he represented: showed that while there was no implied disregard to the poor, yet to relieve spiritual want is a greater boon than to minister to physical necessities. The chief aim should be, to remove the causes of suffering. Our works and gifts are to build up Christ's kingdom. The only way to save the world is by linking it to God through Christ. He made a vigorous plea for an educated ministry and for a local theological school, giving the arguments favoring home instruction. He closed his discourse with a history of the enterprise, the prospective plans for endowments, scholarships, libraries, and an appeal for aid to carry forward this most commendable work.

And again, a week later Brier is in the city at Dr. Scott's church, Calvary Presbyterian on Union Square.

Calvary Church December 12, 1872

Rev. Mr. Brier supplied the pulpit in the morning to present the cause of endowment of the Theological seminary of the Church in this city, and preached a very interesting sermon from Matthew 6:10: "Thy Kingdom Come." In this sermon, Rev. Brier said, "The child sinks more peaceably into slumber after uttering this prayer, which is offered everywhere, by the high and the low, the rich and the poor: and when, in the progress of time and events, it is fully answered by the complete redemption of the race through the gentle influences of the Gospel of Christ, it will cause the conquests, by the sword, of the greatest of earthly monarchs, to sink into insignificance. How great have been the triumphs of the Gospel the last fifty years in Europe, by the overthrow of the temporal, and to a great extent the spiritual power of the Papacy? Now the great continental nations are free in a great measure from its power, and the Gospel in its purity can be preached in all Catholic nations and in Rome itself. The Pope no longer has power to raise his arm against it.

The Jewish people were required to support by their contributions, one of their tribes, as ministers of their religion. It would almost seem that this would impoverish a nation, but it did not. God gave them prosperity, and they prospered under it. But when the nation neglected to pay the tithes, and the priesthood had to leave the offices of religion, to engage in secular labor for a support the nation was impoverished, suffered and languished. It is expensive to support religion, but it is much more costly to protect a people from the vicious portion of the nation.

To counteract the influences of the learned unbeliever, and to elevate the masses, we need a learned ministry. Our Synod has thrice voted unanimously to establish a Theological Seminary, and it has commenced, and now has six students. The four Professors have labored thus far without pay: and to prevent a debt, have expended their own money for textbooks for the students. But this cannot be expected to continue. We must do something on this coast to endow this Seminary, and if we do, we have the assurance that our brethren in the eastern churches will assist us.

Little did he know that the economic climate of the nation was about to abruptly change, with a significant decline in the stock market, the scourge of a summer drought, and crop-devouring locusts that swept across the heartland. This was no time to be raising money, as most people held on to their purses. He continued tirelessly to preach in churches and was the first pastor in California to really call the church to support anything outside itself.

CHAPTER 55

Brier as General Assembly Commissioner

1873

Brier was the Pacific Synod Minister Commissioner to the General Assembly held in Baltimore Maryland, May 15, 1873 to May 30, 1973. This was a high honor for him, and required two weeks of cross country travel, the second since he had made the arduous four-month trek across the peninsula of Panama twenty-three years earlier. He went with an elder from San Jose named James Martin Rogers.

In this letter Brier described an exploring trip through Utah, in which he is allowed to survey the building of the Mormon temple and attend a meeting in which Brigham Young presides.

The *Occident*

May 15, 1873
Brier writes from Utah on the way to New York.

Notes by the way

Dear Occident: To fulfill my promise: Out over the valleys, through Sacramento, rackety crack, up the narrow but not straight way, past cape Horn: the Summit: down swiftly down the Sierras: up the heavy grade to Humboldt: through the never ending sands and sage brush to Ogden we sped. Here is a stop: a quiet spirit pervades: the Utah Railroad runs to suit the other trains: the conductor, a tall thin Mormon, evidently feels that he is doing the Lord's business in carrying pilgrims to Zion: three cars full: one half, the faithful going to the "Conference of the Church of the Latter-day saints?

The grass and fields are green, the heavy waters of the lake as a burnished silver mirror, the snow clad mountains, here, silently sleep, on the shady side, there shimmer and gleam in the Sun's light. Thirty-eight miles from Ogden over a rich thickly settled plain brings us to Salt Lake City.

This reaches from the low marsh—lands of the lake and delta of the river Jordan, by a gradual slope, nearly to the present snow limits of the rugged Wassach Mountains. Ten acre blocks, eight lots each, streets 125 feet wide, little streams of water rushing along artificial stone channels, houses of sun dried brick, neatly painted, thrifty trees, giving to the city a pleasing aspect. In the business part of town it is built up as any other city— Eighteen Thousand Mormons, Six thousand Gentiles. The Tabernacle is in the center of a block, enclosed with a wall of sun dried brick, fourteen feet high, two feet of cut stone, as a foundation, and capped with the same, one foot. "Cannon" the editor of the Desert News, and the great political gun of Utah, formerly of San Francisco, a well—fed, wide awake thrifty, business like, four-wived saint and a delegate to congress showed me though the sacred places. You see," said he, "the idea of the Tabernacle was to make a big umbrella for the people to go under." The roof of that building is a wonder in architecture, self-supporting. It covers an audience room which seats 12,000 people. We went up between the plastering, a roof, and a space eight feet across. The framework bolted in the most substantial manner, stands on numerous stone pillars six by ten feet and about 15 feet high. There are several wide doorways to the main ground seats. The entrances to the galleries are from the outside. These galleries are about 20 feet wide and extend along both sides and the back end of the audience room: across the other end running from the floor up to the height of twelve feet are the seats for the officers.

In the center of this and above and behind each other, are three small half-circle pulpits: behind the most elevated sits Brigham Young, who looks as if well satisfied with the 72 years he has lived—an elegantly dressed old man, the blood retired from his face, his soul seems to have gone to the inner chamber, until some business calls him out, then the blood mounts to his face, his eyes flash, and his natural strength has not abated— others make most of the speeches, and attend to the business, but easily can you see that, that old man, in the back ground made every speech and passed every vote before conference met. In some twenty votes of the people, no one raised a hand in the negative. He is the main spring of Mormondom. When that mainspring breaks, who knows what will be done? The Mormons think the Lord rules, and it wills all is well, but the Gentiles know that Brigham is the lord.

These Mormon leaders are no fools. They have a bank and a cooperative wholesale and retail establishment, filling part of two blocks and $3,00,000.00 worth of goods. The Presbyterians have a small church organization: Mr. Welch the preacher: the congregation numbered 75 when I was there, smaller than usual. The Episcopalians had *communion and 89 went forward. They have a neat chapel and a school. Mr. Welch expects, soon to have a Church on his $11,000 lot: this lot has one acre and a quarter of land, and a house, which rents for $100 per month.*

Above, and three miles from the Tabernacle, is Camp Douglas, from which the city can be guarded by U.S troops. It is independent of our Uncle Sam because of the presence of 400 veteran soldiers. I found your friend and mine, Col. A. S. Hough, comfortably situated and full of hospitality. The officers and their wives are exceedingly pleasant and social. Col. Hough and his Lady spoke of you and your work in the warmest terms: They send much love. I preached at night and was sent back to the city in a four-mule ambulance.

Yours,
W. W. Brier

This was a remarkable letter. Note that he reveals the details of his travels in a very different reporting style. In one sense it is classic Brier. His writing was a blur of dashes, almost a poetry of words, fast-moving images, and observations that are more extreme than the rest of his letters to the Society.

This was the only letter that Brier would publish during his General Assembly trip. There was fruit from the journey. At Baltimore, he was appointed to sit on the Judicial Committee which reviews procedures followed in legal cases in the courts of the church. This committee met over a five-day period, then reported to the overall gathering of two hundred delegates from Presbyteries from around the country. In the committee reports to the General Assembly Committee for Theological Schools, it is reported that W. W. Brier collected $16,542 for the San Francisco Theological Seminary and that an additional $5,000 had been pledged by the First Presbyterian Church of Oakland. Dr. Cunningham had worked on behalf of the seminary to raise $50,000 through churches in Baltimore and Philadelphia on behalf of the school.

CHAPTER 56

A Vanishing Correspondence

During this season of his life, Brier became an elder statesman in the church. His letters to the AHMS office came to an end, as he was no longer supported by them. In the early days of the settling of California, most immigrants were aware that the pioneers were making a difference in the world. They wrote letters that were forceful and fresh. Many people kept a diary to detail the struggle of the overland journey. They wrote letters home narrating the trial and triumph of early days of building a community in California. As all things were fresh and new, families were keen to keep a record. There was happiness to face blessed misery, until the population began to blossom, creating a whole new set of issues.

After twenty or thirty years on the frontier, many did not feel this need for documentation. Families were separated from their identity back east. Those who remained behind were now fully independent. The focus of the nation was in emerging of the stable society. So the number of letters, diaries, and reports to the national office decreased. Brier stopped writing letters to the AHMS, and there are no surviving personal letters from this era. In order to trace the movements of the last chapter of his life, the remaining records we have are the records from the quarterly meetings of Presbytery.

Eureka, Nevada

There were two towns in Nevada to claim the name *Eureka* to reflect the joy of heir discovery of gold in their hillsides. There was an explosive rush and boom from other mining camps. The discovery of lead-silver deposits near Eureka was as spectacular as the first big finds of the gold and silver ore in the country.

But the expansion of the town was slowed by the inferior quality of the materials. It was not until in 1880 that a system was created to grind and bake the material and extract the metal. By 1880 the population was growing to 10,000. The Comstock railroad then came to Eureka. In its heyday it produced $40 million in silver and twenty million in gold bullion. Throughout the 1870's Eureka had the most consistent record of silver production of any Nevada mining town. According to official records, its mines produced between 2 million and 5 million in gold and silver and was the leading producer every year from 1871-1882.

In 1873, the Presbyterian Church was organized by Brier with six members; Rev. W.C. Mc Dougal was assigned as its pastor. A meeting house was soon after erected, and for some time the church continued to grow.

A 1920 photo of the church meeting house.
Photo courtesy of Nevada Historical Society

While it was compared to the Comstock Lode during the years of the big bonanza, it rivaled Virginia City during the early 1880's. As other mining camps fell silent, Eureka's unique reduction works and furnaces transformed millions of tons of raw ore into silver and lead bars, consuming thousands of cords of wood from the mountains. But by the middle of the 1880's, Eureka, like the other camps, felt the pinch of disappearing ore bodies and declining silver prices.

Beginning about 1863 it suffered attrition and desertion as people moved to the better-situated Austin. Sixty years later, Presbytery staff member Otis Linn wrote a letter to recruit a summer work crew to repair the church and manse, saying, "We have a church there and also a manse. I am sending you a picture of both. The manse is not livable. It is like a barn. It has no bath tub, no toilet, ceiling is canvas and house is cold in the winter. If any other church were doing anything, I would say, "withdraw" but no church is doing anything. Furthermore, the property is so run down that unless we fix it up it will be a total loss. Spiritual power is great, and the spiritual response is amazing. Nevada is a mission field. It will always be. This is purely a missionary appeal. Yet there are six or seven hundred souls who need Christ as they need nothing else in the world. If we fix the manse so that a man can live there, there are two other likely mission centers where this man could minister from; Austin 70 miles west and Hamilton 40 miles south east.

Yours most sincerely,

Otis L Linn dated June 5, 1926

CHAPTER 56

Public Education vs. Christian Education

One issue of conviction that pulled at Brier throughout his lifetime was the proper balance between public education and Christian education. He was passionate about every family having access to a public education, believing that Christians should be involved in making the schools available to all students. As one of the leaders in the formation of the seminary and an advocate for the State University at Berkeley, he wanted to advocate for free public educational opportunities. Like many of his contemporaries, he did not want to see the manipulation of the Roman Catholic religion in public schools, but he did want to see that Christians were passionately involved within the institution. They were to be "yeast in the loaf of bread which makes it rise to its God given form."

One example of this desire is in his advocating for a Presbyterian dormitory at the college—for both men and women! "Rev. W.W. Brier introduced a preamble and resolutions in regard to the erection of a Presbyterian Hall at Berkeley, in connection with the State University. The paper was discussed and laid on the table. The model was to have a Christian presence at the University, a residence Hall for Presbyterian men and women to come and study."

As a former Superintendent of Public schools, he could easily see the incompatibility of the state funding Christian schools. He longed that the local public schools would be filled with Christian students from all denominations and would teach significant Christian and moral content. This issue was highlighted during a lengthy debate at the Presbytery over the proposed state funding of Christian schools. Some in the legislature wanted to grant funds for all schools that would allow each municipality to develop along the lines of their prominent religious heritage. Presbyterians were concerned about the Roman Catholic schools gaining an undue share of the funding, since schools like Santa Clara University were in existence long before the gold rush.

In 1873, a gathering of fifty ministers representing the broad Synod of Presbyterian Churches in California debated and passed a resolution to deny state funding for religious education. They were so fearful of Catholic power that the Protestant ministers fought any state funding of vouchers that would give them more power.

"Resolved, that it is the sense of this Synod that while as citizens we are faithful and true in our support to our state Educational institutions, and do claim all and equal right to our share in their benefits, which do and of right belong equally to all fellow citizens: still we hold that it is our inalienable right and our bounden duty to take as efficient measures as are in our power, and such as are at the same time guaranteed to us by our civil government, to raise the standard of education and to secure the training of our youth in the highest mental culture and especially in the knowledge of our holy religion according to our consciences.

But for that and in aid of the religious training of our youth, we neither ask for ourselves, nor will we receive any aid from the State as such, nor do we believe that it is right or constitutional that any moneys of the State should be appropriated to any sectarian or denominational purposes whatsoever. We must give the liberty we ask, and we ask only what we freely give to others." Synod Minutes, October 1873, held at Calvary Church, San Francisco.

The Presbytery records note that Brier was the sole minister to vote *no*, as he expressed his dissent to the principle of this parochial funding.

1874

There is only one reference to Brier in the church records in 1874. The General Assembly Statistical Report lists Rev. Brier continuing at Milpitas Township as the Stated Supply Pastor, with 18 members, and 60 in Sunday school. Synod Minutes, October, 1875, held at First Presbyterian Church, Oakland.

1875

One notable activity Brier engaged in during 1875 is the gathering of information to write a regional history of the Presbyterian Church. He often spoke at meetings of Presbytery and Synod about wishing to gather histories of each congregation, which would then be forwarded to the Presbyterian History Department.

In his leadership role, Brier advocated for the congregations to take better care of their leaders. Pastors of that day were scratching out a living in the pioneer communities. He had seen several friends die in the pulpit, leaving their families destitute and dependent upon the Presbytery. Nonetheless, Brier brought the issue of life insurance before the Synod. "The paper of Rev. W. W. Brier, on the subject of Life Insurance, was then taken from the docket, discussed, and, on motion, indefinitely postponed." The reason the issue was tabled indefinitely is that most pastors did not have the church income to afford such an insurance plan. Synod Minutes, October, 1875, held at First Presbyterian Church, Oakland.

CHAPTER 57

Pleasanton

1876

Rev. Brier had an eye out for the next growing community for planting a Presbyterian Church. He had been making regular trips to Livermore, to visit the congregation but more so to visit pastor Anthony. In the midst of his visits, he was told that a town was growing in the small hamlet of Pleasanton, a few miles southwest on the trail toward Sunol and Niles Canyon's. The opportunity to plant a church there began in a rather unusual manner. Some would say that they were backdoor Presbyterians. Brier had already been canvassing the community leaders regarding the beginning of the Presbyterian congregation. Most notable was the addition of the local college founder, Mrs. Kingsbury of Kingsbury Academy. She had offered the college as a place to meet, but the church group would first have to be chartered. On August 11, 1876, a group of Pleasanton citizens met in Centennial Hall. The stated purpose of the meeting was to form a church, some form of Protestant church. The Presbyterian pastor, Rev. E.M. Stuart, called the meeting to order. They elected a committee to gather the community and voted about the sort of church they would begin.

A few days later, "forty-seven people met to decide the future of their church, on August 15th, and the votes were recorded as Presbyterian, 35, Methodists, 7, Union, 4, Scattered, 1. The vote had been cast. Rev. Stewart conveyed this vote to the Presbytery."

He advised the group to go through the process of incorporating with the County Clerk and the Secretary of State. Five trustees were elected as "Trustees of the First Presbyterian Church of Pleasanton."

Brier coached them into petitioning the Presbytery to be recognized as a church. On September 27 they wrote,

"To the Presbytery of San Jose,

We, the undersigned, desiring the ordinances of God's house, request that you organize us into a church, to be known as the First Presbyterian Church of Pleasanton, to be under the care of the Presbytery of San Jose."

Once they were chartered, it was natural for a church to want to have their own church building. The trustees of the church decided to build a church in general style, patterning after the 'School House, 28'by 44'in size, one story to be set 4'from the ground, from 16' to 18'ceiling, plain belfry, and the whole cost not to exceed $2500 including seating

On October 15th, 1876, the Rev. W. W. Brier and Rev. C.W. Anthony of Livermore, a committee appointed by the Presbytery of San Jose, met to organize the First Presbyterian Church of Pleasanton. Rev. W. W. Brier preached a sermon on John 1:1 "In the beginning was the Word, and the Word was with God, and the Word was God."

"Rev. Anthony of Livermore acted as stated supply from the Board of Home Missions from 1876 to 1880, then resigned to move to Illinois with his wife and children. In 1880 Rev. Brier rode his horse or buggy from Centerville to preach on Sunday nights. He continued the work until June, 1881." [124]

CHAPTER 58

Issues of the Day: "A Champion for the Coolies"

1876

The years would pass quickly. In the providence of the Lord, Brier used the proceeds of his farm in Centerville to plant churches throughout California and Nevada. He employed seven Chinese families to work the farm, while he taught, preached, and traveled around the region.

Brier was often buffeted by the difficulty of living in a rugged pioneer community. He gave himself to virtually any community organization that would provide moral stability; he stepped out to lead the local temperance society, the water district, and the vigilance society. But William Brier could also see through law and order, to the greater issue of true justice. Throughout his ministry, he grew to love the diverse nationalities of California society. From his early days in Marysville, he worked with Chilean, Mexican, and Chinese workers in the community, hired them on his farms, welcomed them into the church, and buried them in the cemetery. Late in his life, he became the focus of a regional controversy regarding the value of Chinese workers.

With the waning of the gold rush, the American economy crashed. Fortune seeking miners returned to San Francisco looking for employment and stability, but were disappointed about the lack of employment and the pervasive presence of Chinese laborers, who scooped up all the physical labor jobs. Since the completion of the transcontinental railroad, there was a diminishing need for Chinese workers to do the tunneling and track laying. After an initial boom of prosperity in California following statehood in 1850, harder times set in. The decade of the 1870's saw depression, bank failures, and growing unemployment, and many people blamed the latter on the Chinese, who gladly worked for low wages. Even though the need for workers declined, the numbers of Chinese men and women coming to this country had actually increased. As Chinese left projects in the rural countryside, they crowded into urban areas in search of community and employment, frequently being forced to live in overcrowded apartments as they cast about the depressed economy. To put the regional problem in perspective, in 1860 there were 8,548 Caucasians in all of Alameda County and 193 Chinese. By 1879, there were 4,386 Chinese living among 57,785 Caucasians spreading across Alameda County. Unemployment skyrocketed in both populations.

Pastor preaches to Chinese Immigrants on the Pacific Mail Steamship.
From Harpers Magazine Illustrators

Chinese immigrants were unkindly referred to as "coolies." The national unrest over foreign-born immigrants worked into a fever pitch by the summer of 1878, with debate flourishing in the newspapers. In late June of 1879, Congress authorized a fact-finding trip to California to gather further information about "*the Chinese Question*." This committee had seven members, representing Senate, Congress, industry, and labor. They were seeking answers to a crafted list of eighteen questions when they opened hearings in San Francisco in early October. The hearing held seventeen meetings, questioning twenty-seven local leaders on the issue of the rights of Chinese immigrants, which took thirty days. Rev. Brier was one of the most colorful leaders interviewed, and what began as forceful advocacy of the value of Chinese workers on his farm captured the focus of the press and nearly ended in a fistfight.

The year was 1879 as Brier emerged as an unlikely champion for the cause of the Chinese laborers. On November 16 Rev. Brier appeared at the luxurious San Francisco Palace Hotel to give testimony before the congressional committee while it sat for hearings in San Francisco. Over his decades in California, he established himself as a passionate and effective orator. Often viewed as conservative and controversial, he was determined to make a difference for the church. Brier made a forceful presentation, provoking the intrigue and anger of the congressmen with his preference for Chinese laborers.

With graying long hair and beard, he looked like a prophet of old. He was medium height with a receding hairline, had a booming voice, was still robust, and was well known as a pastor. He founded many churches and also had served as an elected official for the county. He was known to be provocative in his preaching and storytelling and had a habit of getting excited and forceful when he was agitated, when he felt he was being taken advantage of, or when others were not being treated fairly.

The *San Francisco Examiner* reported, *"A Presbyterian minister named W.W. Brier testified that he has resided in California since 1850. He was engaged in the fruit culture.*

Brier stated, "I regard the moral and physical condition of the Chinese laborers as better than that of any other class of labors. They are temperate, cleanly, and healthy, they all come here to make some money and go back, but after being here some time they become attached to the country. Except in running agricultural machinery they do almost every kind of manual laborers as superior to the white laborers of any other nationality in those departments of labor to which the former devote themselves. I regard the Chinese laborers as superior to the white labors of any other nationality in those departments of laborers to which the former devote themselves.

Congressman Sargent asked, "Can't you teach some young European boys to farm?"

Brier answered, "I have heard of applications for wealthy persons who wished to have their boys learn farming, but I never could afford to employ them. The farmer cannot run a farm with boys. I pay Chinamen a dollar a day and they board themselves. I employ at this time seven Chinamen and one white man. I have 50 acres in fruit, which I sell, in this market. The employment of Chinese had kept up the price of white labor. I could not carry on my business with white labor. Chinese labor has been of advantage to the country. In 1857 I paid one dollar a day less to my white laborers than I do now. Most articles of produce are cheaper now than they were years ago. I cannot see any reason at the present time for restricting Chinese immigration.

Congressman Brooks asked, "Can you not find European boys and girls to do your work?"

Rev. Brier said, "I employ no white girls and boys in my business; I could not get white girls. I am glad that our boys and girls do not have to work in factories. I would not have the

San Francisco boys to work for me. It is difficult to get Catholic girls in the country to do house work, because they do not like to be away from their churches. Almost all the house servants in the country are Chinese. The white servant girls are nearly all Irish and Dutch. Very few American girls do house work as servants."

Congressman Sargent. "Are you an advocate of low wages in California?"

Rev. Brier: "The wages of workwomen have been largely reduced during the last twenty years. I am in favor of low wages. The more laborers put into our country, the more prosperous will be our country at large."

Congressman Sargent—"Do you think that it is to the interest of the country that the capitalist should receive more and more and the laborer less and less?"

Rev. Brier answered—"I think that the encouragement of capital and enterprise is of benefit to the country. I believe the capitalist in California is giving as high wages as they can afford to give. I think the laborers get more than their share of the profits. I consider some of the other nationalities as evil, and do not believe that the restriction of immigration should be confined exclusively to the Chinese. An extreme of Chinese population would be an evil. I think that the cry against the Chinese has been made for political capital. I believe that the Chinese laboring classes amongst us are less corrupt and injurious to us than the laboring classes of other nationalities. There is no anti-Chinese feeling in Alameda County. I should think it would be desirable for Chinese to marry white women, but I think it would be not very good to do. I have attended many Republican meetings in Alameda but never heard any anti-Chinese sentiments expressed there."

Brier continued, "The Republicans advocate anti-Chinese sentiment because they had not the backbone to take the other side. I believe that God had sent this people here for a great and good purpose for the human race. He has sent them to learn something of our institutions and religion, that they may diffuse Christianity over that vast empire."

Congressman Sargent questioned, "Then, taking that view of the case, would it not be better for the Chinese to take California altogether?"

Brier responded: "Well, that might be a very good argument for Congress of the United States, but it would not do in the Presbyterian Synod."

Congressman Sargent offers up a prayer. "We are not sitting as a Presbyterian Synod, thank God. (Laughter ensued) We are sitting here as statesmen. You would give China a chance to take possession of California?"

Brier answered: "If they get the best of us, I do not see why they should not take the State as well as Ireland."

Congressman Sargent (quickly) "We are not talking about Ireland. I have a better opinion of Irishmen that you do."

Brier responded. "I am in favor of restricting the immigration of all foreigners: but I do not see why discrimination should be made (only) against Chinese. They are polite and *obedient, and do not spend their money for whiskey as white laborers do. I would make every Chinaman a voter if he could read and write our language, and pass an examination in the Constitution of the United States even if he had been only two weeks in the country. I think a flood of immigration from France or Germany, or any other country would injure our country.*

I would prefer that a hundred thousand white foreigners would settle in our State than a hundred thousand Chinese. The latter push up the demand for cheap labor, and so improve the country."

General Pixley asked, *"Do you think that you love the Chinese because of cheap farm labor?"*

Brier answered Mr. Pixley—*"If I was a laborer, I would be in favor of cheap wages if the country could be benefited thereby. If Chinese were to purchase fruit orchards, and go into the fruit raising business, I would have to quit and live on the interests of my money."*

Brier's response to the commission created a dramatic stir throughout San Francisco. Some would say that his commending the Chinese created a reactionary environment within the Bay Area, which culminated with massive demonstrations the next night.

Brier's testimony drew newspaper editors to respond to his remarks before the commission. The media attention was a source of embarrassment to him. They worked to humiliate him by suggesting he lacked common sense, or that he was a simple minded "Champion of the Coolies." This editorial by The *San Francisco Examiner* singles out Brier as the instigator of the problem.

Opinion of the Chinese

November 16, 1876

The testimony taken before the Chinese Commission develops a great contrast of opinion on the subject of Chinese immigration. The Mongolians find friends in all quarters, and among people of nearly every condition of life. In respect to the latter, however, there is one important exception. We believe no laborer has yet given his testimony in favor of Chinese Immigration. We have had clergy men, lawyers, physicians, bankers, insurance agents and railroad builders before the Commission: but we believe no man whose labor comes in direct competition with that of the Chinese has yet testified. Possibly the distinguished gentlemen of whom the Commission is composed do not suppose that they can extract much wisdom from a day laborer: but possibly they might get some specific information, which might be of use in a final summing up. Among those who have expressed themselves strongly in favor of Chinese, no one has gone beyond the Rev. Mr. Brier. The gentleman owns a fruit orchard, and his experience with Chinese has caused him to regard the moral and physical condition of that class of laborers as better than that of any other class of laborers. He says that they are temperate, cleanly and healthy. He has discovered, also, that although they all come here to make money, intending to return home in time, they become attached to the country and remain. They do all kinds all manual labor well, except running agricultural machinery.

In the department of labor to which they devote themselves, Mr. Brier regards Chinese as superior to any other nationalities. The witness added that he did not employ any white boys and girls in his business. Girls he could not obtain, and boys he does not want. He adds that he is very glad that our boys and girls do not have to work in factories. We presume that Mr. Brier is to be credited with speaking on these matters as they appear to him. It is not the less to his credit if he had spoken on the unpopular side of this question. But we may venture the opinion that personal interests may have blinded him to the true interests of the State. As a fruit grower and dealer he finds Chinese help cheap and docile, and he speaks of it as it shows itself to him. The business of cheap labor this year is fine if the employment of such labor keeps a more desirable class of immigrants from the State. Can a man professing to be a statesman view, with complacency the introduction of a class of labor, which turns industrious boys and girls into the street or reduces them to starvation wages? That is the point to consider. We admit that certain men make money by employing Chinese. If they did not the question would never have assumed a national importance. It is because they do, and because thereby Chinese are encouraged to come in large numbers, that a proposition to check their coming is urged. It is well for Mr. Brier whose interests are involved, but we presume that the members will weigh it in the scales of common sense.

The controversy prompted the *San Francisco Examiner* to editorialize:

Unjust Comparisons

The investigation now being made by the Congressional Committee of the subject of Mongolian immigration has brought to the front several enthusiastic admirers of the Chinese. We are willing to credit the parties who have made these statements in behalf of their favorites with sincerity, but they are not impartial witnesses. Several are deriving great gain from the employment of Chinese laborers at pauper wages, and desire their presence here that their profits may not be diminished. But the same parties exhibit in their testimony a bitter prejudice against the French, Irish and German laboring classes.

One Reverend gentleman (Brier) thought the Chinese were equal to the French peasantry, in point of morality, but, in reply to a cross-question, he admitted that he had never been in France. Others thought the Mongolians were equal to the Irish and Germans. If the testimony of the parties making such statements was worthy of belief, the Western States, which have made such great efforts to encourage European immigration, should cease their endeavors in that direction, and send to the Flowery Kingdom to bring a laboring element from that region of the earth. They should act upon the advice of the Late Wm. H. Seward, and "bring away their coolies."

The idea dominating the minds of several of the advocates of the Mongolian laborers is that their arrival here would result in their Christianization. That attempt has been made during the last twenty years, with a success so meager that it may be regarded as a failure. But, to convert the few, we have admitted hordes whose presence and practices demoralize society. The cheapness of Chinese labor has deprived of employment large classes of our own people. Honest industry has been driven from many avocations because it could not compete with the low standard of wages at which Mongolians work.

The next day, massive labor demonstrations erupt throughout the city. Brier was clearly a man who inspired passion in his time, today he seems to be an obscure footnote in the history of California.

The following day, the questions from the Commission centered upon the ability to adapt culturally to American ways and their reluctance to cut off the hairstyle known as the Chinese cue. The concern was over the practice of police cutting prisoners hair while they were awaiting trial. The question before the commission was whether the Chinese had the personal right to wear and maintain a cue, a hairstyle of a single braided rope of hair that flowed down the back of the neck and often extended to the middle of the back. Chinese men would wear a cue as a cultural hairstyle, even when they began to dwell long-term in California. This heightened the fears of the European population, who thought those who wore it were making a statement of allegiance to a Chinese foreign government.

Rev. Brier appeared a second day at the commission and was attacked and beaten by a local labor leader, Frank Pixley. This was a remarkable development. General Frank Pixley had been appointed to the Commission on the Chinese Problem to give testimony regarding the danger of the Chinese presence in the city, particularly when they lived in cramped quarters. Frank Pixley was a firebrand who liked to exploit every opportunity to get into the public eye. He was a general from the Civil War, a conservative Republican leader, a labor organizer, lawyer, and soon to become the eighth Attorney General of California. In 1870 he spoke before the Mechanics Union about "The Chinese Problem." This concerned many European communities who thought Chinese were the undesirable element who were taking jobs away from Americans.

After debating the following morning, the commission adjourned for lunch, after prohibiting the cutting of hair before a criminal was convicted of a crime. The commission affirmed it was appropriate to cut hair prior to a lengthy jail sentence but not during simple detention before a criminal hearing. The hearing room cleared quickly, with advocates for both sides of the issue huddling in the courtyard outside the Palace Hotel to discuss the news of the day.

Frank Pixley was angry at the commissioners' conclusions, and Reverend Brier had remained behind to talk with a friend. Pixley yelled across the courtyard lobby in the Palace Hotel, and the two men began to argue. Pixley drew closer, looking as if he were going to strike Brier, then Frank reached out and grabbed him by the beard and slapped his face. The newspapers that day recounted the fight that ensued.

San Francisco Daily Examiner
November 18, 1876

General Pixley's proficiency as a pugilist (boxer) was displayed yesterday at the expense of the Rev. W. W. Brier, the coolie champion. Although Brier was a boxer in his boyhood, he is better with the blow of his tongue now than the blow of his fist. Evidently Pixley is a thorn in the flesh of this Brier.

The altercation was witnessed by several reporters, as the editorial in The *Daily Morning Call* went further in description of the fight.

The Daily Morning Call
San Francisco
Saturday, November 18, 1876

The Two Champion

An incident that is not likely to have the less publicity because it will not go upon the official record, occurred yesterday at the Palace Hotel during the mid-day recess of the Joint Congregational Committee now in session. Rev. W. W. Brier's testimony before the Commission (the Presbyterian clergyman and fruit-grower) has not been of a character to win the admiration of the anti-coolie clubs or the respect of the working boys of California. And Mr. F. M. Pixley, who is not in any danger of being defended in Chinatown, had an argument that was personal enough to be entertaining to a crowd.

Both men are proud of their championship—the one of coolie and the other of white labor. The clergyman charged his opponent with acting from self interests, and the retort was much to the same effect—that the divine was only preaching as he was paid, and that none but men who are making money out of the cheapness and nastiness of coolieism favor this element in the labor market. The conversation then became bitter and exasperating, and eventually the preacher blurted out, "You're a liar sir."

Some of those who heard him say that he repeated this remark. It is certain that Mr. Brier was asked to take the words back. He hesitated about doing so, whereupon Mr. Pixley struck him on the left cheek. The blow brought the divine to his senses. "Mr. Pixley, you know that I cannot resent your blows." The anti-coolie champion answered, "Oh, don't skulk to the church defiant. You are under your cloth. Come out for once and belong to the church militant. You are as big a man as I am. You gave the lie and you've got the blow." This ended the difficulty. Neither party deemed it advisable to court the interference of a policeman.

This editorial included the nickname that he would carry to his old age, the "Champion to the Coolies." Brier was embarrassed by the false report of his violent encounter and responded with a letter to the editor to clarify what happened. In the *Alameda County Independent*, he writes this letter to the editor with his account of the incident. His version of the story is the most complete and the most colorful.

Alameda County Independent
December 2, 1876

Letter to the Editor from the Rev. W.W. Brier

"The other papers caught their items from the Call's newspaper man, and all have presented a one-sided report to throw blame upon me.

The simple facts of the case are these: The question had been up before the Commission of cutting off the Chinamen's cue, when imprisoned for violating the law of sleeping in too close quarters. I remarked to Mr. Pixley as I went out that it seemed hard to cut off the badge of nationality from a Chinaman for an offense so small.

He seemed to be angry because he saw that he had been badly beaten before the Commission, and answered, with an oath, that he would cut all their heads off and would throw them in the Pacific ocean if he could.

I said, "Mr. Pixley you must see from the testimony that a large number of the people of California differ from you in this matter."

He flew into a rage and began to curse the preachers—said they had got up this defense and "we will drive them all out of the country too"

"Now," said I, "Mr. Pixley, you will find men of nerve in this State to stop all this mob movement." After some conversation on this subject, he desiring to insult me as he did from the commencement of my testimony, broke out against the preachers, and said, "Gibson, Loomis, Shearer and you are a G-d,d—d pack of thieves and get your salaries from Boston."

I said, "Mr. Pixley, that's a lie."

He rushed up and said, "Do you call me a liar?"

I said, "No!

He said, "Then you apologize to me!"

I said, "I simply said what you uttered was not true."

He said, "That was not what you said."

I said, "The words were, 'that's a lie!"

He did not seem to want to fight, but to make me believe, he gave no small capital, and provoked me to make an attack, with his friends in the room and mine all gone.

I had no disposition to fight. He began to take hold of my whiskers with his fingers, (I suppose to draw my eyes away from his,) and struck me on the cheek a slight blow, then stepped back to the other side of the room.

I said, "No one but a coward and a brute would strike a woman or a Preacher."

After some other like consoling remarks I went out. The matter was in such a shape that I couldn't escape blame by some.

Some blame me for not knocking him down. If I had, as I might have done, others would have blamed me. I simply held to my principles, never to fight except to repel bodily injury.

W. W. Brier

He was never afraid of a controversial position! He continued to have Chinese laborers on his farm and insisted that Chinese families be buried in the Centerville Church Cemetery alongside other pioneers of the community.

CHAPTER 59

The State of the Church

The duties of the stated clerk included filing a written report to be read to the entire gathering of the Synod when they met once a year. Brier's report on San Jose Presbytery notes,

"The past has been a year of several important changes in the pastorate. Several of our churches receive aid from the Board of Home Missions, and none of them have become self-supporting during the year. This owes in a large degree, to the unsettled state of the population which in turn has its influence in producing an unsettled state of the ministry, both of which evils are however steadily decreasing. The financial condition of the churches is on the whole quite encouraging. The building of a house of worship by one church, the paying of an harassing debt by another, the adoption of the weekly envelope system by others with marked dates, are some of the reports of good progress with financial difficulty, but now of unusual importance.

A steady flow of immigration during the year has largely increased the home Mission population, and the judicious policy pursued by the land-owners in many parts of our State, or offering land in small farms to actual settlers, and especially to colonies, offers to the Presbyterian Church promising fields of labor—in excess of our present ability to cultivate.

There are many difficulties peculiar to the Pacific Coast, with which we have to contend, but none which the Gospel is not able to overcome. The irreligious influence of the early immigration to this coast still makes itself felt. Many are yet drawn neither by the greed of gold, nor by an honest desire for homes. And the love of money proves itself to be the root of all evil. The world had the start in the settlement of the coast, but the church is surely overtaking it: for which all praise be to God." [125]

In the October, 1876, minutes of the Synod of the Pacific Rev. Brier and his committee presented an elaborate report on the districting of each Presbytery and the cost of each church sending a delegate of a minister and an elder. The estimates would be that $2,000.00 would be expended for this annual meeting, and it would be funded by the dues of each congregation, with any fare over $5.00 to be reimbursed by the Presbytery. The burden of connecting with other pastors and elders was remarkable. It was 27 miles by horseback or buggy from Centerville, and for the three-day Presbytery meeting he must have found housing with a family in the area and a suitable stable for his horse.

Brier was also chair of the Committee on Records and Minutes and requested to examine the minutes of the Presbytery of Oregon, which had been delinquent for some time. He wrote, "Two churches have become self-supporting. There is very little church debt, and a growing disposition to contribute to the boards. Although some efforts have been made to hold revival meetings, no great outpouring of the Spirit has been experienced, yet reward has been given for faithful labor."

W. W. Brier Stated Clerk

CHAPTER 60

General Assembly Commissioner

In 1876 Brier was once again elected a delegate to the General Assembly of the Presbyterian Church. The Assembly was held May 18 at Brooklyn, New York, at Tabernacle Presbyterian Church. Brier was appointed to serve on the committee of Home Missions. Further minutes of the Assembly note that he was elected to a third term on the board of directors of San Francisco Theological Seminary.

He is listed again as the stated supply pastor at Milpitas, with 19 members in the church and 30 students in Sunday School. He is also listed as Exploring Agent of the Church.

1877

In 1877 Rev. Brier was elected to a fourth term at San Francisco Theological Seminary. Some historians have suggested that after the initial resistance by SFTS trustees over his failure to raise funds, Brier faded from leadership. This could not be true, as by 1877 he had been on the board of trustees for nine years, and he was elected to another four years.[126]

Coming back from General Assembly, Brier brought many new ideas and much passion to the Home Mission Committee.

"A discussion of much interest was had on the Subject of Home Mission and the necessity of a Presbyterial Missionary. On October 5, 1877, a report reads as follows; The Special committee to whom was referred the matter of the appointment of a Presbyterial Missionary, recommends the adoption of the following memorial to the Board of Home Missions. The Presbytery of San Jose Cal. would represent to the Board of Home Missions that we have large destitutions within our bounds—new regions of very rich lands are rapidly settling up—new towns are springing up—the faithful and able Synodical Missionary

has so wide a field that he cannot give the needed time to these fields of destitution in our bounds. We therefore request the Board of Home Missions to appoint a Presbyterial Missionary, to labor in our bounds—We believe that a larger proportion of the support of such a missionary could be secured in the fields that he should cultivate, than can the Synodical Missionary, and that his work would so interest our churches as to increase their contributions to the funds of the Board."

He added a call for on going support of full-time church planters, called Presbyterial Missionary, *"in each of the Presbyteries of Los Angeles, San Jose, Benicia, and Sacramento, to go into forming communities and remain until churches are organized and houses of worship are built—men of experience in laying the foundations of churches. Unless we enter upon the work with more earnestness, the church in California will relatively go backwards. Should we contribute at the rate on one dollar for each member of our churches, that amount would exceed that appropriated by the Board for our feeble churches during the past year.*

From the report of the Synodical Missionary we learn that nine new churches have been organized, and those chiefly in the small towns and in the country places throughout the State, giving evidence that the world of the churches is spreading, by a natural process, from the larger centers, where the wisdom of former workers had laid the foundation of these results."[127]

An interesting observation from the April 25, 1877, minutes of the Presbytery, is the inventory of the congregations. The twenty churches of the Presbytery are listed: Milpitas, Salinas City, Hollister, San Leandro, Centerville, Alvarado, San Jose, Watsonville, Livermore, Menlo Park, Gilroy, Visalia, Yule Rivers, Bakersfield, Cambria, San Louis Obispo, Arroyo Grande, Mayfield, Pleasanton, and Santa Clara.

It is interesting to note that Brier had chartered seven of them.

The Presbytery of San Jose meeting minutes of April 9th, 1878 recall that, "W. W. Brier, Historian of Presbytery, made a report. The time in which to furnish histories was extended until the fall meeting and he was instructed to notify brethren not present of the fact."

1879

There was a bit of unfinished business that Brier wanted to tackle in his role as stated clerk. He wanted to resolve the legality of who should be allowed to vote on the calling of a pastor to any particular congregation. This was part of the painful past in his experience in San Jose in 1850, where the members who voted in Isaac Brayton were all members of a single family. It also brought back the pain of Brier's experience in Marysville in 1852, when he was voted out by the rallying of some members who had not been attending. At the Presbytery of San Jose meeting on October 4th, 1879: "Rev. W. W. Brier read a paper on the question 'Who should vote in the election of a Pastor.' After much discussion, the Presbytery laid it over for future consideration."

At the same meeting the Presbytery voted an enabling motion which would allow him to begin a new congregation he had already been leading: "*W. W. Brier was appointed to organize a church in Milpitas if the way seems clear.*"

Brier is listed in the *General Assembly Statistical Report* as serving as stated supply Pastor at Milpitas Township, with 13 founding members, and 70 in Sunday School. He was paid $150.00 for his services. He is also listed as stated supply pastor for Livermore Presbyterian Church, which had added 3 members, to a total membership of 14 members.

1881

General Assembly Commissioner.

Rev. Brier in 1880 (age 59)
Photo courtesy of Doug Kinney

Being elected as a commissioner became a natural act for Brier. At one level, he was the natural choice; he had outlasted most of the pastors who came to California, he had no congregational pastoral duties to hold him down from traveling, and he had the farm income to supplement his travel expenses. As the stated clerk of the Presbytery, with fewer than thirty pastors, there were not too many pastors to choose from.

In the 1860's the national church realized that they had a problem with fair representation from pastors on the West Coast. Few ministers or elders could afford the trip to General Assembly on a yearly basis. It was reasonable to expect that congregations east of the Mississippi could pay the expenses of travel to the yearly meeting. It was a hardship for young churches and young presbyteries to be saddled with the extreme costs.

The Presbytery initiated a nationwide per capita travel apportionment, assessed on a membership basis to each congregation. This would then be a pooled fund to reimburse the cost of every delegate's travel expense and became the foundations for a sharing of expenses for the administrative cost of the church.

Brier was elected to be the commissioner to the meeting in Buffalo, New York, and he went again to the Assembly, traveling ten days to reach the East Coast. Along the way home, he would attend the class reunion of his alma mater, Wabash College.

From May 19 to the 28, he served on the Committee of Leave of Absences, which reviewed the status of pastors who are no longer serving congregations, and discerned whether to continue their ordination for the ministry of Word and Sacrament. In his report to the committee, he noted that there were currently 122 ministers serving in churches in California, 7 ministers who had no churches, and over 40 churches without a pastor.

This trip gave him an opportunity to see his family and friends and visit his alma mater, Wabash College.

The years have changed him. He is a mature man walking onto the tree-shrouded campus. This was more than a homecoming for Brier. He returns to his home city and county, even to his own alma mater, as a hero. What greater stature could he have dreamed of when he walked the hallways of Wabash college—the very college which set its goal to train teachers, preachers, and missionaries from the heart of the farmland in northern Indiana?

He had been eminently successful in all four of these arenas. He had worked so intensely in the ministry and returned with a cluster of congregations planted in the rugged soil of California and Nevada. He had a hand in founding schools at every level from the local barnyard school building to the regional college and the College of California. He had been a church leader and elder statesman at the highest levels, as Stated Clerk, Moderator of Presbytery, and Moderator of the Synod. He had been a successful farmer, establishing a productive fruit farm, and had a large year round Chinese crew working his land while he worked to change society for the Kingdom of God.

When he went to school, he made quite a splash. Brier walked into the graduation ceremonies as the conquering hero. In the forty years since his graduation, the Wabash faculty had changed. None of the original teachers remained, but he found little difficulty in establishing his legend at the school. He arrived like a prophet from the western desert, with the flowing gray beard. He was immediately introduced to the student body and asked to say the opening prayer at the commencement celebrations. It was like a homecoming in which his ministry is celebrated. In the Wabash College newspaper, the *Lariat,* from June 22, 1881, there is a note "that the Rev. W. W. Brier, class of 1846, all the way from California, is hand-shaking among old classmates and acquaintances. He invoked the divine blessing at Commencement in a crowded church. Thirty-five years after his graduation, he is nearly 56 yrs old." [128]

His return to California from the East Coast took three weeks. He may have stopped in Indiana to visit friends and family. By April 1880 the Presbytery of San Jose has 949 church members. At end of 1881 there are 996 members. There are 22 churches. This was a very good year. Brier is back in the saddle, not just managing church conflict, but exploring new communities and testing the waters for the establishment of Presbyterian churches. He began doing the most roaming in 20 years since his Nevada days. Brier spent months at a time in the Santa Barbara area, encouraging leaders and chartering congregations as he traveled by train, stagecoach, and buggy. The area was developing rapidly, and he saw the need for many new congregations. And the travel also convinced him that the time would soon come when this region would no longer fit into the Presbytery. At the Presbytery of San Jose meeting of October 6, 1881, he was officially recognized for this traveling role when "Rev. W. W. Brier and the Rev. T. M. Oviatt were appointed Presbyterial Evangelists to labor under the direction of the Committee of Home Missions for one year of 1881-1885."

His visit to General Assembly led to a local, more limited role for him as a Presbyterian. One year later, at the Presbytery of San Jose Meeting on Oct. 3, 1882, Brier and Oviatt were continued as evangelists within the bounds of Presbytery for the ensuing year. He continued to hold multiple roles. In the General Assembly Statistical Report for year 1882, it is reported that W.W. Brier continues as Stated Supply at Milpitas, which has 17 members and 40 in Sunday School.

CHAPTER 61

Signposts on the Frontier:
Women Should Have a Vote!

It would be unfair to discuss crucial issues in the life of the post-gold rush society and the church without highlighting the growing national movement to give women the right to vote. The quest for the vote of women was beginning to gather steam nationally and had its compliment in the life of the church. Free wheeling Californian society seemed to have the best potential for overcoming the barriers to women.

From the years 1850 to 1860 the woman's rights movement was not focused upon getting the vote but simply in gaining the rights to property and family. Intense legal battles emerged to secure equality in the control of property, earnings, guardianship, divorce, and opportunity for education and employment. The churches of both New School and Old School began to embrace these issues as legitimate and worthy of being changed.

There was Presbytery action in 1885 to promote change in the life of women. *"The following overture to the General Assembly was adopted: The action of General Assembly of 1884 in regard to the election of Deaconesses: Since 'in all ages of the church Godly women have been appointed to aid the officers of the church in their labor especially for the relief of the poor and the infirm,' is it not the right and privilege of any of our churches which chooses to do so to elect godly women to act as Deaconess?"[129]*

The church was moving toward change, but it was a slow process. Women in the church often provided leadership through the mission societies, through the study group Presbyterian Women, and through their serving and teaching roles throughout the church. There were three official leadership roles in Presbyterian congregations: trustees, deacons, and elders.

The first official role of women came quite early when the Centerville Presbyterian Church elected Mrs. Clara (nee Hawley) Patterson as a trustee in 1878, a role that seemed uncontested because it dealt with financial matters, not spiritual. Clara was the wife of Ardenwood farmer George Patterson and had been with the Centerville Church since its founding. Clara continued as a trustee of the church following George's death and also during her marriage to Rev. Layson, who served the Newark Presbyterian congregation.

The elders of the church are often viewed as the spiritual leaders. This office was barred to women until the early 1930's. On April 4, 1938 the first two women elders were elected by the Centerville congregation: Mrs. J. S. Bell, and Mrs. Olive Anderson. They both had served a decade as trustees, and they continued for many years as faithful elders.

The leadership of women as pastors in the church came slowly as well. Although Centerville affirmed the role of Sunday School Superintendent for long term leaders like Mary Van Winkle and was the supporter of many single and married women missionaries, they were reluctant to actually call a female pastor. The congregation waited until 1995, when they called the Rev. Marsha Roth as associate pastor for evangelism and discipleship.

One of the first American denominations to advocate and embrace women in leadership, the Presbyterians began to move toward having women in the leadership role of deacons in early 1885. The role of deacons was to provide care in merciful ministries. The Centerville Presbyterian Church did not elect women to the role of deacons due to the small size of the church, with 25 people in worship on Sunday mornings, they did not have elected deacons.

1883

In the *General Assembly Statistical Report* for 1883, noted that Brier was elected to the board of directors of San Francisco Theological Seminary for a fifth term and that he is an evangelist with San Jose Presbytery. During the year Brier traveled up and down the coast, from Santa Barbara to San Jose and through the Central Valley, supporting the pastors and congregations.

The Brier family continued to model a passion for ministry. His nephew, John Brier, was transferred from the Congregational Church in Lodi. At the San Jose Presbytery meeting at Santa Clara, April 3, 1883 "The Rev. John W. Brier was received from the Valley Association, after having been examined in Theology and experimental Religion. "The Presbytery records note that William's son, elder W.W. Brier Jr., was present as well."

1884

In the *General Assembly Statistical Report*, Brier continues to be listed as an Evangelist for the San Jose Presbytery, without a specific church assignment.

This meeting of Presbytery was his final meeting as Stated Clerk. W. W. Brier, F. L. Nash, and Elder Frank H. Babb were appointed to apply to the National Board for the appointment of a Missionary to labor as a Presbyterial Missionary. Presbytery of San Jose Meeting Minutes, Watsonville, April 8, 1884.

We know that the aging Brier was still involved in farming. Yet at this point, he had turned the management of the farm over to his son, William Jr., who had graduated from the university in Berkeley and was involved in teaching at the Alvarado school. In his early thirties, he was already emerging as a leader: he served as an elder in the Centerville Presbyterian Church and was already a delegate to Presbytery.

During these summers, William Wallace Brier was still winning blue ribbons at the Alameda county fair for his apricot fruit and had a number of horses. In the family records is a bill of sale from a neighboring farmer for the purchase of a horse for $100.00.

By 1884, the Brier farm was one of the most noted farms in the area, with mature fruit trees, and crops that would support several people. And yet it was the sunset of his life. It was time to divest, sell off many things. The Lord was not finished with him, or his legacy. He was still a risk taker. He was making the spiritual and social capital work for him and his descendants.

CHAPTER 62

A Surprising Legacy in Porterville

During the 1880's Brier invested a great deal of time saving a church that was struggling in the central California valley. *The History of Kern County* paints this delightful picture of the village of Porterville: "Porterville is a historical town, and one that must be known to be appreciated. By the census of 1890 it had a population of 606, which is increasing rapidly. This prosperous town is situated about twenty-two miles southeast of Tulare City, and on the new railroad line that was recently constructed by the Southern Pacific Company, running from Fresno city on the main line and connecting again therewith at Plano, Kern County. While Porterville is at the base of the foothill, the hills are not near enough to cramp the place, but just enough to give beauty and picturesqueness to the view, and makes the town one of the handsomest locations in the state. The town is about one mile from Tule river and upon the edge of a series of undulates which are becoming highly appreciated."[130]

It makes us wonder what attracted Brier to this town, so remote in the San Joauqin Valley. It may have been that the rail line had just been established through the town, and the town showed more promise than just a dry farming community. In many ways, it may have reminded him of the early days in Centerville. The churches at Porterville and neighboring Plano got back on their feet, grew in membership, and had finally paid off church construction debts. At the next Presbytery meeting it was noted, "Rev. W. W. Brier reported that the churches of Plano and Porterville were both out of debt. Rev Dr. Babb was appointed to prepare a minute expressing the sentiments of the Presbytery with reference to Plano church and thanking Rev W. W. Brier for his efficient services in securing these churches from debt."

The Presbytery remarked about his extraordinary contribution to save this church from failure. "The special thanks of the presbytery is hereby tendered to our Stated Clerk, Rev W. W. Brier for his untiring efforts to save this Porterville church, and for his large donation towards the liquidation of its debt."

This was a crowning moment of glory for Brier. He had thrived as a farmer and a preacher for twenty years since he set foot on the California shore. Yet in that time, following his rejection from Marysville, he established the home farm in Centerville. Many of his colleagues saw this as turning away from his primary calling of planting and nurturing churches. It created wonderful opportunities for him in the later chapters of his ministry. He discovered that he was able to support struggling churches with the farm income he had. When he came across these congregations, he knew that God had called him not only to provide temporary leadership for them while they sought a pastor but also that God had provided so abundantly through his farm that he could share "the fruit of his labors."

Presbytery also voted "That the Committee of Church Erection find out what Sum will Secure the church, free of all debt, the church building at Plano, and to make application to the Board for the amount, with a Statement of its facts." April 13th, 1881, "It was resolved that the Presbytery deem it necessary to save the Plano church, and strongly recommend that the Board of Church Erection appropriate $600 the amount necessary for that purpose, and if they grant this request, we pledge ourselves, as a Presbytery, to do our best to raise at least one half this amount for the Board, during this year."

Plano was fifteen miles south of Porterville, and with the extension of rail lines through the San Joaquin Valley, there was an opportunity to settle communities throughout the valley. Plano and Porterville were thought to be the next breadbaskets for the West Coast. The farms were limited to dry range farming, with insufficient water resources to allow crops to be nurtured for very long.

1885

Rev. Brier in 1885 (Age 64)
Photo from Centerville Presbyterian Archives

In the *General Assembly Statistical Report* for 1885, it was reported that Brier is the Superintendent of the Presbytery of San Jose. Brier oversaw the administrative work of bringing two new congregations into the Presbytery of San Jose. "The first Presbyterian Church of Arroyo Grande and the Mayfield Presbyterian Church were received under the Care of Presbytery by their request, presently by the W.W. Brier." [131] Mayfield was in the present day neighborhood of Stanford University, and Arroyo Grande is in Santa Barbara County.

CHAPTER 63

Declining Health

1886

Brier's last Presbytery meeting was in January of 1886. He was absent at the April 5 meeting of Presbytery. Family records state that he had a brain illness, and struggled for the next fourteen months before his death. In those days, it was common to describe a stroke as a sudden onset brain illness. The patient was often cared for at their home. The Presbytery makes note of his illness in the minutes from their meeting of March.

The following resolution was adopted: *"Whereas the Presbytery has learned with deep sorrow of the feeble health of the Rev. W. W. Brier, the only one of the original members of this body now connected with it and recalls with deep and grateful interest his long and faithful service in building up the cause of Christ on this coast, therefore resolved that we unite in earnest pray to God on behalf of our beloved brother and send our esteem to his family the assurance of our deep and earnest sympathy."*

The *San Francisco Examiner* of May 13, 1886, noted a wedding that took place in Centerville, the Trumbull/Brier wedding at the residence of W.W.Brier in Centerville. This would be the wedding of his youngest daughter, married on the farm. It is curious that it did not take place in the Centerville Church, but on the family farm. The minister was not listed, which suggests that it was not W.W. Brier himself. One logical explanation is that since William Brier was stricken and in bed, the family moved the wedding to him so he could be present.

William Wallace Brier died when he was sixty-six years old. He left a legacy in his five children, and a significant legacy in his family farm. But an even greater legacy in the spiritual life of the congregations he planted and nurtured. His obituary was recounted in the *Occident* June 8, 1887, just five days after his death.

"Another of that heroic band of pioneer ministers who first unfurled the banner of the Cross on the Pacific Coast is gone.

Reverend W.W. Brier died at his residence near Centerville on Friday, June 3, 1887, after a lingering illness. He was born near Dayton, Ohio, November 6, 1821. He moved to Indiana with his parent when five years old. After completing his preparatory studies he entered Wabash College, and graduated in 1846. He entered Lane Seminary under the tuition of Dr. Lyman Beecher and was graduated there having been licensed to preach in 1848, and for two years preached at Romney, Indiana. On December 19, 1849 he was married to Elizabeth Naylor of Crawfordsville. He then came to California, in 1850 under the appointment of the American Home Missionary Society and settled in Marysville.

When his health failed in that climate in 1852 he came to the Santa Clara Valley, and settled near Centerville where he has resided ever since. He organized and built the churches of Centerville and Alvarado, of which he was the pastor for the first eight years. In 1860 he resigned in order to accept the appointment of District Secretary for Home Missions in California and Nevada.

Brother Brier's funeral was attended on Sabbath, June 5th, by a large concourse of his brethren, friends and neighbors. Rev. Dr. Alexander, an old friend and a former pastor of the family, conducted the services.

He was ably assisted by Rev. H. H. Dobbins and J. Lundy, present minister of the Centerville church. The music rendered by the choir was tender and appropriate. Dr. Alexander in his address alluded very feelingly to his early acquaintance with the deceased soon after his arrival on this coast, at San Jose in 1869. He spoke of the many sterling qualities of the man, the frank and open candor of his disposition, the steadiness and fidelity of his friendships, the robust vigor of his physical, and intellectual powers, the life-long zeal and energy of his devotion to Home Missions. When asked by the Secretary of that day, where he would like to go, his reply was, "Give me the hardest place you have." He was in a sense the father of San Jose Presbytery. Not only to the Churches of Centreville and Alvarado, but those of Livermore, Pleasanton, and Milpitas allowed their existence to him, as did also the churches of Marysville and Placerville, and perhaps others in Sacramento Presbytery.

A great deal of this labor was performed gratuitously and often at his own expense.

And he was a liberal contributor to the funds of the church, and especially to the Home Board. In the last year of his life he established, largely at this own expense, a depository of the Board of Publications in this city, which does his son conduct. One of the last acts of his life was a gift of one thousand dollars toward the endowment of the Theological Seminary, of which he has been a Director from the beginning.

Brother Dobbins referred to Mr. Brier's courage, and his disposition to encourage and strengthen the weak. As instances, he mentioned how came the relief of the churches of Gilroy, Watsonville, Salinas, and Porterville when in a weak and discouraged state. He spoke of his ready sympathy with the suffering and distressed, and his thorough integrity and honesty in financial and business transactions. He alluded to his unvarying friendship with the deceased for fifteen years.

Mr. Lundy spoke very briefly of the kindness of the deceased to him as a student, and as a young and inexperienced minister, and of the benefit of his fatherly counsels.

Mr. Brier was one of the most faithful of all our ministers in his attendance upon the judicatories of the church. He was Moderator of the Synod of Alta California at San Jose in 1859, and Moderator of the (reunited) Synod of the Pacific in the same place in 1871. For many years he was Stated Clerk of the Presbytery of San Jose. No minister of the coast represented one presbytery in the General Assembly so often as he did.

After a life of toil and self-denial, our brother has crossed over the river to rest under the shade of the trees, and to behold the King in his beauty.

Mr. Brier came of a sturdy Scotch heritage. As a preacher he was strong and vigorous, uncompromising with error, and often eloquent. Brother Brier leaves a widow and five children, for whom he was enabled during his life to make a comfortable provision. Three of his daughters are happily married, his son and one daughter remaining at home unmarried. All have received a good and liberal education, and the Brier Mansion has long been known for its pleasant and generous hospitality."

His death was announced at the Presbytery the next October, and a rare written memorial to him was entered into the minutes of the October 8, 1887, meeting. *"The great Head of the Church, having translated into heaven our Brother Rev. William Wallace Brier since our last meeting: we as bereaved co-presbyters would put on record our high appreciation of his personal worth and of his great usefulness as one of the pioneer ministers of this coast. We would emphasize his fidelity to this Presbytery of which he was one of the original members, and whose meetings he never failed to attend when it was possible for him to do so. He organized not a few of the churches under the care of this presbytery. He bore them all upon his heart and aided many of them with his counsel and his money. Though he rests from his labors, his works follow him. To his family we extend the assurance of our warmest sympathy and our fervent prayers."[132]*

CHAPTER 64

Epilogue : The Earth Shook, the Sky Burned

At the moment the clocks stopped on April 16, 1906, Mary Brier Moores was fifty years old. She was born in San Jose to pioneer parents Elizabeth and William Wallace Brier, who came in the 1850's in search of the golden souls of men and women who would be claimed for the Presbyterian Church.

Mary was still grieving over her father's death in 1887. Most of his personal effects were left with her brother, who had made a career of teaching and farming in the Centerville area. After moving to San Francisco, she had gathered some mementos from the family home in Centerville but had not looked at them since her mother Elizabeth had moved to Los Angeles.

But her world changed on that clear morning. The great earthquake split the earth in two, and with it separated all of western American history into what happened before, and what happened after the quake. In the early hours after the quake, tens of thousands of residents crowded the city street corners and accounted for the damage to their buildings and the dead in their neighborhoods. But then a more menacing threat began to loom on the horizon. A fire began in a restaurant, which led to the nickname of "the ham and eggs fire" that started as a single fire and built into a inferno that consumed most of the city as it swept from midtown to the eastern shore of the San Francisco Bay. Firefighters found they were helpless against its advance.

By late morning the families were given false assurance that the fire might turn on itself, and they would be able to return to their apartments by the next morning. But it was not to be. The earthquake had reduced many apartments to kindling. Others were steadfast, but filled with broken glass, toppled bookcases, torn draperies that fluttered outside of open windows. Residents had fled the buildings in haste but now stood in awe of the billowing plumes of smoke that filled the sky like a curtain of Black Death, sweeping block-by-block across the city. Panicked residents re-entered the buildings to rescue what valuables they could carry, but there were no wagons available, as the operable wagons were attempting to unload valuable records in the financial district. Most roads were blocked with rubble anyway, with the cobblestone pavement ripped open and rippled by the earthquake. Making recovery more treacherous, live overhead electric wires from the streetcars lay tangled throughout the narrow city streets.

The fire brought the entire population of San Francisco to a standstill. It if was not the trauma of the earthquake, it was the powerful aftershocks that left everyone with a feeling of terror. Time was running out. The wind from the fire blanketed the neighborhood in soot. In a matter of minutes, it became clear to the residents that they would need to evacuate their apartments. In the course of April 17 and April 18, there were not enough hours in the day to evacuate many of the valuables. Residents scrambled onto the streets with whatever they could carry.

Charles and Mary Moore owned an apartment at 1518 Larkin Street, near the corner of Sacramento Street and Larkin. After the trauma of the quake, the Moore family evacuated to the nearby city park, to assess the damage. Smoke rose quickly over the neighborhoods to the north. They watched from their high vantage point. The fire started in the west, near the corner of Hayes Street, and the flames spread toward the east, consuming over 200 city blocks, or nearly a third of the city. Residents in the north east and north west part of the city, whose homes were in the triangle of three hills, (Russian Hill, Nob Hill, and Telegraph Hill) thought their homes would be spared from the flames as the fire rushed down to the bay water's edge and burned out. But the next day, the flames began to roar again, this time roaring from the inland bay westward. The fires spread twenty blocks before consuming the Moore apartment, and continued on another six blocks before the fire was put out near Franklin Street.

The depth and detail of their loss was not apparent at first to Mary Brier Moore. There were so many things that she was sorry about: her photographs, her collection of English teacups, and her cultivated orchids. But as the days went on, she began to grieve over her many other losses. She grieved the most over the loss of her family trunk and over the complete loss of her father's records and manuscript of the history of the Presbyterian Church in the gold rush era.

Just a few weeks earlier, she had been sifting through her father's trunk when she discovered a sheaf of papers that had yellowed in the nineteen years since his death. William Wallace Brier was working on a definitive history of San Francisco and San Jose Presbytery during the gold rush, when he experienced a debilitating stroke. He was disabled and languished in the upper bedroom of his Centerville farmhouse for over a year.

We have evidence of this loss from San Francisco Seminary professor of history Edward Wicher who wrote,

"It is, unhappily, impossible now to trace all the activities of some of the pioneers of 1849 and 1850. Mr. Brier was himself appointed the historian of the Synod of Alta California in 1858, and it would appear that he prepared a large amount of historical manuscript. This manuscript was completely lost until shortly before the fire of 1906, when his daughter, Mrs. Moore, discovered it among some old possessions. But before it could be used, it was destroyed in the great fire shortly after the date of finding. If it still existed it would probably make clear to us several points upon which now we have no light."[133]

With Brier's records destroyed by the fire, this book is an attempt to reconstruct what was lost, not as a definitive history of the Synod, but as a reconstruction of Brier's inspiring ministry.

Modern Day Analysis of the Churches Brier Planted.

The Brier family Bible lists the following churches he planted.

The current membership of these 29 congregations he founded or served is listed.

Indiana Churches

Romney	1848	Closed
Wea Presbyterian	1848	Closed
West Point	1848	Closed
Hickory Cross	1849	Closed

California Churches

Marysville	1850	220
Grass Valley	1852	Closed
Centerville	1853	725
Eden	1854	Closed
Santa Cruz (Congregational)	1857	375
Alvarado	1860	Closed
San Leandro	1864	263
Red Bluff	1860	100
Brooklyn Oakland	1860	Closed
Alameda	1864	142
Gilroy	1860	723
Watsonville	1863	172
Milpitas	1871	662
Livermore	1871	723
Pleasanton	1871	602

Porterville	1870/1890	83
Salinas	1869/1872	1742
Nevada		
Virginia City	1860	83
Carson City	1862	514
Elko	1870	313
Eureka	1873	Closed
Austin	1864	Closed
Pioche	1874	Closed
Gold Hill	1862	Closed
Hamilton	1869	Closed

Current membership of the churches he served   7,442

Centerville Presbyterian Church congregation
Celebrating the 150th anniversary of its founding.
Pastor Greg and Marsha Roth are in photo dressed as Rev. and Mrs. Brier
Photo by permission of Dianne Wood Photography

"To Him who overcomes I will make a pillar in the temple of my God,
and he will go out no more."

ENDNOTES

1   *Wabash College The First Hundred Years*, James Osborne, and Theodore Gronert, p. 106

2   ibid, p. 91

3   Family Records, including the Obituary for William Wallace Brier, in the Crawfordsville, Indiana newspapers following his death in 1888 remember his attendance "under the tuition of Lyman Beecher at Lane."

4   *The Autobiography of Lyman Beecher,* ed. Barbara M. Cross, volume 2, p. 167 as quoted in Rugoff p. 78

5   *A Plea for the West*, Henry Ward Beecher p.11

6   *A Plea for the West*, Henry Ward Beecher p.47

7   *Student Handbook* from Lane Seminary 1845, p 51

8   *Brier letter To AHMS* March 1, 1849/ American Home Missionary Society Archives, Amistad Research Center at Tulane University

9   *Brier letter to AHMS* Unnumbered/ American Home Missionary Society Archives, Amistad Research Center at Tulane University

10   *Brier Letter to AHMS*, letter #1650 American Home Missionary Society Archives, Amistad Research Center at Tulane University

11   *Brier Letter to AHMS*, March 1, 1849/American Home Missionary Society Archives, Amistad Research Center at Tulane University

12   *Brier Letter to AHMS*, Unnumbered in file dated August 22, 1849/ American Home Missionary Society Archives, Amistad Research Center at Tulane University

13   *Brier Letter to AHMS*, dated 25 November, 1849/ American Home Missionary Society Archives, Amistad Research Center at Tulane University

14   *A Plea for the West*, Henry Ward Beecher, p. 86

15   *Henry Ward Beecher*, p. 86

16   *Crawfordsville Journal,* November 3, 1888

17   *Crawfordsville Journal,* November 3, 1888

18   *AHMS Administrative Letter,* #1631/ American Home Missionary Society Archives, Amistad Research Center at Tulane University

19   *AHMS Administrative Letter,* # 1799, AHMS to Douglas/ American Home Missionary Society Archives, Amistad Research Center at Tulane University

20   *AHMS Administrative Letter,* #2113/ American Home Missionary Society Archives, Amistad Research Center at Tulane University

21   *AHMS Administrative Letter/* American Home Missionary Society Archives, Amistad Research Center at Tulane University

22   *AHMS Response Letter,* # 2299/ American Home Missionary Society Archives, Amistad Research Center at Tulane University

23   *Gold Rush Album,* p. 112

24   *Gold Rush Album,* p. 113

25   *Panama Route,* by Kembler, p.172

26   *Gold Rush Album,* p.116

27   *Brier Family Oral History.* When I met with Mary Louise Brier Facca, a descendent of Elizabeth Brier in Red Bluff, California area, nearly 151 years after the Briers crossed Panama, she told me the family story about Elizabeth ruining her shoes, not knowing why she walked across the Isthmus. The power of the oral tradition is strong indeed.

28   *The Panama Route to the Gold Fields,* p.42

29   *San Francisco Ship Passenger Lists,* Louis Rasmussen, Vol 1

30   *Letter from Willey to the AHMS,* May 27, 1850/ American Home Missionary Society Archives, Amistad Research Center at Tulane University

31   *Missionary Life California Life Illustrated,* Taylor p.63/ American Home Missionary Society Archives, Amistad Research Center at Tulane University

32   *AHMS Reference Letter,* # 00813/ American Home Missionary Society Archives, Amistad Research Center at Tulane University

33   *California Historical Quarterly,* p. 44

34   *AHMS Microfilm Letter* From Willey January 9, 1851/ American Home Missionary Society Archives, Amistad Research Center at Tulane University

35   *More Gleanings from Alta California.* Mary Dean Walsworth p.1

36   *AHMS Microfilm letter,* # 00813/ American Home Missionary Society Archives, Amistad Research Center at Tulane University

37   *AHMS Microfilm letter,* # 00824/ American Home Missionary Society Archives, Amistad Research Center at Tulane University

38   *AHMS Microfilm letter,* # 2158/ American Home Missionary Society Archives, Amistad Research Center at Tulane University

39   *AHMS Administrative letter,* #2158/ American Home Missionary Society Archives, Amistad Research Center at Tulane University

40   *More Gleanings from Alta California,* Alsworth, Mary Dean, 1851

41   *Brayton to the AHMS Board,* April 1850/ American Home Missionary Society Archives, Amistad Research Center at Tulane University

42   *California Historical Quarterly,*

43   *AHMS Response letter,* Microfilm #2316/ American Home Missionary Society Archives, Amistad Research Center at Tulane University

[44] *AHMS Microfilm letter,* #00854/ American Home Missionary Society Archives, Amistad Research Center at Tulane University

[45] *Marysville Herald,* November 14, 1851

[46] *Benton letter to AHMS* October 13, 1851/ American Home Missionary Society Archives, Amistad Research Center at Tulane University

[47] *AHMS Microfilm letter,* # 00861/ American Home Missionary Society Archives, Amistad Research Center at Tulane University

[48] *Rev. Willey Letter to the AHMS,* 4th May 1852/ American Home Missionary Society Archives, Amistad Research Center at Tulane University

[49] *AHMS letter to Willey* June 22, 1852/ American Home Missionary Society Archives, Amistad Research Center at Tulane University

[50] *The History of Santa Clara County Pioneers*

[51] From City of Fremont Museum of Local History file on E.L. Beard.

[52] From City of Fremont Museum of Local History File on E.L. Beard

[53] *History of Washington Township.* p. 147

[54] Wood, M.W. *A History of Alameda County California,* Oakland, 1883 p.102

[55] *The Centennial Year Book of Alameda County California,* William Halley 1876, p. 566

[56] *A History of Alameda County,* Woods, M. W., p. 121

[57] *History of Deciduous Fruits In California,* H. M. Butterfield July 1938 Official Publications of the California Fruit Exchange, Sacramento, XIV

[58] *Historical Sketches of Southern Alameda County,* Shin, Charles Howard. Alameda County Historical Society Articles June 8-Nov 19, 1889, reprinted 1991, p.191

[59] *Centerville Presbyterian Church,* A history compiled by Elder Donaldson, 1950

[60] *History of Alameda County,* Woods M. W., p. 85

[61] ibid, p. 86

[62] ibid, p. 87

[63] From *The History of Washington Township,* p.138

[64] Letter Provided by the Brier Family, 1999

[65] *The History of Washington Township,* p. 126

[66] Letter provided by Brier Decendant, Jean Roath, 1998

[67] *Brier letter to AHMS,* #01085/ American Home Missionary Society Archives, Amistad Research Center at Tulane University

[68] *Hoozier Zion,* p. 74

[69] *Brier letter to AHMS,* #001007/ American Home Missionary Society Archives, Amistad Research Center at Tulane University

[70] *Brier letter to the AHMS,* #01520/ American Home Missionary Society Archives, Amistad Research Center at Tulane University

[71] *AHMS Microfilm letter,* # 01536/ American Home Missionary Society Archives, Amistad Research Center at Tulane University

[72] *AHMS Microfilm letter*, # 01526/ American Home Missionary Society Archives, Amistad Research Center at Tulane University

[73] *Original Session Minute book, 1853*, Centerville Presbyterian Church

[74] ibid p. 94

[75] *The San Francisco Picayune*, July 11, 1851

[76] AHMS speech, *God and Country*

[77] *History of Washington Township*, p.100

[78] *AHMS Microfilm letter*, #01532/ American Home Missionary Society Archives, Amistad Research Center at Tulane University

[79] *AHMS Microfilm letter*, # 01536/ American Home Missionary Society Archives, Amistad Research Center at Tulane University

[80] *AHMS Microfilm letter*, # 01974/ American Home Missionary Society Archives, Amistad Research Center at Tulane University

[81] *The Pacific Newspaper*, June 15, 1856

[82] Letter Provided by the Brier family, 1999

[83] As quoted in *"Horace Bushnell and the Virtuous Republic*, Howard Barnes, 1991, p.375

[84] *Brier letter to the AHMS, Microfilm # 01979/* American Home Missionary Society Archives, Amistad Research Center at Tulane University

[85] Ibid

[86] *Brier letter to the AHMS, # 01979/* American Home Missionary Society Archives, Amistad Research Center at Tulane University

[87] *AHMS Microfilm letter*, # 02209/ American Home Missionary Society Archives, Amistad Research Center at Tulane University

[88] *Alameda County Marriages, 1855-1863 Book A* Film # 844, Hayward Historical Museum Library, p. 448

[89] *California Firsts*, Rockwell D. Hunt, Fearon Publishers, San Francisco, 1934

[90] *AHMS Microfilm Letter* #0245/ American Home Missionary Society Archives, Amistad Research Center at Tulane University

[91] *Amador-Livermore Valley Historical Society, Newsletter*, May 1985

[92] *The Bay of San Francisco, Its Cities and their Suburbs,* Library of the California Historical Society, Abijah Baker, Biography

[93] *The Centennial Year Book of Alameda County California.*, William Halley

[94] Reminiscences of a Private Life. Being a Narrative of a Portion of the Life Experiences of Mrs.Charlotte (Hawley) Cornell", New York, 1893.

[95] *AHMS Microfilm Letter* #02744/ American Home Missionary Society Archives, Amistad Research Center at Tulane University

[96] *AHMS Microfilm Letter* #01536, letter 25 / American Home Missionary Society Archives, Amistad Research Center at Tulane University

[97] *George Washington Patterson*, Kennedy, p. 47

[98] *History of the Congregational Church of Santa Cruz*, p. 21

[99] Taken from hand-typed manuscript from local Historian Betty Lewis, found at the Pajaro Historical Society

[100] *History of the First Presbyterian Church in Carson City, Nevada, 1861-1997*, Including a list of Pastors serving during the church's lifetime. Victor Goodwin and Wilbur Wieprecht, 1997, p.2

[101] *History of Nevada*, Sam Davis, p. 587

[102] *History of the First Presbyterian Church of Virginia City*, held at the Presbyterian Historical Society, Philadelphia, Pa.

[103] *Nevada Ghost towns and Mining Camps*, Stanley W Paher, p. 166

[104] Quoted in *First Presbyterian Church, Carson City, Nevada, 1861-1997*, Victor Goodwin, and Wilbur Wieprect. p. 37

[105] *Faith is the Victory, The History of the First Presbyterian Church of San Leandro*, p.2

[106] ibid p.1

[107] *Our Heritage:History of First Presbyterian Church of Alameda*, p.1

[108] Wicher, *The Presbyterian Church in California*, 1848-1900

[109] Clyde Arbuckle, *History of San Jose* p. 256

[110] *Synod of Pacific* Minutes, p. 17

[111] *Sagebrush and Steeples*, p.23

[112] *The Silver City*. p.125

[113] *The History of Nevada*, Sam Davis p. 585

[114] *History of Alameda County*, Woods, p. 56

[115] *Bicentennial Record*, p. 3 as footnoted in Hadsel and Coote. P.28

[116] *San Francisco Theological Seminary*, Hadsel and Coote, 1999, p.28

[117] *The Presbyterian Church in California 1846-1900*, Wicher, p.123

[118] *San Francisco Theological Seminary*, Hadsel and Coote,1999, p.28

[119] *History of Santa Clara County*, p.647

[120] *Making of the Seminary*, Alexander, p. 11

[121] *Christian Seed*, Hogue, p. 21-22

[122] *The History of San Francisco Theological Seminary*, Hadsel and Coote, p.29

[123] *Synod Minutes*, May, 1874 p.17

[124] *The Story of Our Church, 1876-1951 First Presbyterian Church Pleasanton*

[125] *The Occident*, May 3, 1877

[126] *Synod of the Pacific Meeting Minutes*, May 1874

[127] *Synod of the Pacific Minutes*, October 1877, p. 23

[128] *The Lariat*, Student Newspaper of Wabash College, June 22, 1881

[129]

[130] *The History of Kern County*, 1895

BIBLIOGRAPHY

Abbott, Lyman, *Henry Ward Beecher, A sketch of his Career*, American Publishing Company, Hartford Conn., 1887

Alsworth, Mary Dean, *More Gleanings for Alta California*, Vital Records Published in California's first Newspaper, 1851. Dean Publications, R22040 El Canto Circle, Rancho Cordova, CA

Arbuckle, Clyde, *History of San Jose*, Smith and McKay Publishing Co. 1995

Barker, Malcolm E. *More San Francisco Memoirs, 1852-1899: The ripening years*. Londonborn Publications, San Francisco, 1996

Barrows, Susana and Robin Room, *Drinking: Behavior and Belief in Modern History* University of California Press, 1991

Benton, Joseph Augustine, *In Memorial: Funeral Messages Upon His Death*. San Francisco Pacific Theological Seminary, 1892

Beilharz, Edwin A, and Carlos U. Lopez We were 49rs. Chileans in the Gold Rush, Ward Ritchie Press, Pasadena, CA, 1976

Biographical Record and Portrait Album of Tippecanoe County, Indiana Chicago: The Lewis Publishing Co., 1888

Bullard, Asa, *Fifty Years with the Sabbath Schools*, Boston. Lockwood, Brooks and Company, 1876

Butterfield, H.M., *History of Deciduous Fruits In California*, July, 1938 Official Publications of the California Fruit Exchange, Sacramento, California Volumes XIV

Clark, Clifford E, Jr., *Henry Ward Beecher: Spokesman for a Middle Class America* University of Illinois Press, Urbana, 1978

Delgado, James *To California by Sea: A Maritime History of the California Gold Rush*, South Carolina Press 1990

Drury, Clifford Merrill, *William Anderson Scott "No Ordinary Man."* The Arthur H. Clark Company, Glendale, CA 1967

The Presbyterian Panorama One hundred and fifty years of National Missions History, Board of Christian Education, Philadelphia, 1952

Elsmere, Jane Shaffer *Henry Ward Beecher, The Indiana Years 1837-1847*, Indiana Historical Society 1973

Beecher, Lyman *The Autobiography of Lyman Beecher* The Belknap Press, Harvard, Cambridge Mass. 1961

Cammack, Eleanor A. *"Notes on Wabash River Steam Boating: Early Lafayette."* Indiana Magazine of History 1954

Country Club of Washington Township Research Committee. *History of Washington Township.* N. P. 1904, reprint and 2nd ed., Palo Alto: Stanford University Press, 1950

De Hart, R.P. *Past and Present of Tippecanoe County Indiana*, 2 vol. Indianapolis: B.B. Bowen, 1965

Edwards, Ben F. *100 Years of Achievement and Challenge, A Brief History of the First Presbyterian Church of Oakland*, California, The Centennial Committee of the First Presbyterian Church of Oakland, CA, 1953

Earley, Logan. *History of Indiana-Tippecanoe County-Wabash Valley*, vol 3 Dayton, Ohio: National Historical Association, 1928

Ferrier, William Warren, *Pioneer Church Beginnings and Educational Movements in California*, Berkeley, California, 1927

Ferrier, William Warren, *Congregationalism's Place in California History*, Berkley Press, 1943

Flexner, Eleanor *Century of Struggle: The Woman's Rights Movement in the United States* The Belknap Press of Harvard University Press, Cambridge Mass 1959

Frazer, James W. *Pedagogue for God's Kingdom, Lyman Beecher and the Second Great Awakening. University Press of America*, 1985, Lahnam, MD.

Gilroy's First Century of Incorporation 1870-1970, A History of the City, City of Gilroy, Published June 25th, 1975- Gilroy, California

Goodykoontz, Colin Brummitt *Home Mission on the American Frontier, with Particular Reference to the American Home Missionary Society*, Caxton Printers, Caldwell, Idaho, 1939

Hadsel, John, and Dr. Coote *History of San Anselmo Seminary*, 1999

Halley, William. *The Centennial Year Book of Alameda County*, California, Oakland, California, 1876

Hays, Rev. George P., *Presbyterians: A Popular narrative of their origin, progress, doctrines, and achievements*, J.A. Hill and Company, Spokane, 1892

Hickok, Rev. Laurens P. *Sermon: A Nation Saved from its Prosperity only by the Gospel.* Published by the American Home Missionary Society, New York, May 1853

Hirrel, Leo P. *Children of Wrath, New School Calvinism and Antebellum Reform*, The University Press of Kentucky, 1975

Hogue, Harland *Prophets and Paupers :Religion in the California Gold Rush 1848-1869.* International Scholars Publication. 1999

Hurt, Douglass R., *The Ohio Frontier, Crucible of the Old Northwest, 1720-1830*, Indiana University Press 1990

Ignoffo, Mary Jo, Gold Rush Politics, *California's First Legislature*, California State Senate, Sacramento, CA. and the California History Center and Foundation, 1999

Kennedy, Keith E. *George Washington Patterson and the Founding of Ardenwood.* California History Center and Foundation, Cupertino, California, 1995

Kleinke, Julia A. *125 Years, A History of the First Presbyterian Church of Livermore, California 1871-1996*, Published by Garrett B. Drummond, 1995

Kriebel, Robert C. *Old Lafayette, 1811-1853 Based Upon Historical Columns from the Pages of the Journal and Courier.* Tippecanoe County Historical Association, 1988

Lender, Mark Edward, and Martin, James Kirby, *Drinking in America: A History,* The Free Press, MacMillian, New York, 1978.

Lewis, Betty, *Watsonville Yesterday.* Mehl's Colonial Chapel, Copyright 1978

Loofbourow, Leon, *From Steeples among the Sage A Centennial Story of Nevada's Churches,* The Historical Society of the California-Nevada Annual Conference of the Methodist Church 330 Ellis Street, San Francisco, CA, Larkin Press, 1964

Maffly-Kipp Laurie F *"Religion and Society in Frontier California,* Yale University Press, 1998

Marsden, George *The Evangelical Mind and the New School Experience: A Case Study of Thought and Theology in the 19th Century America.* New Haven and London, Yale University Press, 1970.

Mc Can, William E, and Edgar J. Hinkel, editors. *History of Rural Alameda County*, 2 vols., WPA Project 165-03-6504, Oakland, California, 1937

Merritt, Frank Clinton. *History of Alameda County*, Volume 2, Chicago: The S. J. Clarke Publishing Co. 1895

Mosier, Page and Dan *Alameda County Place Names,* Mines Road Books, Fremont, Ca 1986

Miyakawa, T. Scott, *Protestants and Pioneers Individualism and Conformity on the American Frontier,* University of Chicago Press, 1964

Pegram, Thomas R., *Battling Demon Rum: The Struggle for a Dry America 1800-1933.* Ivan R. Dee, Chicago, 1998

Pond, William C., *Gospel Pioneering: Reminiscences of Early Congregationalism in California 1833-1920.* The News Printing Company, Oberlin, Ohio, 1921

Paul, Rodman W. *"The Beginnings of Agriculture in California: Innovation vs. Continuity,"* California Historical Society Quarterly, 52:16-27

Rasmussen, Louis, J. *San Francisco Ship Passenger Lists,* Genealogical Publishing Co. Inc, Baltimore, 1978

Rudolph, L.C. *Hoosier Zion, The Presbyterians in Early Indiana,* Yale University Press 1963

Rugoff, Milton, *The Beechers, An American Family in the Nineteenth Century,* Harper and Row, 1981

Sandoval, John S, *A Century of Fremont in the East Bay*, Number 7 in a Series. Hayward, California: Chapel of the Chimes. Undated.

A Century of Mission San Jose in the East Bay, Number 12 in a Series. Hayward, California: Chapel of the Chimes. Undated.

Shaffer, Harry E. *A Garden Grows in Eden, The Centennial Story of San Leandro.* San Leandro Historical Centennial Committee, San Leandro, California. 1965

Schorr-Hind, Carolyn *Whither Thou Goest*, Western Journal Press: Conrad Mollmath and Co, Printers and Publishers/ San Mateo, CA. 1985

Slosser, Gaius Jackson, *They Seek a Country: The American Presbyterians.* Macmillan Company, New York, 1955.

Taber, Stephen L. *Pioneer Community of Faith, Old First Presbyterian Church 1849-1999* Published by Old First Presbyterian Church, 1999

Taylor, William, *California Life Illustrated*, New York by Carlton and Porter 1858

Wicher, Edward Arthur, *The Presbyterian Church in California 1849-1927*, The Grafton Press, NY 1927

Williams, Albert, *A Pioneer Pastorate*, 1885

Willey, Samuel H., *Two Historical Discourses occasioned by the close of the First Ten Years Ministry in California.* Town and Bacon, San Francisco, 1859.

Wood, M.W *A History of Alameda County California*, Oakland, 1883 p.102

Woods, James. *California Pioneer Decade of 1849 The Presbyterian Church.* Rev. Leo Brown, Publishing, Reedley, CA 1981

Regional Histories

Memorial and Biographical History of the Counties of Fresno, Tulare, and Kern California Chicago: The Lewis Publishing Company, 1881

History of Santa Clara County, California, Geography, Geology, Topography, Climatography, and Description, Alley, Bowen, and Co. 1881

Watsonville Yesterday, Betty Lewis, Mehl's Colonial Chapel, Watsonville CA 1978

Letters and Privately Published Histories

Barrett, Richard, *History of First Presbyterian Church of Pleasanton*, 2002

The Story of Our Church. 1876-1951 First Presbyterian Church of Pleasanton, California.

A Century of Christian Witness, History of First Congregational Church of Santa Cruz, CA Published by the Church Historical Committee, 1982

Benton, Joseph Augustine, *In Memorial: Funeral Messages upon his death.* San Francisco Pacific Theological Seminary, 1892

Gilroy's *First Century of Incorporation 1870-1970, A History of the City* City of Gilroy, Published June 25th, 1970, Gilroy, California.

History of the First Presbyterian Church of Virginia City, Nevada

Kleinke, Julia A. 125 Years, *A History of the First Presbyterian Church of Livermore, California 1871-1996*, Published by Garrett B. Drummond, 1995

Cornell, Mrs. Charlotte Hawley *"Reminiscences of a Private Life. Being a Narrative of a Portion of the Life Experiences of Mrs. Charlotte (Hawley) Cornell"*, New York, 1893, belonging to Mrs. Clara May of Decoto, California.

Brier letter to the American Home Mission Society, September 1, 1860

Synod of Pacific Minutes, Book and Job Printer, C. W. Gordon Steam, October, 1877, pp 23

Synod of Pacific Minutes October 1879, Pacific Press Publishing House, Oakland Ca

Synod Minutes, Alta Presbyterian Church, 1861-1890

Daughters of the American Revolution family Genealogical record, Brier family, page 50

History of the First Congregational Church of Santa Cruz, 1982

History of the First Presbyterian Church of Marysville, 1850-1975 Helen Turner Shaver and Doris Shaver Lynch published by the 125th Anniversary Committee, 1985

History of the First Presbyterian Church in Carson City, Nevada, 1861-1997, Including a list of Pastors serving during the church's lifetime. Victor Goodwin, and Wilbur Wieprecht, 1997

125 Years: /A history of the First Presbyterian Church. Livermore California 1871-1996 By Julia A Kleineke, Expanded and updated by Garrett B. Drummond 1996.

History of San Anselmo Seminary, 199, Harry Hadsel, pp29

Lewis, Betty, *Watsonville Yesterday,* Mehl's Colonial Chapel, Copyright 1978

Synod of Pacific Minutes, Book and Job Printer, C. W. Gordon Steam October 1877, pp 23

Synod of Pacific Minutes, October 1879, Pacific Press Publishing House, Oakland CA

A Brief History of Centerville Presbyterian Church, Material Compiled by Donaldson circa 1945

A Woman's Perspective of History by Mrs. George Wright 1975

The Centennial History, First Church Livermore.

Some Presbyterian Beginnings on the Pacific Coast, By Clifford M Drury, 1958 p. 4, Draft copies held at San Anselmo Theological Library

A History of Centerville Church. Material written by George Wright 1953

The Brier Family, by Charles Templeton Brier, undated.

Kolberg, George *"A Continuing History of the Centerville Presbyterian Church"* Centerville Presbyterian Church, 1995

Taken from letter from local historian, Bernadette L. Eyselee, February 16, 1967,
     Quoted from Pacific Rural Press, XV March 22, 1879, p. 200, California History
     Quarterly, 1966/ 60:45
Synod Minutes, Alta Presbyterian Church, Years 1861-1890
Memorial and Biographical History of the Counties of Fresno, Tulare, and Kern, Chicago,
     The Lewis Publishing Company, 1898
History of Santa Clara County, California, Alley, Bowen, and Company Publishers,
     San Francisco, 1881

Newspapers

The *Marysville Herald*, May 17, 1851, Cited in *California Historical Quarterly* 1936
     vol 15, page 43
The *Marysville Herald*, February 14, 1851 ibid, page 44
The *Marysville Herald*, November 1851. ibid, page 45

ACKNOWLEDGEMENTS

I began this work as a weekend research project, and it stretched into a ten-year journey. It is true, that if I knew how long it would take, I may have never agreed to take it on.

Along the way, many people provided me with pieces of a treasure map.

Library after library revealed further details the Brier story. I am grateful to Brenda Square, Director of Archives and Library at the Amistad Research Center at Tulane University for granting me permission to publish Brier's letter. Mike Peterson, research librarian at San Francisco Theological Seminary gave me access to numerous files by the respected historian, Dr. Clifford Drury, which helped me uncover an overview of Brier's career.

I owe special thanks to members of the Brier extended family who shared their photographs, letters, and artifacts from Elizabeth and William Brier. Brier family sources included Mr. Doug Kinney, Mrs. Elizabeth Thomson, Mrs. Marice George. Mrs.Jean Roathe, and Mrs. Mary Louise Faca.

Church historians that made helpful additions were Gerald Drummond of Livermore, Bill Steig, of the Wabash Avenue Presbyterian Church, R. Scott Sherman of the Tehama County Genealogical and Historical Society, Alice Thorn of the Presbytery of San Jose, and Maynard Clark, First Presbyterian Church of Virginia City, Nevada.

Fremont historian Phil Holmes, and a member of the Centerville Presbyterian Church, encouraged me to continue the search until I exhausted every clue. My father, Al Roth, and Richard Barrett from Pleasanton read the manuscript in its early form, and made helpful comments. Editors Jane Mueller, and Anitra Dark gave me advice on crafting the story, and Shirley Strong dedicated hundred of hours correcting inconsistencies in the manuscript. I would not have been able to finish without their help.

My greatest debt of gratitude is to my wife Marsha, and my children Amanda and Joe, who sat with me in research libraries, and visited many of the Brier churches in California and Nevada.

It is a humbling task to reconstruct a life, long forgotten. Oftentimes I wondered what evidence will remain of my ministry, one hundred and fifty years from now. It must be the grace of God that multiplies our earthly efforts, as is evidenced by the legacy of the Rev. William Wallace Brier.